ARMS AND
THE WIZARD

*Lloyd George and
the Ministry of Munitions,
1915-1916*

R. J. Q. ADAMS

CASSELL
LONDON

CASSELL & CO. LTD.
35 Red Lion Square, London WC1R 4SG
and at Sydney, Auckland, Toronto, Johannesburg,
an affiliate of
Macmillan Publishing Co., Inc.,
New York.

First published 1978

ISBN 0 304 29916 2

Photoset and printed in Great Britain by
Lowe & Brydone Printers Limited
Thetford, Norfolk

THIS BOOK
IS DEDICATED TO
THE MEMORY OF
MY PARENTS

CONTENTS

PREFACE

With the coming of the Coalition Government, formed by Prime Minister Herbert Henry Asquith in May 1915, a new Department, the Ministry of Munitions, was created to overcome the serious shortage of armaments which had been allowed to occur. Lloyd George, the statesman who had made the munitions crisis his personal cause, was placed in charge. During his year in that office, he brought about the organization of the productive capacity of the nation for munitions production, and the British Army was no longer to fear another 'Shells Scandal'.

As the subtitle suggests, this book is an examination of the role of Lloyd George in the creation of this revolutionary Department of State and in the policies which came to identify it.

Arthur Marwick, who has written so vividly about the First World War, has counselled:

> Aside from the broad highway of change, the historian is concerned with the limited, the specific and the unique; he has at times the sacred duty to be parochial.

It is hoped that in pursuing this 'sacred duty' the present author has added a further chapter to history dealing not only with Great Britain's efforts to win the First World War, but also with her struggle to survive in the modern world.

It is perhaps worth noting here that throughout this book, the author has referred to the participants in the story of the Ministry by the names they bore at that time: Lord Addison, then, is called Dr. Christopher Addison; Lord Beveridge is known as Sir William Beveridge, and so forth. The author has also resisted the urge to employ the elegant but somewhat outdated custom of peppering the text with 'as he was then', or the like, to explain this nomenclature. Likewise changes in status and rank are generally not included among the chapter notes.

R. J. Q. ADAMS
College Station, Texas
1977

BIBLIOGRAPHICAL NOTE

This study is based upon several collections of papers, public and private; upon the contemporary newspaper press and the *Parliamentary Debates*; as well as upon a number of published sources. The purpose of the footnote references is not only to show the sources of quotations or to provide evidence for the author's conclusions, but also to direct the reader who wishes to pursue further the lines of thought developed in these pages. It is felt, therefore, that a monumental listing of page after page of secondary sources is unnecessary. Perhaps this statement can also be considered a defence against critics of the large number of footnotes which begin with the words 'See . . . ' or 'In this regard . . .'.

The most useful primary sources which the author was privileged to consult include, in the first place, the large collection of the papers of the Ministry of Munitions, on deposit at the Public Record Office, London. The most informative portion of these are the documents catalogued by the Historical Records Section of the Ministry, just before and in the years immediately after the end of World War I, for use in writing the *History of the Ministry of Munitions,* the 'official' record of the lifespan of the Department. Among the departmental papers are many documents germane to the writing of the *History* itself, including vast amounts of correspondence among the authors and editors, draft chapters of the sections of the *History* and the like, which are very useful to a modern student of the Ministry. These are, of course, in addition to the great volume of papers of the production and administrative departments of the Ministry of Munitions.

The papers of the Cabinet (including its War Council, Dardanelles

Committee and War Committee), the Board of Trade, the War Office, the Home Office and the Treasury were useful in examining the efforts of the British Government to overcome the munitions crisis before May 1915, and in understanding, after that date, the development of the policy of Centralism and Control under the leadership of the Ministry of Munitions.

Among the private collections consulted by the author, of first importance are the papers of David Lloyd George, now deposited in the House of Lords Record Office since the closing of the Beaverbrook Library. They are perhaps more useful for the period leading up to the advent of the Ministry and for the early months of the lifespan of the Department than for the later period. If one seeks evidence of the sparkling energy, the intolerance of 'red tape' and the hatred of 'established practice' which characterized the first Minister of Munitions, one will find it in these letters and papers. Also useful are the collections of papers of Lloyd George's Cabinet colleagues, who were in one way or another interested parties in the creation and operation of the Ministry. Of particular interest are the Asquith Papers (Bodleian Library, Oxford), the Bonar Law Papers (House of Lords Record Office), the Balfour Papers (British Library), and the Kitchener Papers (Public Record Office).

Among those who worked closely with Lloyd George at the Ministry during this period and left substantial collections of papers were Dr. Christopher Addison (Bodleian Library, Oxford) and Sir William Beveridge (British Library of Political and Economic Science). A small collection of the papers of Sir Frederick Black, the second Director General of Munitions Supply, is contained within the papers of the Ministry at the Public Record Office, London. Although not technically an archival source, since it was published in 1971, but worthy of note is the diary of Miss Stevenson, Lloyd George's long-time secretary and trusted confidante, whom he married in later years (*Lloyd George: A Diary by Frances Stevenson*: edited by A. J. P. Taylor). There were few Ministry secrets which Lloyd George did not reveal to Miss Stevenson.

ACKNOWLEDGMENTS

I must express my thanks to the following individuals and institutions who made available to me materials without which this study could never have been completed: to Professor A. J. P. Taylor, F.B.A., Honorary Director of the Beaverbrook Library—the closure of which all who worked in its pleasant confines will long mourn—(Lloyd George and Bonar Law Papers); to the British Library Reading Room, Newspaper Library, Colindale, and Manuscripts Room (Balfour Papers); to the Bodleian Library, Oxford University (Addison and Asquith Papers); to Lady Liddell Hart and to the Liddell Hart Centre for Military Archives, University of London King's College (Liddell Hart Papers); to the British Library of Political and Economic Science (Beveridge Papers); and to the Public Record Office, London (Kitchener Papers and Ministry of Munitions, Cabinet and other Departmental Papers). I would also like to record my gratitude to the staffs of the many libraries where I sought materials; in addition to those named above, I would like to thank the librarians of the Hoover Institution, Stanford University, the University Library of the University of California, Santa Barbara and the Sterling C. Evans Library of the Texas A&M University in America, without whose efforts my attempts to write British history in the United States would have been quite hopeless.

For permission to quote materials, to which they hold copyright, I wish to thank the Dowager Viscountess Addison, the First Beaverbrook Foundation, the Curators of the Bodleian Library, the British Library Board, and the Controller of H.M. Stationery Office. If I have unwittingly infringed upon the copyright of any persons or institutions, I hope they will accept my sincerest apologies and notify me of the oversight.

I wish to acknowledge my debt to the University of California, Santa Barbara and to the Texas A&M University for financial assistance which, in part, made these researches possible.

It would be impossible to thank adequately all those who aided me in my work on this book. In many ways, an essay of this kind is a group effort, in which the author shares the birthright with his friends, colleagues and students who contribute so materially to its development. I would like to single out for special thanks Lady Liddell Hart and Mr. and Mrs. John Grigg, who opened their homes to me during the summer of 1975, and shared their insights into the character and career of Lloyd George. Professor Alfred M. Gollin originally suggested to me the topic of the Ministry of Munitions in a chance meeting in a stairwell in Ellison Hall at the University of California, Santa Barbara; he also directed this work through its first stage—as a doctoral dissertation. His sage advice and guidance often extracted me from snares of my own creation. Mr. George Dangerfield, formerly of the same university, taught me much of what I know about the art of writing history—the sole limitation on this exercise was not how much he could teach, but how much I could learn. To him I gratefully record my thanks. These men and Mr. John Grigg, Professor Roger A. Beaumont and Professor James Startt read all or part of this manuscript in one or another of its incarnations. For their suggestions and criticisms, I am very grateful.

I would also like to thank Mr. Patrick Annesley, formerly of Cassell and Company, who originally had faith in the 'publishability' of this study, and Dr. M. W. B. Orange and Miss Mary Griffith, who took up the arduous task at Red Lion Square of seeing this book through to completion. For his confidence in the viability of an American edition of the book I am pleased to thank Mr. Frank Wardlaw.

My sometime assistant Mrs. Barbara Moyer aided me greatly in the preparation of the *Appendixes,* and Miss Cyndi Colson typed the manuscript with great care and skill. I am indebted to both of them for their help.

Finally, I wish to thank Mrs. Marcia Jane Adams, who read

every word of this essay a dozen times and whose good sense weeded out extraneous prose, and Master Ian James Tucker Adams, for their support and sacrifice during the long process of converting a vague idea into a printed book.

The author is solely responsible, of course, for any errors of fact or interpretation.

One

BUSINESS AS USUAL

I

When Herbert Henry Asquith created his Coalition Government in May 1915, David Lloyd George surrendered his post as Chancellor of the Exchequer to the former Home Secretary, Reginald McKenna.[1] Instead, he became Minister of Munitions of War, the office considered by many to be the most significant in the inter-party arrangement for a better conduct of the World War. In these anxious days Lloyd George's place in history was already assured. He was the father of what would, in future, come to be called the Welfare State; he was clearly the most exciting figure in British politics since the time of Joseph Chamberlain.

Ten months after the outbreak of the War the curious situation had come about that the man who was once considered the most famous radical pacifist in the nation had agreed, had even demanded, that the responsibility for producing the vast amounts of warlike stores needed by the British Army be taken from the War Office and placed in his hands. He was moved to act because the professional soldiers of that Department had failed to do so.

On 1 August 1914, three days before Britain entered a state of war with the Central Powers, the Master General of the Ordnance, the Officer charged with the supply of munitions to the Army, communicated to the Prime Minister, who was also then Acting Secretary of State for War:

Present ammunition in equipments and reserve have been held to be sufficient to meet the requirements of the E.F. [Expeditionary

Force] in the field for 6 months, but unless orders are placed I cannot guarantee that there will not be a deficiency when the first six months of the war are over.[2]

In a very few months after this message was sent it became clear that the battles of the World War would consume many times these estimated amounts of munitions in a few weeks of artillery siege. Indeed, the cost of the orders contemplated by Major-General Sir Stanley von Donop,[3] the Master General, totalled £1,641,000, and that figure would seem as nothing when compared with the gigantic sums soon afterward spent on military stores.

No nation, even the best prepared, entered the War adequately provisioned for the murderous trench warfare which characterized it. The greatest failure of the War Office and its Ordnance Department was not merely that they were less well prepared than France or Germany, but rather that these professional soldiers never understood what had to be done to produce the unprecedented quantities of munitions which were needed.

When he left the confines of the Treasury to take up the new Ministry's work in Whitehall Gardens, Lloyd George meant drastically to change that situation. He had no master plan, nor was he rich in expertise in the field of munitions manufacture. He knew, however, that War Office methods had failed and that something different had to be tried if the British Army were not to be effectively neutralized for want of munitions. That *something* entailed an end to the *laissez-faire* attitude which allowed the private and public sectors of the nation's economy to remain separate during the War. It certainly included, as well, the realization that the highly professionalized outlook of the soldiers in charge of the supply function of the War Office was altogether too narrow and inflexible ever to produce an acceptable solution. He rejected what appeared to him to be a commitment to routine-mindedness and began the greatest experiment in Government organization of national resources, the first great modern essay in State control, in the nation's history.

To understand the need which drove him and others to this unprecedented decision, we must first examine the attitudes and practices with which Great Britain entered the War. To comprehend the path taken by the Ministry under its first chief, we must understand the failure which preceded it.

II

On 31 July 1914 the German Government dispatched two ultimata: they sent a demand to St. Petersburg that Russian mobilization, begun the day before, be stopped immediately. To Paris they sent an exaction of French neutrality in the event of a Russo-German conflict. Both, of course, were rejected, and Europe made ready for general war. While it was not then completely certain that Britain would enter such a conflict, the Government did take certain measures to prepare the nation for its uncertain future. Anticipating upset in world finance and desiring to prevent too great a strain on the reserves of the Bank of England, the bank rate was raised on 31 July to 8 per cent, and to 10 per cent on the following day. The payment of certain bills of exchange was postponed for a month, postal orders were declared legal tender, and the Bank Holiday, begun on 1 August, was extended to the 6th. Withdrawals from deposit accounts were rationed to prevent a run on the banks. There was, however, no financial crisis in August 1914, and, within a week or two, the banking establishment was functioning normally.[4]

In the interests of national security, from 1 to 3 August Royal Proclamations prohibited wireless telegraphy on merchant ships in British territorial waters, the flying of private aircraft within the nation and the export of a specified list of warlike stores.

In addition, the Government assumed responsibility for the purchase and supply of sugar. Fully two-thirds of this necessary foodstuff consumed in Britain had traditionally come from the Central Powers, and the War made it necessary to find new sources. There was little adverse comment on this break with the Free Trade tradition, and Britons went on buying sugar, albeit at slightly dearer prices, as they had always done.[5]

Save for the assumption of responsibility for risks to wartime merchant shipping, there was but one other major preparatory action with which the Government made ready to face the World War. With the quite reasonable explanation that their action was necessary for the swift embarkation of the Expeditionary Force to the continent, the Government took control of rail transport in the nation. This authority was vested in a board of directors of the great railways, and this so-called Executive Committee of Railway Managers was authorized to assure share-holders in the various companies that profits on the average of the three business years previous to the coming of the War would be guaranteed by the State.[6] This even greater breach of *laissez-faire* principles was also accepted by Britons in the flurry of activity as the nation girded its loins. In the end, the experiment in railway management by the State proved acceptable.

These steps were the only major non-military ones taken by the Government to prepare the nation for the holocaust which lay ahead. War began at 11.00 pm (German time) on 4 August 1914. Six days later Parliament rose, and the nation waited, somewhat impatiently, for victory.

If these measures seem few in number, their intent was sufficiently vast—they were meant not to bring the meaning of the War home to the nation, to declare that the realm was in danger, but, rather, to prevent that feeling. They were intended to ensure what seemed to be the deepest desire of the nation, best typified by the slogan popular in those first weeks of War: 'Business as Usual'. This phrase, often displayed outside a shop which had experienced a fire or suffered some other calamity, bespoke the aspiration of Britain to aid her friends and punish her enemies with as little upset to British life as possible. It would not be many months before only the memory of that feeling lingered. It was not to be that kind of War.[7]

The people of Great Britain, like the citizenry of all the warring nations, can hardly be blamed for their lack of foresight in the matter. They merely reflected the beliefs of their leaders that the fighting would be short-lived. The Germans had their glorious military tradition and their flawless Schlieffen Plan; the French had their magnificent army and a general staff committed to *revanche;* the British had their B.E.F., with all the swiftness and mobility its architect, Richard Burdon Haldane, could give it. The Great War would surely, it was almost universally believed in August 1914, be over by Christmas; and then the nations could get on with the peace. This great illusion did not survive the autumn of the year.

III

The Government remained almost unchanged.[8] There was one important addition, and it was this man, almost alone among the 'birds of paradise' on the Government bench, who saw the error in the short-war delusion. Lord Kitchener of Khartoum had been seconded to the War Office. In March 1914, the former Secretary of State, J. E. B. Seely, had left that office in disgrace, the scapegoat of the unfortunate Curragh incident. While Asquith himself took the portfolio temporarily, the coming of the War made the appointment of a full-time War Minister a necessity. Quite coincidentally, Kitchener, the hero of Omdurman, the greatest living soldier of his day, was on leave in the capital. On 3 August the Prime Minister ordered the Field Marshal to remain in London; on the 5th he decided to appoint Kitchener to the vacant post. The appointment was met with 'universal acclamation':

> Lord Kitchener was more than a national hero [Asquith's daughter wrote many years later]. He was a national institution . . . There was a feeling that Kitchener could not fail. The psychological effect of his appointment, the tonic to public confidence were instantaneous and overwhelming. And he at once gave, in his own right, a national status to the Government.[9]

On 6 August, a day before his first Cabinet, the new War Lord prompted the Government to authorize an increase in the size of the Army by 500,000 men, and the drive to bring recruits to the colours was begun under Kitchener's aegis. In that first meeting with his new colleagues, seated at the right hand of the Prime Minister, he announced, no doubt to the shock and horror of several of those Liberals: 'We must be prepared to put armies of millions into the field and to maintain them for several years.'[10] The Field Marshal saw clearly that the War would not be over by Christmas—or for several Christmases yet to come, for that matter. In the early days of August 1914, he was almost alone in seeing this: by the close of the year, among men of affairs, that opinion had become almost universally accepted.

Once the B.E.F. had taken its place on the French left, it found itself directly in the path of the German Army—a force, in that sector, almost three times its own size. On 22 August, the Battle of Mons was fought, and the British Army initiated a retreat halted on 5 September and followed a day later by the opening of the Battle of the Marne. Three days later, it was the turn of the German Army to begin a general retreat. The alternate retreat and advance tactics of the opponents ended, however, with the terrible First Battle of Ypres, fought between 12 October and 11 November 1914. First Ypres was a confused and confusing engagement, fought in wooded and marshy ground, largely by young inexperienced reservists on the German side and, after the regulars had taken terrible losses among the Allies, by cooks and orderlies on the British. With the close of the battle German hopes for a swift victory in the West passed away, and with those dreams of conquest died also traditional open warfare on the Western Front. Winter set in almost immediately after the end of First Ypres, and it found both contending forces dug in in trench lines from Switzerland to the sea.

The German Army, and with it the Schlieffen Plan, were stopped, but the cost was great. The B.E.F. virtually sacrificed itself in that battle. One in ten of those who crossed to France had been killed, and more than half the original Expeditionary Force were among the casualty lists. While enough senior and junior officers, as well as non-commissioned officers, remained to form the nucleus of a new and far larger British Army, the fact remained that by mid-November 1914 the professional Army which made up the Expeditionary Force had all but ceased to exist. 'The courage, skill and discipline with which it fulfilled its duty,' one historian of the period has written, 'have never been surpassed.'[11]

Kitchener's decision to increase the size of the Army, made all the more necessary by the sanguinary results of First Ypres, set the stage for what was surely his greatest triumph of the War. The overwhelming answer of the young (and sometimes not-so-young) men of Britain to the famous Alfred Leet poster of Kitchener's stern visage and outstretched finger—a poster which greeted them in every public place—was both clear and quick to come. By mid-September, the half-million additional volunteers for whom Lord

Kitchener had called had been signed up. In fact, the recruiting officers could not deal with the hundreds of thousands who were flocking to the colours in the certain knowledge that Kitchener indeed 'wanted them'.

Whether real or mythical, the greatest moments in the creation of the legend of a military hero are, of course, those on the victorious battlefield. Yet there were probably few among the multitudes who admired Lord Kitchener who realized that it was not the broad sweep of strategy or the incisive decisions of tactics which had brought him to the highest place in the Army: rather, it was his talent for conducting a campaign of economy, in terms of manpower, supplies and equipment, and, consequently, of money. His mind was not unlike that which military tradition often identified with the Royal Engineer—unexciting but thorough—and his 'methodical wearing down of the enemy' was his great contribution to the military arts. Lloyd George once compared his mind to a lighthouse beacon: at times it illuminated things in a blinding clear light, and then it would turn away, leaving only 'inutterable darkness'.[12] The Field Marshal had been the first to see the need of an army of continental proportions, the first to anticipate the great length of the War. Once the trenches had been dug from the Swiss frontier to the sea in the autumn of 1914, however, the beacon turned away, leaving all in shadow.

Kitchener was sixty-four years of age when he took up his new burden, and he had spent his whole adult life on the frontiers of the Empire in the service of his nation. He was tall and straight and magisterial in his bearing and, at first, the lonely brooding figure of the War Lord was held in awe by many of his new colleagues. None doubted his right to join their number. Kitchener was not a politician; in fact, the public generally saw him as above the partisan feuds of party politics. There seemed, as well, a supreme logic in bringing the nation's greatest soldier to conduct the affairs of the War Office in this time of peril. The mystique, however, began to wear thin for some of his Cabinet colleagues in a few brief months. As a general officer must, Kitchener had learned to make decisions in solitude and to communicate them to his subordinates in expectation that they would be carried out to the letter, without question. Such procedure is an absolute

necessity to an army; in parliamentary government it usually leads
to disaster. The whole concept of Cabinet responsibility was lost
on the Field Marshal.[13]

Kitchener felt his authority to conduct the War ought to be
complete. He had been summoned against his better judgement to
take his new post, but once he had accepted it, he meant to act
as the War Lord the nation called upon him to be. For months he
laboured with the acquiescence of his colleagues and to the best of
his great abilities, but the tragedy for Britain was that no man
was equipped to run such a war alone. The hero of Omdurman,
despite his great gifts, was no exception. As he himself admitted,
once the war of movement was ended in November 1914, in the
so-called race to the sea of trench-building: 'I don't know what is
to be done . . . this isn't war.'[14] He was, of course, wrong; it
was war to the death. The beacon of Lloyd George's epigram, however, did brilliantly illumine the terrible problem which even it
could not solve. Commenting on the decision for intervention by
the politicians, he said: 'Did they remember when they went
headlong into a war like this, that they were without an army, and
without any preparation to equip one?'[15]

The armies raised in Kitchener's name appeared with little
trouble; indeed men were no problem. Yet before the War entered
its second year, it was clear to many that all the efforts of the
Secretary of State and the War Office had failed to 'equip' them
once they had come forward. The great beacon could reveal the
problem, yet it could not solve it.

Another of Britain's greatest warriors, the man who has rightly
been called the greatest naval mind since Nelson, once wrote of
the experience of war: 'My own humble idea is that "men are
everything and material nothing", whether it's working the War
Office or fighting a fleet.'[16] If warlike stores, the 'materials' of
Admiral Sir John Fisher's reference in 1903, was 'nothing' at that
time, the World War demonstrated that beyond doubt the military
arts had changed. For, while the War was certainly fought and
won by the men in the trenches, the question of how best to
supply the gigantic amounts of military equipment they required
came very soon to be of overpowering importance. While supply
of these instruments of warfare did not receive the very highest

attention of the Government until the spring of 1915, the story of the attempts to provide them began much earlier.

IV

The South African War had done much to make uneasy Britain's entry into the new century. It had revealed to her own people, and to friends and enemies abroad, that the British Army was unprepared and ill-equipped to perform as an effective instrument of her foreign policy. 'Britain's Imperial authority,' Alfred Gollin has written, 'had been exposed to ridicule.'[17] The victories of the colonial wars of the nineteenth century seemed most unimpressive when the British Army faced the well equipped and highly trained Boer units. The surprise was not that Britain had finally triumphed in such a war, but, rather, that it had taken so long. Something had to be done.

In July 1902 a man reached the highest rank in British politics who meant to rectify these matters. A. J. Balfour succeeded his uncle, Lord Salisbury, as Prime Minister. Keenly interested in military affairs, he set to work to overhaul the defence machinery of the Empire. While his two successive War Secretaries did not accomplish much at the War Office, Balfour's efforts did bear fruit in other spheres. Perhaps the most famous of the innovations begun during his premiership were the reforms worked in the Navy by Admiral Sir John Fisher, all aimed toward making the Fleet better armed and manned and more modern than any other navy in the world. An attempt at centralizing defence thinking was also embodied in the recreation of the Committee of Imperial Defence, which had formally existed since the Boer War. Balfour remade it into a loosely structured body of politicians and service advisers which concentrated its attentions on preparing the nation to meet the next war.

Several Royal Commissions were also appointed during Balfour's Ministry to enquire into defence matters; most germane to our history was the committee of Admiral Fisher, Sir George Clark and, as chairman, Viscount Esher, which examined the organization of the War Office itself.[18] No doubt influenced by the ideas of Fisher, they called for an end to the post of Commander-in-Chief and its replacement at the top of the organizational pyramid by an Army Council of service and civilian members, not unlike the arrangements at the Admiralty. The report of the Esher Committee was presented in 1904 and this recommendation was immediately accepted. Lord Roberts, the last Commander-in-Chief, was retired and the first Army Council was appointed.[19]

The second recommendation of the Committee which we must notice was equally far-sighted and every bit as necessary: it called for the creation of a General Staff along the lines of those possessed by the other Great Powers. The suggestion was also accepted by the Balfour Government, but was not implemented before that Cabinet fell from power. The concept was not lost, however, but was left to the Liberal Government which took power in 1905 and to the great talents of its War Minister, R. B. Haldane. In time, then, an Imperial General Staff was created.

The Esher Committee dealt also in its investigations with the administrative machinery which governed the supply of warlike stores to the Army and they were not pleased with what they discovered. This significant function had, from the fifteenth century, rested with a Board of Ordnance and the ministerial office of Master General of the Ordnance. In 1855, as a result of another unhappy wartime experience and another period of much-needed military reform, both the Board and the Master General's office were swept away and complete responsibility in the matter of provision of munitions devolved directly upon the Secretary of State for War.[20] The Esher Report advised that this consolidation enacted after the Crimean War had outlived its purpose. The task of equipping a twentieth century army required, they suggested, an officer of executive ability and technical expertise to devote his full attention to the problem of munitions supply. Acting upon this recommendation, the Government re-created the office dissolved fifty years before (including its rather archaic title) and created an Ordnance Board of munitions experts chosen from both services to advise him. The new Master General, of course, was not to enjoy ministerial rank, yet it was understood that the Army Council and the Secretary of State for War were to delegate to him full charge of munitions supply authority.

While these reforms were real improvements, they were not sufficient to see Britain through a war of the scale of the 1914–1918 conflict. No provision had been made to supply a large army. Moreover, any campaign in which the British Army might take part was presumed to be like that of the 1899–1901 War. Furthermore, the Russo-Japanese War, which should have contained lessons for British military thinkers, brought about no substantive changes in munitions supply procedures at the War Office— neither did the adoption, thereafter, of a new pattern of quick-firing artillery which employed more ammunition than previous guns.

The reason [Sir Llewellyn Woodward wrote] was, as usual, lack of money, but the General Staff do not seem to have pressed strongly for larger reserves and wider sources of supply. If they thought of a Continental war, they invisaged it as lasting only for a short time.[21]

While all the military minds which turned to war in August 1914, with a few exceptions, expected a short conflict, those in Paris and Berlin had made preparations for munitions supply which could be expanded to meet the contingencies of a long one. The Esher Report was based upon conditions at the turn of the century, and the fault in British military preparedness lay with the men who did not further develop those recommendations and alter and expand them to keep pace with the events of that important decade. To be sure they were, after 1905, faced with a political climate in which military expenditure was a highly controversial issue. For several years, however, they had a Secretary of State of proven genius. Had they pressed upon him the need for better organization of munitions supply, perhaps the task of 1914 and 1915 might not have been so great. Indeed, once the holocaust was upon them, these same men, charged with supplying armaments to hundreds of thousands of troops in France and holding *carte blanche* authority to purchase or make warlike stores, were unable to see the futility of their methods. Their failure was so great that only a total recasting of the organization for munitions supply could hope to meet the requirements of the hour.

There were two principal sources of munitions for the Army and Navy, as there had been for many decades. One of these was the complex of state-owned works called the Royal Ordnance Factories.[22] They consisted of the small arms factory at Enfield, which made rifles, pistols and sidearms; the gunpowder factory at Waltham Abbey, which manufactured explosives; as well as the newest of these armament works, the Royal Aircraft Factory at Farnborough. This last-named, given the nature of its product, had been in operation only about a decade when the War broke out. It was, in fact, more of a laboratory than a factory. Designs were laid down and experiments carried on at Farnborough; the actual manufacture of aircraft, however, was largely carried on by contractors.

The most important source of munitions among the publicly-owned workshops was the Royal Arsenal at Woolwich, which was, in fact, not one but many workshops grouped together in the ancient riverside borough. Woolwich had had a Naval Dockyard from Tudor times until the advent of the ironclad closed it in 1869. A gun-carriage shop had been opened there in 1683, but the Royal Arsenal dated only from 1805. It was, in 1914, an enormous, conglomeration of buildings and workshops and was equipped to manufacture almost all types of heavy armaments: guns and mountings, gun-carriages and heavy shells, as well as virtually any other form of armament not obtainable from the other factories or limited, by patent, to private manufacture. It was, at the time of the outbreak of the Great War, almost the sole facility for shell-filling (the addition of explosive and propellant charges to artillery shells) in the nation. In addition, it was the major producer of most armaments for the Army.

The other principal source of munitions to the Forces in Great Britain consisted of the private armaments manufacturers. These firms, sometimes called the War Office List companies, Vickers Armstrong, Cammell Laird, the Coventry Ordnance Works and Beardmore, among others, had long been in the armaments trade and were felt by the Ordnance Department of the War Office to be sufficiently expert to satisfy Army standards.[23] While the War

Office List firms produced only about 20 per cent each of guns and shells for the Army in the years before the First World War, they were considered by the War Office to be the only alternative to the Royal Arsenals for the provision of warlike stores should the State factories become overburdened.

The procedure for the supply of munitions to the Army, after the resurrection of the office of Master General of the Ordnance, worked in the following fashion. Once the officers of units of the Army had determined their needs, these were passed along through the ascending chain of command to the War Office. The Secretary of State, the official recipient of these demands, would pass them along to the Ordnance Department and its Master General, who would authorize the supply of stores from reserves or arrange for their manufacture within the Royal Arsenals to patterns approved by the experts of the Ordnance Board. If further *matériel* was required, the Director of Army Contracts was charged with obtaining quotations from the War Office List firms. His recommendations were then made to the Secretary of State and the Army Council. 'After due discussion,' one critic of this system wryly commented, 'a contract would eventually be placed.'[24]

This rather cumbersome procedure worked quite well in peacetime and would have functioned adequately in the colonial wars which were Britain's only military ventures after the middle of the nineteenth century. The World War, however, proved to be more than the system could bear. Yet none of the men to whom the vast wartime decisions fell, neither statesmen nor soldiers, saw it in August 1914.

Perhaps the problem of the Ordnance Department, in its inability to overcome the munitions shortage which appeared in the autumn of 1914, began with its outlook. Its chief, Major-General Sir Stanley von Donop, and his colleagues and subordinates never surrendered the view that only professional soldiers were qualified to express opinion on a matter so technical as the supply of munitions to the Army. The World War, however, was a conflict of unprecedented scale; it was a war of nations, a war of peoples, not a contest to be rapidly decided by armies which could afford such a limited over-professional attitude.

The ordnance specialists never came to understand this matter of scope, of the great size of the war they were called upon to fight. Their failure to deal with the problems thrust upon them proved all but fatal to the Army which they had served for their entire adult lives. The Master General was, beyond doubt, well qualified to comment on the purely technical questions involving munitions design and quality. Yet he and his department did not understand the kind of war they faced.

The extent of their failure was not limited to their refusal to supplement the established armaments makers with the many willing and talented engineering firms who sought to aid in the manufacture of munitions components. Nor was it confined to their unwillingness to share their problems with the Cabinet or its committees created to aid them. The great shortcoming of the men who commanded the Ordnance Department was not simply that they could not produce sufficient numbers of shells and guns; rather, their chief weakness was a failure of imagination, an inability to conceive of the problem which faced them, outside the narrow framework of tradition and precedent to which they bound themselves. Sir George Riddell, the newspaper–proprietor who observed all and learned much, confided to his diary when the War was but a month old:

Von Donop and the others who are at the head of Ordnance know all about guns, but have no wide view of a situation.[25]

In the Great War, knowing 'all about guns' was simply not enough. Men with the 'wide view', as Riddell called it, with the vision and force to carry this important task to a successful conclusion could not be found on the highest levels of the War Office or the Ordnance Department.

Two

THE WAR IN WHITEHALL

I

Field Marshal Lord Kitchener was not long at his new post before he discovered the unprecedented need for munitions at the Front. His desk was crossed almost daily by requests from G.H.Q. in France for greater and greater quantities of the tools of modern warfare. He wrote to Field Marshal Sir John French, the Commander-in-Chief of the British Expeditionary Force, as early as 31 October 1914:

> The supply of ammunition gives me great anxiety . . . Do not think we are keeping munitions back. All we can gather is being sent, but at present rate of expenditure we are certain before long to run short, and then to produce more than a small daily allowance per gun will be impossible. I hope to increase the ammunition being sent today.[1]

Later that same day he wrote again to the Field Marshal suggesting that he encourage the French Commander, General Joffre, to bring up more guns and shells as a measure to increase the effectiveness of Allied attacks. Despite the terrible tolls of dead and injured which the earliest battles of the War wrought on the B.E.F., the success of the recruiting campaign in Britain had already eliminated concern at the War Office for any possible shortage of manpower in the trenches. The same confidence did not exist in regard to the provision of munitions; Kitchener enquired of his Commander in this second letter: 'Are more men, *or anything I can send* required by you?'[2]

In order to regulate what was felt to be excessive expenditure of shells—Kitchener always dreaded the spectre of 'waste'—and to stave off the terrible possibility of the B.E.F. running out of ammunition, the War Office implemented a policy of rationing the number of shells fired by the British artillery. Kitchener's most recent biographer has written:

> The allowance, for example, of 18-pounder ammunition was reduced from twenty to ten, and, on the second Army's front after the Battle of Ypres, to two rounds per gun per day. The ration of 4.5 [inch] howitzer ammunition sank at one time to two rounds per gun per day along the entire front, and the ration of 6-inch howitzers was sometimes as low as six rounds.[3]

Yet, so far as the Government was concerned, the Secretary of State for War carried out his monumental struggle in silence. He neither volunteered this information to his colleagues on the War Council[4] or in meetings of the Cabinet, nor was he candid when questioned about it.[5] He laboured, along with the Master General of the Ordnance, to overcome the munitions problem. But it was, for him, exclusively a War Office matter. The politicians who came to suspect it and, later, to know of it, found little welcome for their interest among these high-ranking officers.[6]

II

A number of politicians became interested in rumours about shortages in munitions which had begun to circulate in Whitehall; Lloyd George made it his cause. He was fifty-two years old when the War began and could look back upon a career which was a model in its time for younger politicians of radical leanings. Though he had entered Parliament a quarter of a century earlier with neither a great name, nor a secure fortune, nor powerful friends, he rose rapidly within his party.[7] While in Opposition, he became known as a tireless critic of the wealthy and landed classes. He cast himself in the role of champion of his beloved Wales and of all the poor and powerless. Once in office, after December 1905, he further distinguished himself. Though his official position as seen by the leader of his party might not have been so sure, he was clearly recognized in the public eye as the chief lieutenant of the Prime Minister by the beginning of the second decade of the twentieth century.[8] His Insurance Act, his bold 'Radical Budget' and attack on the House of Lords, his land campaign, had secured his place as a Liberal champion and a scourge of the Opposition.

Because of the years of his controversial 'Pro-Boer' campaign, when he supported the cause of the Dutch-speaking republics against what was, to him, British aggression, Lloyd George was still considered by many to be the most important radical pacifist in Great Britain. Yet, in 1914, he was to emerge as one of the greatest wartime leaders in Britain. This contradiction was more apparent than real. He opposed the Boer War because he felt it was capricious, stupid, unjust, and a gross misappropriation of public funds which could otherwise have paid for social reforms.[9]

In August 1914 he was again faced with the decision to support or oppose a war. This conflict, however, was different: Britain's entry into the affair was motivated by reasons less base than those of 1899, he felt. Britain also would find herself on the side of the underdog, for Belgium was cast, this time, in the role once played by the Boer Republics. The tremendous sense of outrage expressed by the British people at this invasion, as well as his desire to avoid repeating the difficult path he followed more than a dozen years before, helped to persuade him to join the war party. In addition, the Chancellor of the Exchequer in 1914 saw that his future— whatever political future he might have—lay with supporting the War. These reasons swept away all doubt and he went to war with a fervour which, within a few months, rivalled that of any Tory half-pay colonel.[10]

Also of importance in the conversion of the great radical into the man of war was the very nature of the office he held. The Exchequer was, most certainly, of tremendous importance in times of war, as it was in more normal circumstances. He had, within a month of Britain's entry into the War, spoken of the importance of finance in winning a modern conflict.[11] Yet the formulation of war budgets and attempts to press monetary aid upon unwilling generals were not enough to satisfy Lloyd George. He began to crave action soon after the War began and he found a ready and fertile field in the sphere of munitions supply. Before the turn of the year 1914 'Lloyd George's restless, inventive mind,' Peter Lowe has written, 'was looking beyond the tasks of the Treasury . . . and towards . . . the mobilization of resources to wage [the War] effectively.'[12]

Lloyd George did not stray from the familiar paths of the Treasury in his first attempts to increase the production of munitions. In an effort to increase the productive capacity of the established armaments makers, the 'trade' as they were known to the War Office, on 30 September 1914 the Chancellor placed at the disposal of the Master General of the Ordnance the sum of £20 million. He discovered, however, that helping the unwilling Major-General von Donop was no easy task: fearing a great onrush of supplicants for the funds which the Treasury offered, the Master General chose not to inform the armaments firms of their availability.[13] Undeterred, Lloyd George went on to give the Ordnance Department virtual *carte blanche* approval for the purchase of the needed stores. He struck down the ancient practice of Treasury approval of military expenditure at one blow, and the result was still failure. Before the autumn of 1914 was past, rumours of munitions shortages were circulating in Whitehall.

Sir George Riddell noted in his diary on 13 October 1914:

> Von Donop and the others seemed surprised that they could have any money they required. L. G. said to them: 'What are ten, twenty, or thirty millions when the British Empire is at stake? This is artillery war. We must have every gun we can lay our hands upon. We are sadly deficient in guns now. You have never asked me for more money.'[14]

This offer to approve virtually any purchase by the Ordnance Department of the War Office continued so long as Lloyd George remained at the Treasury, and still the guns and shells did not appear.

III

In September 1914, when Field Marshal French's 18-pounder field guns, the very backbone of British field artillery at that time, were firing at an average rate of fourteen rounds per gun per day and receiving but seven rounds per gun daily from Great Britain,[15] Lloyd George requested that a Cabinet committee be appointed to look into the 'guns, shells and rifles question'. The suggestion, however, was met with hostility by Lord Kitchener, to whom such committees were a waste of time and energy. In addition, he resented the attempts by the politicians 'to encroach upon what he considered to be the military domain'.[16] The great prestige of the Field Marshal doomed the plan; there was no Cabinet committee created in September 1914.

The Chancellor was undeterred, however, and by 12 October he got his way. The chairmanship of the so-called 'Shells Committee' was thrust upon Kitchener by the Prime Minister. Serving with him were Lloyd George; Winston Churchill, the First Lord of the Admiralty; Walter Runciman, the President of the Board of Trade; Reginald McKenna, the Home Secretary; Lord Lucas, the President of the Board of Agriculture; and Lord Haldane, the Lord Chancellor. 'The War in Whitehall,' Frank Owen has written, 'was about to begin.'[17]

The Shells Committee, despite the hostility to its existence of its own chairman, immediately set to work to examine the supply of armaments. Despite the title which it came to bear, the group's greatest work was not in the field of shell supply, but rather in their work to increase the amount of artillery with French's armies. Although Lord Kitchener was already planning to put seventy divisions in the field, they discovered that Major-General von Donop had ordered only 900 18-pounder field guns, enough for twenty-four divisions, for delivery by 15 June 1915. The Committee, pressed by Lloyd George, increased the order by 2,100 guns and shortened the contract delivery period by one month. Meeting with the representatives of the four largest armaments firms in Britain, the Committee secured the agreement of these manufacturers to increase their facilities in order to meet these large orders promptly. The State, it was agreed, would underwrite the costs of this expansion.[18]

The Shells Committee was also able, to a degree, to breach the Ordnance Department's prejudice against the incursion into the manufacture of munitions of firms who were not on the War

Office List. In order to hasten delivery of these large new contracts, the Committee set up an Armaments Firms Committee of representatives of the Government and the War Office List companies to distribute contracts for munitions components among other engineering shops. By May 1915 and the creation of the Ministry, more than 2,500 such firms were involved in some facet of arms manufacture.

The Shells Committee, in the end, satisfied neither the attackers nor the defenders of War Office administration of munitions supply. To Lord Kitchener it was an annoyance, and he finally succeeded in bringing its 'interference' to an end by announcing that he could no longer find time to attend its meetings. While, in the first weeks after its creation, Lloyd George was pleased with the work of the panel, his satisfaction did not last long.[19] Before the end of the year, the Chancellor was again seriously concerned about the provision of armaments to the Forces.

The Shells Committee served two important purposes, however. In the first place it staved off a Cabinet crisis precipitated by the disagreement between Kitchener and Lloyd George. In the second place, those who suspected the maladministration of the Ordnance Department came to be armed with valuable experience and evidence during the three months in which the Committee existed. The Chancellor, and those in whom he confided, came to understand the weaknesses in the methods of the Master General's Department and they moved closer to the conclusion that only greater organization of the industrial capacity of the entire nation would overcome the Army's appetite for munitions.[20]

By early 1915 the Secretary of State for War was free of the bothersome meetings of the Shells Committee; Major-General von Donop was left in charge of the orders which had been placed, and no further official action was taken by the Government until March. By then, the lessons learned by the Chancellor of the Exchequer prompted him again to raise the munitions question.

IV

The next phase of the 'War in Whitehall' opened in February 1915. On the 22nd, Lloyd George laid before his Cabinet colleagues a memorandum concerning the supply of warlike stores. With his newly gained experience in munitions supply matters fresh in his mind, he analysed first the capacity of the enemy for the manufacture of armaments. The Central Powers had begun the War with a vast advantage in military establishment. He suggested further 'that they have undoubtedly made better use of their manufacturing resources for the purpose of increasing their output. Germany is the best organized country in the world and her organization has told.'[21] The Chancellor saw certain advantages which fell to the Allies, however:

> The manufacturing resources at the disposal of the Allies are enormously greater than those which Germany and Austria can command . . . and the seas being free to them can more easily obtain material. I do not believe Great Britain has even yet done anything like what she can do in the matter if [sic] increasing her war equipment. . . . All the engineering works of the country ought to be turned to the production of war material. The population ought to be prepared to suffer all sorts of deprivations and even hardships whilst this process is going on.

The memorandum pointed out that the steps necessary to overcome the no longer deniable munitions deficits constituted a gamble which the politicians had to take:

> If it turns out that my estimate errs on the side of pessimism the worst that happens will be that we shall spend a considerable amount of money, we shall have caused a considerable amount of inconvenience to the population. But all that is nothing compared with the disaster of having to face another year of war with inadequate preparation. This the public will never forgive after the warning we have received nor ought they to be expected to forgive.

This memorandum was nothing less than a declaration of war on the 'quartermaster mind' at the War Office—that inflexible routine-mindedness of Major-General Sir Stanley von Donop and the Ordnance Department—and, even more important, on the wartime viability of Liberalism itself. The old tenets of *laissez-*

faire and individualism, the politics of Gladstone and, perhaps, even Asquith himself, simply would not serve to guide Britain through the crisis of twentieth-century war. Only central organization of the nation's industrial and manpower resources, only a firm commitment to state control of the productive capacity of Great Britain would supply the needed tools of war. The greatest radical in the nation had come down firmly on the side of the proponents of what one historian has called National Efficiency,[22] and he meant to have his way.

Among those who felt as the Chancellor did was the former Prime Minister and erstwhile leader of the Conservative and Unionist Party, A. J. Balfour. Within a fortnight of reading the memorandum of 22 February, he wrote to Lloyd George encouraging him in his efforts at organization for war production:

> The position seems to me to be most unsatisfactory, and unless you will take in hand the organisation of the engineering resources of the country in the interests of military equipment, I do not see how any improvement is to be expected.[23]

The pre-War political battles in which these two figures had been opponents were put aside. They now pulled together in another great struggle. Lloyd George replied to his friend later the following day, 6 March 1915, and described a remarkable meeting held the previous day at Number 10 Downing Street. With the Prime Minister, the Chancellor and the Secretary of State for War, were Lord Crewe; Major-General Sir Stanley von Donop; the industrialist, Sir George Gibb; and the principal labour negotiator of the Board of Trade, Sir George Askwith. Acting as secretary was Lieutenant-Colonel Maurice Hankey, the Secretary of the Committee of Imperial Defence.[24] The major topic of discussion was the munitions question, and the decision of the meeting—at any rate, the decision as Lloyd George interpreted it—is worthy of our closest attention. Lloyd George wrote to Balfour:

> An executive committee is to be set up for the purpose not merely of supervising existing work but for organizing our engineering reserves for the purpose of increasing the output [of munitions]. Kitchener absolutely refuses to hand over the whole

output of munitions of war for Admiralty and War Office alike to the Executive. . . . He clearly means to retain complete control over this executive himself, and I fear he is on the look-out for a tame chairman who will carry out the directions of the War Office instead of acting on his own initiative. . . . Nothing can remedy this state of things except the placing at the head of the new Executive of an energetic fearless man who will not be cajoled and bamboozled by Von Donop nor bullied by anyone else.[25]

But in early March, after this meeting was held, Lloyd George's confidence that substantive action was to be taken in reshaping the nation's capacity for war production was premature. There was no such 'Executive' created for several months. The tension between the Chancellor and the War Lord increased in these weeks to the point that Asquith, fearing a break between the two ministers, broached the possibility of a compromise. He had in mind the creation of a Directorate of Army Contracts, with Lloyd George in charge. The possibility intrigued Edwin Montagu, who was coming to share Lloyd George's views, to the extent that he actually prepared a scheme for the operation of the proposed office.[26]

The Contracts Department, however, was stillborn. Lloyd George was unwilling to give up his Cabinet post unless the War Office surrendered to the proposed Director of Contracts sufficient powers actually to control munitions supply. Lord Kitchener would not hear of such an arrangement and the Contracts Department was never heard of again.[27]

Frances Stevenson revealed to her diary her feeling that perhaps the rigidity of Kitchener and the mooted compromises of Asquith had pushed Lloyd George too far: 'I fear,' she wrote on 26 March 1915, 'he is going to wash his hands of the whole business.'[28] While the anger of the Chancellor of the Exchequer was considerable, in the end he did not abandon his concern for armaments production. Before the end of March 1915 these matters underwent further changes.

The supreme faith which the politicians had once had in Lord Kitchener was gone by March 1915. His prestige among the people, however, was largely unimpaired, and he was still able to fend off direct attacks such as these on his prerogatives as War Minister. While Lloyd George has been among the first to notice the growing munitions problem and some of its causes, by this time he was not the only politician to be aware of it. The Prime Minister, of course, had shown concern in this sphere. Andrew Bonar Law, since 1911 the leader of the Conservative Party, was conscious of the growth of such suspicions among the backbenchers of his own party. Kitchener was coming to discover in these weeks that he would have to act to prevent the loss of his control over the provision of munitions to the Army.

V

At the meeting at 10 Downing Street on 5 March, the Master General of the Ordnance gave his explanation of why munitions deliveries had fallen far behind contract delivery dates, subsequently leaving the British Army in France ill-armed for battle. The reason was that there was a great shortage of skilled labour. As Lord Kitchener was himself to explain several months later, had there been an abundance of such labour, the orders placed by the Ordnance Department with the Royal Arsenals and the War Office List firms would have provided for all the needs of the B.E.F.[29]

Now the problem of labour supply was a very real one, which, as we shall see in another chapter, was exacerbated by War Office policies laid down early in the War. Kitchener now seized upon the labour shortage as the issue which would prove he could clean his own house without the aid of the proponents of Control— politicians such as Lloyd George, Balfour and Montagu. He turned for advice and aid in overcoming this matter of labour supply to George Macaulay Booth, the shipowner, industrialist and son of the pioneer social scientist, Charles Booth. Since the outset of the War, Booth had acted as unofficial adviser to the Secretary of State for War on matters of supply. After 20 March 1915 Kitchener called upon him to direct all of his energies toward overcoming the shortage of labour in the armaments factories.

The Secretary of State appointed on 31 March, and officially announced on 7 April, the War Office Armaments Output Committee, which was to be the vehicle through which Booth was to accomplish his task. The already overburdened Kitchener was the titular chairman of the Committee and it did not want for other important members, but the actual work of the body was left to Booth.[30]

George Macaulay Booth had seen even before the constitution of the Committee that the problem of munitions supply went far beyond the shortages of skilled labour. Likewise, he understood that the shortage of armaments would never be overcome so long as the Ordnance Department relied largely on the established munitions manufacturers for the production of weapons.[31] Despite being poorly armed himself, with an inadequate staff and insufficient authority, Booth set to work almost singlehanded to reshape the supply function of the War Office. He had not long to wait, however, for powerful help in his important work.

The Prime Minister, at this same time, had found what he felt to be an acceptable answer to the pressures placed upon him by the Chancellor's demands for a hand in the supply of munitions. A meeting, attended by Asquith, Balfour, Churchill, Montagu, and of course, Lloyd George was held on 22 March 1915. 'The discussion was quite a good one,' Asquith wrote to a friend, 'and we came to some rational conclusions.'[32] The following day he wrote to Lord Kitchener that, as a result of his talks with his colleagues and especially Lloyd George, a new Cabinet committee was to be created to 'mobilize' potential as well as existing sources of armaments supply. The new committee was to have the right to place contracts on its own authority and was, of course, unlike Booth's committee, to derive its powers from the Cabinet rather than the War Office.[33]

This proposition was nothing less than a direct assault on the War Office prerogative to provide munitions in its own way and the Secretary of State perceived it in just this fashion. It was a counterblast to Kitchener's Armaments Output Committee and he wrote in answer to the Prime Minister demonstrating his displeasure: he wanted no interference with what were clearly War Office procedures.[34]

Lloyd George, in his own reply to Kitchener's objections, made it abundantly clear where he, and those who agreed with him, stood: no one, he said, sought such a huge task, and the politicians would accept it only in hope of aiding the already overworked Kitchener. 'But unless the Committee really succeeds in co-ordinating and pressing forward the work which has already been done, then it had better not be appointed. We would simply have a great deal of responsibility, no end of work and absolutely no power to be of the slightest use to you or anyone else.'[35]

Asquith wrote on 28 March 1915:

There is a truly royal row on the stocks between Kitchener and Lloyd George in regard to the proposed Committee on Munitions. Neither is disposed to give way. K. threatens to give up his office and L. G. to wash his hands of the whole business, leaving on record all sorts of solemn protests and warnings.[36]

Asquith met the antagonists on 6 April and he announced his final decision the next day.

He wrote to Kitchener on the 8th that he had appointed a committee to be made up of Lloyd George, who was to be chairman; Balfour; Montagu, the Chancellor of the Duchy of Lancaster; Arthur Henderson of the Labour Party; Major-General von Donop and George Macaulay Booth, representing the War Office; Sir Frederick Black, the secretary, and another unnamed representative of the Admiralty, 'to ensure the promptest and most efficient application of all the available resources of the country to the manufacture and supply of Munitions of War for the Army and Navy. It has,' he added, 'full authority to take all steps necessary for that purpose.'[37]

Lloyd George was delighted and wrote to Balfour that Asquith 'has appointed our Committee not merely to look into the question of organizing the resources of the country for war munitions, but with full authority to take any action they think necessary.'[38] At last, he felt, he would be free of the deadening influence of the Ordnance Department and its Master General over his attempts to organize the nation for war production. His satisfaction, as it had been on 5 March, was premature.

The Treasury Committee, as the Lloyd George group was popularly known, was not a success. It did not receive the coopera-tion of the War Office, as its chairman had hoped, in its attempts to supply armaments to the British Army. Its efforts were met only with the obstinate refusal of the Secretary of State for War to delegate any authority to the civilian body. Kitchener maintained that he could not share with the Committee the military secrets which he possessed and, hence, the short life of the Treasury Committee was characterized by frustration for its members and tension within its parent body, the Cabinet.

An example of the secrecy and obstructiveness of the War Office which so irritated the members of the Committee and helped to bring on the munitions shortage in the first place, may be found in the memoirs of Sir William Beveridge, who had been co-opted to the Committee early in its lifespan. Lloyd George had requested certain statistical returns on munitions production— figures the War Office had failed to volunteer to the group which had Cabinet authority to increase munitions production. Beveridge recalled speaking with the Master General of the Ordnance as they withdrew from the meeting:

> 'I'll get him the figures,' said von Donop, 'but they will delay production of shells for two days. The statistics are absolutely secret, known only to me. I'll have to spend two days with a slide-rule on them myself, instead of getting on with my job.' This was the organization [wrote Beveridge] with which we faced Germany at the outset of World War I.[39]

Lloyd George came quickly to the conclusion that no Cabinet Committee, no matter how broad its charge, could ever overcome the munitions shortage. George Macaulay Booth, though he never lost his admiration for Lord Kitchener, soon agreed. Within two months of the creation of the Treasury Committee, Lloyd George would finally get his 'Executive', the Ministry of Munitions. It would take nothing less than the wholesale reconstruction of the Government and a break with the traditional tenets of Liberalism. It would contribute, though none saw it in 1915, to the break-up of the Liberal Party itself. To better understand this important step it is necessary, however briefly, to stand aside from the question of munitions supply and to examine the sphere of party politics in the spring of 1915.

Three

THE MAY CRISIS

I

Before the close of the first month of the War, representatives of the Liberal, Conservative and Unionist, and Labour Parties met and agreed to a truce. The political battles which had raged for the previous decade were, it was implied, to be set aside until Britain had triumphed on the battlefield. While in fact the agreement only committed each party to avoid fighting by-elections, it was meant to do much more. The truce was a declaration of the cessation of 'Politics as Usual' until the end of the War.[1] By the late winter and early spring of 1915, however, though the truce remained in effect, certain members of the Opposition had come to see both the agreement and the Asquith Government as liabilities in the War effort.

The reasons for this growing factiousness were many: the controversy which raged between proponents and opponents of military conscription, the squabbles over strategy and tactics, the debates over the Dardanelles venture and the old partisan animosities which refused to disappear all did little to promote harmony between Government supporters and the newly-muzzled Opposition. Perhaps the paramount reason, however, why many Tories, and certain Liberals as well, grew restless under the leadership of Asquith was their lack of confidence that traditional Liberal methods could ever win such an untraditional war. These men were proponents of greater State control over the nation's material and human resources in the interest of victory.

Among the most zealous of Asquith's opponents were the members of the Unionist Business Committee, a Tory 'ginger group' surrounding the economist-politician, W. A. S. Hewins. Incensed with what they felt to be the Government's clear failure to supply the necessary munitions to guarantee victory on the Western Front, these men, in early May 1915 prepared a motion of censure against the Government. Only the authority of the Tory Leader, Bonar Law, crushed their rebellion against the Government and preserved the truce among parties.[2]

On 12 May 1915, one day before this abortive insurrection, the Liberal member for Pontefract, Frederick Handel Booth, asked the Prime Minister at Question Time whether, in light of the great challenge before the nation, 'he will consider the desirability of admitting into the ranks of Ministers leading Members of the various parties in this House?'[3] Asquith assured him that it was not at all in contemplation at that time.

Asquith answered Handel Booth's question truthfully. Within a week's time, however, the attitudes expressed by the two party leaders in these two episodes in May of 1915 changed drastically. Two events intervened to alter their judgement and the entire future of British politics: the public exposure of the munitions shortage and the resignation of Admiral of the Fleet Lord Fisher, the First Sea Lord.

II

The relationship between Fisher and his political chief, Winston Churchill, had become strained over the latter's enthusiastic support of the Dardanelles campaign. The resolution of the War Council on 14 May to strengthen the naval detachment in that zone convinced the First Sea Lord that Churchill planned to rush the Turkish fortifications—in short, to do the Army's work at the expense of dangerously weakening the Grand Fleet. On the following day, Britain's greatest living sailor resigned. He wrote to Churchill on the 16th:

YOU ARE BENT ON FORCING THE DARDANELLES AND NOTHING WILL TURN YOU FROM IT—NOTHING—I know you so well! I could give you no better proof of my desire to stand by you than

my having remained by you in this Dardanelles business up to
the last moment against the strongest conviction of my life. . . .[4]

The irate retirement of the old admiral was received by the Tory
Party with anger and frustration, and the desire for revolt which
had been stifled on 13 May was sure to flare up again with a new
strength when the news became known. Alfred M. Gollin has
written:

> In the first place, the admiral was the darling of the Tories in
> the House and in the country. They relied upon him to preserve
> the Navy and all that depended upon it in time of War. At the
> same time the Tories disliked Churchill.[5]

Churchill, who had not only abandoned the party of his heritage
but had risen to power and influence among the Liberals, was an
apostate to loyal Conservatives. The vision of him at the Admiralty
without the restraining influence of the greatest naval mind since
Nelson, was more than they could bear. If such a Tory nightmare
were allowed to materialize, it would have precipitated a back-
bench revolt against the truce of parties which even their Leader,
had he so desired, could not have stayed. Not only did Bonar Law
share the opinion of his party colleagues of the two naval per-
sonages, but he was also charged with the task of maintaining a
unified party. The possibility was real that his tenure at the head
of his party might not have survived another attempt to quieten a
Conservative uprising against the political armistice—either
Churchill must go, he decided, or the truce of parties was doomed.[6]
Early on the morning of 17 May 1915 Bonar Law called upon
his erstwhile enemy of Tariff Reform and Home Rule days, Lloyd
George. Despite their partisan battles, the two enjoyed, as Lloyd
George recorded in his *War Memoirs,* 'terms of greater cordiality . . .
than is usual between political adversaries who are taking a
strenuous part in party conflicts. . . .'[7] When the news of Fisher's
resignation was confirmed, the Tory leader expressed in the gravest
possible terms that his party would never accept continuation of
the truce so long as Churchill remained at the Admiralty. Bonar
Law also cited the discontent among many Tory Members at the
rumours of a munitions shortage and at the disappointing results

of the Dardanelles campaign. The Chancellor of the Exchequer and the Leader of the Opposition came to the conclusion that only one solution could stave off a brutal and divisive party battle: a coalition Government. Lloyd George left Bonar Law and went next door to 10 Downing Street to present the situation to the Prime Minister. Asquith immediately agreed to the reasoning of his colleague.

Lloyd George, Asquith and Bonar Law then met briefly in the Cabinet Room at Number 10, where, after a quarter-hour conversation on that Monday morning, the last Liberal Government in British history was doomed.

The resignation of Lord Fisher was, to be sure, the major cause of the political crisis of May 1915. Since the publication of Lord Beaverbrook's *Politicians and the War* in 1928, this interpretation has forced aside all others.[8] However, it would be a mistake to ignore totally the role played in this episode by the so-called 'Shells Scandal'—the revelation in the newspaper press of the shortage of armaments of the British Army on the Western Front. It too, had a part in the political drama which brought to life both the Coalition Ministry and the Ministry of Munitions.

The efforts of the War Office, despite the aid of Lloyd George's Shells Committee, toward increasing the output of munitions had not been adequate in the eyes of Field Marshal Sir John French. After the Battle of Neuve Chapelle in early March 1915, the Commander-in-Chief decided to begin a different sort of campaign to force the politicians to meet his demands for *materiel*. Sir John was also angered by the Dardanelles venture. The Commander-in-Chief of the B.E.F. was, of course, a committed 'Westerner' in that he felt the attempt to breach the enemy's flank at the Straits was an enormous waste of men and equipment desperately needed on the Western Front.[9] He became convinced that Kitchener neither understood nor appreciated his plight; he was equally sure that the Prime Minister, Herbert Henry Asquith, would never overrule his War Minister and give the munitions supply question the attention it deserved. Asquith's great speech at Newcastle on 20 April 1915, in which he declared that the munitions supply at Neuve Chapelle was sufficient—and cited Lord Kitchener, who, in turn, strangely enough, was citing

French as his source of this assurance—was what finally moved the Commander-in-Chief to act.[10]

Field Marshal Sir John French turned to political intrigue and he hoped to employ the newspaper press literally to force the politicians to heed his wishes. In this connection he gained a powerful ally in 'the greatest figure who ever strode down Fleet Street', Lord Northcliffe. The great Press Lord wrote to Sir John on 1 May 1915:

> A short and very vigorous statement from you to a private correspondent (the usual way of making things public in England) would, I believe, render the Government's position impossible, and enable you to secure the publication of that which would tell the people here the truth. . . .[11]

Sir John French turned, however, not merely to a 'private correspondent', but to the Military Correspondent of Northcliffe's *Times,* Lieutenant-Colonel Charles à Court Repington. Repington had once served on Kitchener's staff at Omdurman. He had left the Army in 1902 after involvement in a divorce case and went on to a second career as a military journalist. Those affairs of thirteen years earlier had not endangered the Colonel's friendship with Sir John. Repington had, in fact, visited his headquarters on several occasions, although, officially, newspaper correspondents were barred from the Front.

On 12 May 1915, after the British failure at the Battle of Festubert, Repington dispatched a telegram to his editor, the former Milner 'Kindergartener', Geoffrey Dawson. It was published on the 14th, and left no doubt as to the author's interpretation of the outcome of the engagement: 'The want of an unlimited supply of high explosive,' he wrote, 'was a fatal bar to our success.'[12] His later denial of collusion with the Commander-in-Chief is made more suspect by the curious superscription borne by the despatch: 'This letter is marked "passed by censor", but he will not have seen it.'[13] Thus was born the 'Shells Scandal' campaign of the Northcliffe press—a series of articles attacking the Government, and particularly the Secretary of State for War, for their inaction in overcoming the obvious shortage of munitions at the Front.

Sir John French supplemented these activities with a second plan. He sent his secretary, Colonel Brinsley FitzGerald, and his A.D.C., Captain Frederick Guest, to London. Their task was to lay before Balfour, Bonar Law and Lloyd George a memorandum which contained the figures of French's demands for high explosive shells, and the actual figures of deliveries received from Britain by the B.E.F. They accomplished this between 12 and 14 May.[14] The newspaper accusations came as no surprise to these statesmen; neither did the general tone of French's secret memorandum. The actual facts, however, were unknown to any of these men until this time.

What role did the munitions shortage play in the reconstruction of the Government? In the first place, we must realise that neither the need of the British Army for more plentiful supplies of armaments, nor the revelations by the Northcliffe Press that this was so, brought about the end of the Asquith Liberal Government. Bonar Law was inspired to call on Lloyd George on the morning of 17 May 1915 by the Fisher resignation crisis; Lloyd George was moved to recommend the idea of a multi-party Government to his chief because of Bonar Law's revelation of Tory anger over the Fisher affair and because he saw it as an opportunity to bring to life his munitions 'Executive'. The Coalition was born in the visit the Tory Leader and the Liberal Chancellor paid to the Prime Minister on that Monday morning in May 1915. The decision for the reconstruction of the Cabinet was made among these statesmen before the 'Shells Scandal' campaign began in earnest.

Asquith had his own reasons for agreeing so readily to the Coalition scheme. It held the very real potential for solving several of his problems; it was also the path of least resistance for him in a time of trial, both political and personal. A Coalition Cabinet, dominated by himself, would more effectively muzzle the more factious Tories than had the party truce. It would preserve, perhaps until the War was over, national unity and quieten criticism in the House and in the press.[15]

Coalition also held a charm for Asquith in that it would prevent the crisis then raging over the Fisher–Churchill battle, the munitions shortage and the Dardanelles affair, from toppling his

Government. Though no direct evidence exists to support the contention, it is likely that Coalition would allow the replacement of the no-longer-infallible Lord Kitchener.

There is another side to the Prime Minister's behaviour in these days: on 12 May, two days before Lord Fisher made his decision to resign and Repington's despatch was published, a personal relationship which was very dear to Asquith came to an end. For almost a year he had enjoyed a pleasurable and consoling (and largely epistolary) relationship with Venetia Stanley, the twenty-eight year old daughter of Lord Sheffield. On the eve of the great political crisis, she wrote to the Prime Minister that she had decided to marry Edwin Montagu and that their relationship was at an end.[16] The effect of her decision on Asquith was devastating. He wrote to her on 17 May, the very day when he acquiesced to Lloyd George's and Bonar Law's call for Coalition:

> I am on the eve of the most astounding & world-shaking decisions—such as I would never have taken without your counsel & consent. It seems so strange & empty & unnatural: yet there is nowhere else that I can go, nor would I if I could.[17]

Asquith, though he would regain his spirit before his tenure as Prime Minister was over, had tired of the fight. This grave personal loss had surely made the easy answer more palatable.

The need for warlike stores, and especially for high explosive artillery ammunition, did play a role in the reconstruction of the Government, however. It helped to poison the atmosphere at Westminster and drove deeper the wedge between Asquith's loyal supporters and men who wished a more vigorous prosecution of the War. Some of these men were among the scores of M.P.s and peers who had taken commissions and seen service in France or the Dardanelles. Some had brothers and sons and friends who had. Some simply believed the rumours which freely circulated by May 1915.

If the munitions shortage did not cause the fall of the last Liberal Government, it certainly did help to create a climate of opinion of distrust and hostility. The news of the Fisher resignation, when introduced into such a volatile atmosphere, was like a time fuse, making some kind of explosion inevitable. It was the existence of such tensions which caused the Tory Leader to move as quickly as he did and which helped to bring about the end of Asquith's Liberal Cabinet.

Northcliffe's 'Shells Scandal' press campaign had far less to do with the political crisis. With the exception of the Repington despatch and an accompanying editorial, the real press campaign did not begin until 21 May, several days after the Coalition had been agreed on and two days after it had been announced in the House of Commons. The publication of news about the need of ammunition was, however, not unimportant. It served two purposes: in the first place, it stirred up public interest in the subject of munitions supply. It helped to make clear to many the importance of the shortage and helped, furthermore, to orient the public to the unprecedented solution which was soon to follow. Second, through its publicity, it aided in making that solution possible: it helped to create an atmosphere agreeable to the new Ministry of Munitions and its first chief, Lloyd George.

III

May 1915, was, of course, not the first time an emergency munitions authority had been suggested by Lloyd George. He was not, however, the only political figure to voice such an idea. As early as September 1914 a scheme 'to commandeer the entire manufacturing potentialities of the Empire' was sent to Lord Kitchener by way of Lieutenant-Colonel Hankey.[18] The War Lord himself, though his ardour for the creation of such an office surely cooled later, had hinted early in the War that it would be a fine idea to press the President of the Board of Trade into service as a kind of Joint-Secretary of State for War, with special responsibility for supply. Nothing came of this idea either.[19] In a previous chapter we have seen Asquith's flirtation with the notion of creating a Ministry of Contracts.

However, during the first ten months of the War, only two governmental bodies had acted to aid the War Office to further munitions production: Lloyd George's two committees. By May 1915 the second, the so-called Treasury Committee, was already proving itself unable to accomplish the task set for it. Frustration with Kitchener and the Master General of the Ordnance,[20] who refused to be candid and to fully cooperate with the Committee, as well as his political instincts which told him that reconstruction was the right time to create the new munitions 'Executive' he had long sought, prompted the Chancellor of the Exchequer to write to the Prime Minister on 19 May that continuing existing arrangements would be a 'farce':

A Cabinet Committee cannot have executive power: it can only advise and recommend. It is for the Department to act. They have not done so, and all the horrible loss of life which has occurred in consequence of the lack of high explosive shell is the result.[21]

By this time there was no answer to Lloyd George's arguments, save surrender: only a Department of State could take the executive decisions which the emergency required. However, Kitchener's unimpaired popularity in the country, made manifest by the indignant reaction to the attacks upon him by the 'Shells Scandal' campaign, made it impossible to appoint a more dynamic Secretary of State for War. The only answer was the creation of a new Department.

While others, Bonar Law in particular,[22] could have made claims against that new office, there was in fact only one man who was the obvious choice to become the first Minister of Munitions—Lloyd George. The way was at last cleared for him to give vent to his great ambition to cut through War Office 'red tape' and to overwhelm in a sea of energy the 'Quartermaster mind' of its munitions supply departments. The frustration born of ten months of struggle with that Office and its titanic chief seemed to be over. Kitchener himself sent a magnanimous letter of congratulation.[23]

On the very day that the announcement of the establishment of the Ministry of Munitions was made public, Lloyd George took up his new duties at the temporary headquarters of the new Department, 6 Whitehall Gardens. This rather grand town house had once been the London home of William Ewart Gladstone, and the shade of the founder of the Liberal Party and life-long guardian of its virtues was no doubt disquieted by what came to pass there in the three years which followed. On 26 May 1915, however, all that lay in future; waiting for neither Royal approval nor statutory authority, the former Chancellor of the Exchequer took up his enormous responsibilities. There was, he felt, no time to waste.

Four

THE MEN OF PUSH AND GO

I

Lloyd George found 6 Whitehall Gardens to be a large, rather old-fashioned house, which had only just been vacated by a well-known art dealer. While it was far from ideal for its new purpose, the structure sheltered the Ministry of Munitions, for virtually the only time in its lifespan, with space to spare. The Department staff consisted at this time, 26 May 1915, only of Lloyd George; Sir Hubert Llewellyn Smith, the Secretary of the Board of Trade who had come from that Office to assist in setting up the new Department; Dr. Christopher Addison, who had been Parliamentary Secretary to the Board of Education and was to serve in the same capacity at the Munitions Office; and the Minister's two secretaries, Miss Frances Stevenson[1] and J. T. Davies.

In the drawing-room of the great house chosen to serve as the office of the Minister of Munitions, Lloyd George found only two tables, a chair and a number of mirrors hung on the walls. Soon thereafter, workmen from the Department of Works arrived, insisting that even that meagre supply of furniture had to be removed as it was not rightfully the property of the new Ministry. He prevailed upon them to leave the few pieces until the headquarters could be properly furnished, which they did.[2] Thus began the greatest innovative Department of State of the entire period of the War.

Lloyd George had triumphed in the struggle to breathe life into the Ministry of Munitions. A central authority for the provision of warlike stores had been created and the problem which now faced its chief was this: How was the shortage of armaments to be rectified? This challenge was a formidable one, and Lloyd George concluded that his first task was to discover exactly what was needed —knowing that there were munitions wanted was not enough.[3] It had to be determined where these needs existed and which were the most pressing, in the immediate and long-run. Equally important was the need to ascertain the nation's capacity of the elements needed to produce munitions: machinery, raw materials and labour.

As answers to these questions were being brought to light, a staff capable of understanding these problems would have to be assembled. Indeed, Lloyd George would have to discover the so-called 'men of push and go'[4] of his oft-quoted phrase—men capable of vast exertions, both mental and physical, necessary to overcome the great test before them. Finally, an organization of awesome power and complexity had to be created, disciplined, and set to the great task which had already defeated men whose careers had been spent mastering the complexities of munitions production.

Each of these duties was staggering in its magnitude, and each cried out to be begun at once.

II

Once the decision to establish the Ministry had been taken, it became immediately necessary to define clearly its powers in order to prevent conflicts of authority with existing Departments. The pressures of wartime made lengthy deliberations impossible, so this was accomplished in great haste. On 25 May Sir Hubert Llewellyn Smith met Sir Reginald Brade, the Secretary of the War Office, to discuss the matter of demarcation of duties. Sir John Simon,[5] the Home Secretary in the Coalition Government, was assisting the new Department at this time and drafted a memorandum of his own conversation with the Secretary-designate of the Ministry of Munitions.[6] At this early stage of negotiations, Brade conceded the wisdom of Llewellyn Smith's desire for the broadest possible definition of 'munitions of war': 'all armaments, ammunition, and explosives and other instruments of war as cannot be separated from the above', in order to give the new Department the broadest possible power. Further, the two civil servants suggested the transfer to Ministry control of the Royal Arsenals, the Ordnance Board and the Inspection Department headquartered at Woolwich.

On the sensitive matter of relations between the Ministry and the War Office, they suggested that the older Department retain control over demand for the various natures of munitions, as well as for their distribution. Problems arising over this division between the demand and supply functions were, it was felt, inevitable; hence, they suggested that such matters be referred to a small Cabinet Committee of the Prime Minister, the Minister of Munitions and the political heads of the two service Departments.

Two days later, on 27 May 1915,, Llewellyn Smith met Sir Charles Harris, the Assistant Financial Secretary of the War Office, to discuss further what had come to be identified as the 'transfer of functions'. Sir Charles' memorandum of the meeting indicates that the War Office had concluded that fewer powers than those discussed two days before required transfer.[7] Only the 'organization and general control [of the Arsenals] as distinct from actual management', it was suggested, were needed by the Ministry. 'This would avoid throwing upon the new Department,' Sir Charles Harris advised, 'direct responsibility for conducting in detail the expenditure of many millions with the corresponding accounts etc.' The modified War Office attitude allowed for the transfer of their Ordnance Department Contract Section, however, Sir Charles suggested that it might be possible to divide the authority of that department in order to keep 'payments and accounting' under War Office control.

In the same vein, this memorandum indicated that the War Office preferred to retain control over the Arsenals, the Inspection Department and the Ordnance Department. The Secretary of State for War and his Master General of the Ordnance meant to maintain unimpaired as many of their powers as possible, despite the new Ministry.

On the same day, a meeting of the Treasury Committee was held and certain preliminary agreements between the new and the old Departments were reached. Close cooperation between them was recognised by both as absolutely necessary. Furthermore, it was agreed that the Inspection Department and the Contracts

Department of the War Office should eventually be transferred to the Ministry of Munitions. No date for the change was specified, however, and it was foreseen that the transfer might be best done 'gradually, if necessary'.[8]

On 31 May 1915 Major-General Sir Percy Girouard, who, soon after the appointment of the War Office Armaments Output Committee had come to share responsibility with George Macaulay Booth for that Department's efforts to increase munitions production, presented a memorandum to the Treasury Committee. In it, he suggested the immediate transfer to the Ministry of Munitions of the Armaments Output Committee staff he and Booth were assembling at the War Office, of the explosives procurement organization set up by Lord Moulton which operated under the nominal authority of the War Office, of the Contracts and Finance Departments of the War Office and of the 'general administration' of the Royal Arsenals.[9]

The first phase of the transfer of functions did not end until 5 June 1915, when these negotiations finally brought temporary agreement between the two Departments. On that day, a lengthy letter was addressed by Sir Hubert Llewellyn Smith to the War Office which set forth the actual responsibilities the Ministry of Munitions was prepared to assume.[10] It called for the eventual transfer of the Contracts and Labour Branches of the War Office, the Royal Arsenals, the High Explosives Department of Lord Moulton, the Armaments Output Committee staff assembled by Booth and Girouard, the Inspection Department at Woolwich and 'any other services arranged thereafter'. It was understood at Whitehall Gardens that all of these powers were not to be transferred at once; controls over both the Arsenals and the Inspection Department, for example, were to be retained in War Office hands 'for the present', and no date for transfer of authority was specified. The two Departments of State agreed that all payments due on munitions contracts would continue to be made by the War Office and that the salaries of Ministry officers, civilian and military, transferred from other Departments should continue to be borne by those other Departments.

The transfer of functions of May and June 1915 was neither successful nor long-lived. The War Office officials who negotiated

for that Department saw the new Ministry of Munitions as a
kind of super-supply department, an offshoot of their own Office.
They conceived of it as a convenient robot, powerful but brain-
less, which would perform certain specified functions only when
it received demands for certain natures and quantities of warlike
stores. That view was, of course, mistaken. However, it was not
the only misconception made during these early days of the
Ministry of Munitions. Both the War Office and the new Department erred: the War Office officials were unwilling to release
sufficient powers to the Ministry, despite the broad charge to the
new Department to supply warlike stores. The Ministry, for their
part, had failed to demand sufficient authority to allow them to
accomplish their task. The older Department was suspicious and
uncooperative; the newer one was inexperienced and unsure of its
own powers. Months of wrangling over demarcation of authority
lay ahead, as we shall see; and the final transfers of authority would
not come until late in 1915.

The Ministry of Munitions Act, which created the new Department, received the Royal Assent on 9 June 1915 and it reflected a
wider view of the charge of the Ministry than that exhibited
by these civil servants in their negotiations. Within a short
while, Lloyd George, Dr. Addison, and the other men of Whitehall
Gardens began to strip away the controls over munitions production retained by the War Office. In the Order in Council of 16 June
1915, which officially installed the Minister in his new post,
allowance was clearly made for this broader view of his duties:

> It shall be the duty of the Minister of Munitions to examine into
> and organize the sources of supply and labour available for the
> supply of any kind of munitions of war, the supply of which is in
> whole or in part undertaken by him, and by that means, as far
> as possible, to ensure such supply of munitions for the present
> war as may be required by the Army Council or the Admiralty
> *or may be otherwise found necessary.*[11]

This Order, composed to suit the new Minister of Munitions,
provided a clear notice that Lloyd George had no intention of
presiding over a docile and obedient instrument, designed to be
played upon by the generals. The later battles over the transfer of

authority will be discussed in greater detail in a later chapter. It is sufficient to note at this point that as the Minister of Munitions decided further powers were required for the production by his Department of munitions, those powers were acquired by the Ministry. That Department grew until, by mid-1916 and the close of Lloyd George's tenure as Minister, it controlled virtually the entire process of armaments production: from research and development, procurement of raw materials and machinery, supervision of both private and State factories, to the provision to the War Office of finished guns, shells and other warlike stores.[12]

III

While the first decisions were being made in regard to the powers of the Ministry, there was much else to occupy the minds of the small staff at Whitehall Gardens. Given the nature of the crisis in the Munitions sphere, the attitude of the Minister was typical of his dynamic but impulsive mind: everything must be done at once. While Miss Stevenson and J. T. Davies groaned under the weight of correspondence from self-styled 'men of push and go', and Dr. Addison set to work on the gigantic task of measuring the actual gulf between munitions requirements and supplies, the Minister himself took to the public platform with a message of urgency, of sacrifice and cooperation. Lloyd George's most telling criticism of the Ordnance Department of the War Office had been that they had allowed the most highly industrialized nation in the world to fall behind in the race to produce armaments. They had failed, he repeatedly said, to organise the industrial capacity of Great Britain for the production of war *matériel*. In June 1915, then, he went to the manufacturing centres to call for greater efforts from directors, managers, foremen and workers alike. The munitions crusade was their struggle, he said; without them, it could only fail.

Lloyd George once defined oratory as 'moving speech, not moving to tears, not moving to admiration. That is rhetoric, it may be even literature, but it is not oratory. Oratory is the moving of man to action.'[13] He travelled, between 3 and 12 June 1915, to Manchester, Liverpool, Cardiff and Bristol to do exactly that: to move men to action.[14] Lloyd George had been born into an age which valued oratory, which indeed, demanded it of its politicians. He had, since childhood, cultivated and laboured over his own speaking skills, and in this flying tour of the industrial districts the fruits of his labour were displayed at their best.

He made clear to his listeners that, as Minister of Munitions, he could be no protector of the traditions of the past. Neither could they be: 'When the house is on fire,' he said, 'questions of procedure and precedence, of etiquette and time and division of labour must disappear.'[15] The four great speeches bore a common message: victory depended upon munitions, munitions depended upon national organization, and successful organization depended upon the sweeping away of all obstructions through collective and personal sacrifice. Such sacrifice might be of profits, trade union regulations or personal comfort, but all were equally important to securing the goal of victory.

His powerful words were meant not to plead with these men and women to endure the hardships brought on by the Great War, but rather to make clear to them that they were themselves part of the world conflict. He was in a position, he told them, to provide the industrial leadership which the nation had wanted for almost a year, but only they could make the industrial effort a success. To the Minister of Munitions, each workman was a private soldier, each skilled man a corporal or sergeant and every foreman and manager an officer in a vast industrial army engaged as directly in the World War as the thousands then under the command of Field Marshal French.

IV

Dr. Addison recorded in his diary on 30 May 1915:

> The Ministry of Munitions is going to be no sinecure. The job we have to undertake is almost appalling in its magnitude. Hitherto there seems to have been no head, no co-ordinating force, and apparently nobody from whom authority could be derived without endless delay.[16]

The Ministry of Munitions Act and the appointment of Lloyd George supplied the authority and the 'head'—however, as Dr. Addison was to discover, the weeks after his diary entry were to demonstrate that bringing together a body to follow the commands of the 'head' was also a staggering task.

The Minister realized that the immediate need of his Department was for men of proved executive ability to implement the decisions reached at 6 Whitehall Gardens. Recognizing this fact, he reached a conclusion of great significance for the future of the Department and the War effort in general. He envisaged nothing less than a veritable team of captains, for he meant to choose his chief assistants in each possible case from the highest levels of the business community of Great Britain. While it might, on the surface, appear peculiar that the man who had for some years worn the mantle of the greatest radical champion of the poor in the nation should come to such a conclusion, it is a contradiction more apparent than real. Lloyd George, since his first steps into public life, had opposed the power and privilege of inherited wealth; he was not, however, dedicated to the reduction of all private fortunes themselves. He admired the successful businessman —particularly the self-made man of wealth—for his efficiency, his dynamism, his energy.[17] The routine of governing held no charm for Lloyd George in time of peace; in the crisis of wartime he considered it absolutely suicidal. With his decision to throw open the new Ministry of Munitions to men of this type, talented outsiders, 'men of push and go', he hoped to cut through the morass of routine and established practice which he termed 'red tape'.[18] The implementation of this decision worked a civil service revolution and it was in no way more obvious than in the departmental organization of the Ministry of Munitions.

What was then termed the 'scope of the Department' was very much in the minds of the founders of the Ministry in these early days at Whitehall Gardens. At the 27 May meeting of the Treasury Committee, the subject was discussed at length. After several false starts,[19] a working scheme of departmental organization was presented on 1 June 1915, by George Macaulay Booth and Sir Percy Girouard of the Armaments Output Committee staff. They suggested that, under the general authority of the Minister, the work of the Department be divided among three equal heads, each reporting directly to the Minister: the first, an administrative chief, was to be responsible for 'office organization, political work, co-ordination and labour questions'. Secondly, a Controller General of Explosives Supply was to take charge of the extant Explosives Department and continue its work; it was assumed that Lord Moulton would simply take the new title and Departmental affiliation and carry on his efforts. Finally, they envisaged a Controller General of Munitions Supply, who was to take charge of the staff assembled at the War Office by Booth and Girouard and to exercise general authority over the actual production programmes and departments responsible for the manufacture of warlike stores. The plan was developed and presented in a revised and detailed form three weeks later.

On 25 June a further revision of the scheme was worked out, and it became the basis of the organization of the Ministry of Munitions. The most substantive changes involved the last of the three divisions. Sir Percy Girouard was placed in charge and styled Director General of Munitions Supply; the nucleus of his department was based upon the staff he and Booth had begun to build at the War Office. Under him were to be three Deputy Directors General: his associate, George Macaulay Booth, was to take charge of local organization for munitions supply, of labour matters and of the collection of statistics and intelligence information. Eric Geddes, who had left the Managing Directorship of the North Eastern Railway on the recommendation of Sir Edward Grey to become one of the first 'men of push and go', was to control the production of artillery; and Glyn H. West, who had served under Girouard while the latter directed the great Elswick works of the firm of Armstrong Whitworth, was charged with responsibility for the production of artillery ammunition, machinery and materials. This scheme was adopted and became the basis for the organization of the Ministry of Munitions.[20]

In late July, Sir Percy Girouard left the Ministry, and his place was temporarily filled by Major-General Sir Ivor Philipps, the Military Secretary to the Ministry of Munitions. On 29 July Sir Ivor addressed a letter to the Minister in regard to what he felt to be the rather disturbing lack of coordination between the various departments as they were developing under the leadership of the Director General of Munitions Supply:

> The chief question which requires consideration is the relation of the various Departments to one another and to the Ministry . . . but briefly the points at issue are, whether each of the Departments of Supply shall be separate and distinct, taking their orders from the D.G.M.S., or whether each Department shall be controlled by a technical expert and the commercial and business control be centred in two assistants to the D.G.M.S.
> I think it is essential that the head of each Sub-Department should be a technical expert but that in the case of the head of the Department it is immaterial whether he is an ordinary businessman or a technical expert, provided we continue to secure the services of such men as you now have at the head of the various Departments.[21]

Sir Percy Girouard, himself a former engineer officer and manager of a huge armaments works, had championed the cause of technical experts within the Ministry of Munitions. He also had grave misgivings about the distribution of armaments sub-contracts among engineering firms inexperienced in munitions production.[22] Within two months of Girouard's move from the War Office Armaments Output Committee, under the congenial wing of Lord Kitchener, to the Munitions Office, Lloyd George concluded that the first Director General of Munitions Supply would have to be replaced.

There are, in this unfortunate affair, insights both into the character of these two men and into the mode in which Lloyd George meant to conduct his new Ministry. Sir Percy had enjoyed a successful career as an engineer-officer under Kitchener in the Sudan and as Governor in both Northern Nigeria and the East African Protectorate before going to Armstrongs in 1912. He was a man of immense talent and ambition, and he possessed a rather high degree of self-esteem. Unfortunately, two of Girouard's characteristics which made the deepest impression on Lloyd George were his concern for his own position in the Ministry hierarchy and his seemingly limitless officiousness.[23] It was, however, his energetic and constant support of munitions experts which brought him down. On 19 July 1915 he wrote to Lloyd George insisting that the directors of each of the divisions of the Munitions Supply Department must be chosen from among such men. 'I trust that any scruples which existed have been removed and that all Departments at once will be placed under the control of experienced Munitions managers.'[24]

Three days later, Lloyd George wrote to Sir Percy advising him that it would be well if he sent a formal letter declining the offer of appointment as Director General of Munitions Supply. Though he remonstrated and objected to such an unorthodox procedure, Girouard was summarily informed on the 24th to turn over his office immediately to Sir Ivor Philipps.[25]

There are several conclusions which may be drawn from this episode: in the first place, Lloyd George meant to brook no interference with his conduct of the Ministry he had battled to create. Next, he was unimpressed by the credentials of men who enjoyed reputations as munitions experts because of long years of experience in and about armaments works. His struggles with Major General von Donop had long before convinced him that such expertise was of limited value unless accompanied by the ability to solve administrative problems quickly and successfully. Finally, it underlined the Minister's decision to rely on men of proved executive ability to do the work on the new Department. The removal of Sir Percy Girouard cleared the way for the influx of Lloyd George's 'men of push and go', as administrative ability came to be the sole test for appointment to the major executive posts in the Ministry of Munitions. There was, to be sure, no shortage of technical expertise, but those expert in armaments production engineering usually served as lieutenants to the administrators on the highest ranks of each department.

As we have seen, among the first Deputy Directors General of Munitions Supply, only one had come from the armaments firms, Glyn H. West, who had been Sir Percy Girouard's deputy at the Elswick works. In July a fourth D.D.G.M.S. was appointed. Charles Ellis, of the shipbuilding firm of John Brown and Company, relieved Eric Geddes of responsibility for the provision of guns and gun equipments. Another significant staff change occurred in August: Sir Ivor Philipps left the Ministry to command a division in France and his place was taken by Sir Frederick Black, formerly the Director of Naval Contracts at the Admiralty. He immediately assembled a staff of experts to advise him: Sir H. F. Donaldson, the Chief Superintendent of the Royal Ordnance Factory, Woolwich; Colonel F. F. Minchin, the Chief Inspector, Woolwich; Samuel Hardman Lever and E. D. Chetham-Strode for, respectively, financial and legal matters, and Dr. R. T. Glazebrook, the Director of the National Physical Laboratory, for scientific matters.

Sir Frederick Black did not, despite his similar title, replace Sir Percy Girouard. The first Director General of Munitions Supply envisaged his position as largely independent in directing the policy of the Ministry in organizing the nation for armaments manufacture. Lloyd George considered his efforts, like his evaluation of his position, amiss. The second Director General did not make the same mistake. Sir Frederick Black carried out the policies of his Minister and he remained in his post until long after Lloyd George left the Ministry.

Among the many businessmen who flocked to the Munitions Supply Department were Leonard W. Llewellyn, the Managing Director of the Cambrian Coal Combine, who directed the Raw Materials Department; Alfred Herbert, who headed the machine-tool firm which bore his name and became responsible for the provision of such devices for the Ministry. Ernest W. Moir, of S. Pearson and Sons, the engineering firm which had built many of the nations' greatest docks and harbours, was first placed in charge of machine-gun production but later headed the Munitions Inventions Department. With the transfer of control over the Royal Ordnance Factories in August 1915, management of the vast complex was vested in Vincent Raven. He had no munitions experience but gained the confidence of Eric Geddes while the two had worked together at the North Eastern Railway. Among these experienced manufacturers, the Ministry placed another businessman as the head of the Ministry Finance Department, Samuel Hardman Lever, who was one of Britain's best-known chartered accountants.

In January 1916 the responsibility for the production of machine-guns, small arms ammunition and rifles, as well as responsibility for salvage, was taken from the overworked Geddes' section and placed under the authority of a fifth Deputy Director General, the businessman Arthur Duckham.

The other major departments of the Ministry also reflected Lloyd George's proclivity for 'men of push and go', not all of whom came from the world of business. In 1914, for example, soon after the outbreak of the War, a committee under the chairmanship of the eminent scientist-jurist Lord Moulton, was created to increase the supply of high-explosives for munitions production. Moulton was not at all pleased with his attachment to the War Office; in June 1915 his organization was absorbed into the Ministry of Munitions where he received both the aid and the authority he required to arrange for the production of sufficient quantities of explosives.

Lord Moulton became Director General of Explosives Supply, with Sir Sothern Holland as his Deputy. This section of the Ministry, as we shall see in a future chapter, was allowed full authority to pursue its important charge independently. As its technical purpose dictated, it took on a decidedly scientific-technological colouring in its staffing practices.[26]

Lord Moulton was not the only eminent lawyer to join the Ministry. Sir Maurice Sheldon Amos, Professor of Comparative Law at the University of London, came to Whitehall Gardens to head the Priorities Department, which was charged with overseeing the distribution of raw materials to the Ministry Departments.

After the initial organization of the Ministry was accomplished, another manufacturing section, the Trench Warfare Supply Department, was created. It resolved itself into two divisions by the autumn of 1915: the supply division actually arranged for the production of mortars, grenades and other such devices and was headed by the financier and banker, Alexander Roger. Research and development of these stores was carried out by a separate division under Brigadier-General Louis Jackson.[27]

A Department of Statistics was established under a Cambridge don, Walter T. Layton, and Departments of Munitions Inventions, headed, as we have seen, by E. W. Moir, and Munitions Design, under Major-General John P. DuCane, were created when these functions were wrested from the War Office in the autumn of 1915.[28]

If not a Ministry of all the talents [Lloyd George wrote many years later] it was undoubtedly a Ministry of all the industries— war and peace, production, transport, law, medicine, science, the Civil Service, politics, and poetry—and all at their best. It was a wonderful array of talent. It was a formidable battery of dynamic energy. But I saw that unless firmly controlled and carefully watched there would be constant explosions which would make the whole machine unworkable.[29]

The Ministry of Munitions was so obviously unorthodox that its need of special and careful management was unmistakable to the Minister or to any acute observer. It was a Department of outsiders, not brought along over years of Civil Service experience; and many of these men were far more accustomed to giving orders than they were to carrying them out. Hence, Lloyd George kept the closest personal watch over the 'push and go' inmates of Whitehall Gardens and Armament Buildings. He granted access to his own office to all department heads and many sub-department chiefs, a practice frowned upon in more traditional hierarchies. The authority of the Secretary of the Ministry, Sir Hubert Llewellyn Smith, was, of course, diminished in comparison to that which most permanent secretaries in Departments of State enjoyed. Like Sir Frederick Black, however, Llewellyn Smith accepted the fact that he served a very unusual Department in which such strange practices were commonplace.

Surrounded by men accustomed to making great decisions at a moment's notice without reference to precedent or superior authority, who were in no way prone to the 'red tape' methods of Government Departments, who often preferred the telephone to the written memorandum and whose greatest motivation was, often, competition, Lloyd George made his system work only because of the force and power of his own will and because of the overwhelming public confidence which he then enjoyed. The problems to which such a system of personal authority were prone did not fully reveal themselves until after his departure from the Munitions Office. The secret ingredient which made this curious system work well was the Minister himself.

The staff of the Ministry of Munitions continued its unabated growth until the end of the World War, but it was certainly the decision of the first Minister to secure the services of the best production and executive and intellectual talent available, without regard for tradition, which lent the notes of dynamism and excitement which forever characterised the story of that Department.[30]

V

Lloyd George's experience with the Shells and the Treasury Committees had shown him that one of the weaknesses of War Office procedures for munitions supply was its failure to gather adequate statistical information on the production of military goods. Only the Master General of the Ordnance, it seemed, possessed current information on munitions production at any given time.

This dearth of concrete evidence had been a great source of frustration to the Minister during the months before the Ministry was organized, and he meant that the same weakness should not be present in the new Department. Almost immediately after the Ministry first took up residence at Whitehall Gardens, he set the Parliamentary Secretary of the Ministry, Dr. Addison, to the huge task of amassing the actual figures which would expose the true depth of the shortage of *matériel*. Addison chose to assist him the head of the Statistics Department, Walter T. Layton, a university economist who had been on temporary duty at the Board of Trade before joining the Ministry and who was both a talented administrator and a brilliant statistician. Addison later said of him: 'He and the assistants he got together would tear the truth out of almost any mass of figures, and I never knew them to be guilty of hiding it when it was unpleasant.'[31]

These men plunged into the sources of munitions information; they unearthed and presented their preliminary findings on 5 June and a more comprehensive report on the 9th. The news was devastating and the Prime Minister forbade the printing and circulation of the reports. Cabinet Ministers, including the Minister of Munitions himself, were required to come to Addison's room to read it.[32] At this time, Lord Kitchener had come to the conclusion (though he had by no means confided it to Lloyd George) that Great Britain would have to place as many as seventy divisions into the field for the campaign of 1916, but Addison's paper made quite clear that the military stores on hand and those which realistically could be expected in the near future were pitifully below what would be needed for such an army. Lloyd George's worst fears were realised: Addison's report showed that the War Office could indeed raise a modern army but had failed properly to arm it.

There existed, for example, enough guns of small calibre, largely 18-pounders and all less than 4.5-inch bore, for twenty-eight divisions; enough 4.7-inch and 60-pounder guns for thirty-one divisions; and enough 4.5-inch and 5-inch howitzers for only seventeen divisions. Even if the massive arrears in deliveries had not existed, at the rate of delivery in June 1915 it would have been years before enough artillery pieces existed to equip the army of continental proportions contemplated. The few orders given for very heavy artillery, pieces above the 6-inch bore, had not begun to materialize[33] and they were far too modest for a force of seventy divisions. Having seen the facts made clear, as they never had been before, Lloyd George saw how small were the efforts of his two committees when held up in comparison to the size of the job which lay ahead.

The statistics of artillery ammunition were even more disturbing: War Office requirements called, in theory, for forty-two days' supply of shells 'on the lines of communication', and only the 6-inch guns were fully supplied to these limits—and there were only eight such guns in the field—60-pounders had but twenty-two days' supply, 18-pounders twelve, and most other calibres only enough for seven or eight days. The supply of shells which existed and the rates at which they were being produced allowed enough ammunition, either shrapnel or high explosive, for approximately half of the meagre number of guns which already existed, given the tremendous rates of expenditure required by trench warfare.

The figures for rifle supplies were even more dismal. In the spring of 1915, Great Britain 'nominally' possessed 1,433,000 rifles. After subtraction for garrison duty, home defence, and reserves, there were but 538,000 rifles available for duty with the B.E.F.—enough for approximately thirty-three divisions. Output at home was, at that time, only 12,000 per week, and orders placed abroad for 130,000 had netted nothing. It was hoped by the War Office that one million might be available, if orders materialized, for overseas duty by February 1916.

The German Army had demonstrated that in trench warfare the machine-gun gave the defensive position a great advantage. In regard to that important device the picture was also bleak indeed. The War Office forecast a requirement of 13,000 guns in the field—requiring an annual output of 26,000 guns, as the life expectancy of such pieces was estimated at this time to be about six months—for the near future.[34] In June 1915, domestic orders existed for only 3,344 guns, and deliveries were seriously in arrears. Two thousand more guns had been ordered from abroad just before the creation of the Ministry. As well, continuations of existing orders had been given by the War Office for 200 additional guns. Yet, between August 1914 and May 1915, only 1,115 machine-guns had been delivered—enough for twelve divisions on a modest scale.

Deliveries of mortars and other trench warfare supplies were negligible. Grenades, for the most part, were improvised at the Front by the soldiers themselves.[35] While the War Office requirements called, for example, for 70,000 grenades to be delivered daily, only 2,500 were actually sent to France each day. Orders for trench howitzers and mortars equalled only about 15 per cent of requirements at that time, and deliveries were almost nil.

The sole bright spot in this distressing picture dealt with the production of explosives. As we have seen, this function had, early in the War, been placed in the hands of a special committee headed by Lord Moulton, which was absorbed into the Ministry in June 1915. Indeed, shell production was so far behind schedule— due generally to a shortage of necessary components or to inefficiency in shell filling at Woolwich Arsenal—that there was an uncomfortable surplus of explosives. Dr. Addison once said of the early success of Moulton's committee that it was like coming to a place of 'open space and light' in a dense and forbidding forest. This brief respite from their worries was little enough for Dr. Addison and Walter Layton when compared with the general tone of dire necessity which dominated the munitions survey they produced.

On 7 July 1915, at a conference of British and French leaders held at Calais, Lord Kitchener announced his intention to place a seventy-division army into the field for the coming campaign. As we have observed, neither the guns nor the ammunition existed for a well-equipped army of one-half that size. The responsibility for producing those armaments, by that time, was no longer within the province of the War Lord, for it lay with the new Ministry of Munitions.

The official historians of the Ministry have written: 'The circumstances of his appointment and the failure of the supplies arranged by the War Office to meet the needs of the army gave [Lloyd George] a very special position.'[36] The reception given his speeches on his tour of industrial districts in early June demonstrated the reliability of that view: the Minister of Munitions found himself able to ask much of the nation and to assume that great efforts would be given in return. The statistical picture sketched by Addison and Layton showed the dimensions of the problem; Kitchener's announcement at Calais demonstrated the great demands which would soon thereafter be made on the Ministry. A staff was in the making, and the time had come to put the talents and enthusiasm of those men and of the industrial power of Great Britain to the test. The first task to which the Minister set his developing munitions machine was the organization of this industrial might for the production of military stores so desperately needed by the B.E.F. It had been Lloyd George's contention for many months that this was the sole method by which the munitions crisis would be solved—the time had come to prove that he was right.

Five

NATIONAL ORGANISATION FOR MUNITIONS SUPPLY

I

Lloyd George's efforts with his Shells Committee and George Macaulay Booth's experience as adviser to Lord Kitchener had led each of them to the conclusion that the British Army would not be adequately armed until the industrial capacity of the nation was organized for armaments production. In March 1915 munitions supply was still very much under the control of the Secretary of State for War and for that reason Booth enjoyed a singular advantage over the Chancellor of the Exchequer: Lord Kitchener trusted him. Booth's patience, unlike Lloyd George's, was never stretched to the breaking-point in his dealings with the great soldier whom he sincerely admired. He worked constantly, however, at this time to bring the Secretary of State for War around to the viewpoint that the sources of munitions supply had to be broadened greatly. Lloyd George admired Booth's tact, his ability to play the 'conciliator', and at no time was that gift more useful to their common goal than in the period before the formation of the Ministry of Munitions.

Booth believed, like the Chancellor, that many engineering firms in Great Britain, though they lacked experience in munitions manufacture, could convert their workshops to the production of components for various armaments.[1] This opinion was shared by hundreds of managers and owners of engineering works throughout the country.[2] Inactivity in the War effort had spurred a group of manufacturers in Leicester, in late February and early March 1915, to meet and discuss what they could do to convert their engineering shops for shell production. They applied to the War Office for assistance and advice in their efforts, requesting a meeting with a representative of the Ordnance Department to discuss the matter.

The Master General of the Ordnance was suspicious of the plan, though he did not veto it out of hand. A meeting was scheduled in Leicester for 23 March and Major-General Mahon was invited to attend as the Ordnance Department's representative. Only five days before the meeting however, the Director of Artillery, Major-General Guthrie Smith, announced that the War Office would send no representative to Leicester and, furthermore, would allow no more munitions subcontracts until the labour needs of the War Office List firms were met.

By 16 March Lord Kitchener had already suggested to Booth that the group which came to be called the Armaments Output Committee was soon to be formed. Hence, Booth's position at the War Office was quite secure. Fully supported by Lloyd George, he lent his influence with the Secretary of State toward restoring Major-General Mahon's appearance at Leicester. One day before the scheduled meeting, Booth succeeded in doing so. The Leicester Committee met the general and, after the Ordnance Department's control over munitions production was undermined, first by Lloyd George's Treasury Committee and later by the Ministry of Munitions, this local Munitions Committee became the model for many others throughout the nation.[3]

Unlike the sub-contractors encouraged by the first Cabinet Committee on munitions in late 1914, the Leicester businessmen wished to make complete shells. The tacit War Office recognition of their ambitious efforts, signified by Major-General Mahon's attendance at their meeting, was a very considerable victory for what was then generally called 'contract spreading'. It was a breach, though perhaps a small one, in the War Office wall of prejudice against the employment of inexperienced munitions makers. The fissure eventually gave way to a torrent of such manufacturers, as, under the auspices of the Ministry of Munitions, jewellers, bridge-builders and motorcar makers came to produce munitions. As we have noticed, Booth's War Office Committee came to be attached to Lloyd George's Treasury Committee; in May 1915 both, in turn, were absorbed into the Ministry of Munitions, which from the outset was totally committed to widening the sources of armaments supply.

II

In mid-April, even before the official constitution of the War Office Output Committee, Booth was actively at work pursuing the charge Kitchener had given him: to increase the labour force in the workshops of the established armaments makers. Always a proponent of contract spreading, Booth also secured War Office permission to encourage local organizations such as that in Leicester. In the early days of the Committee, the industrial districts of the nation were designated either 'A' or 'B' areas. 'A' areas were those in which one of the major armaments sources was located. In order to increase the labour supply to these factories, all workmen housed within a twenty-mile radius of these establishments were, in theory, to be reserved for work there. In the 'B' areas, workers were to be available for alternative organization for munitions supply or for transfer to 'A' areas.[4] Booth was convinced that this system was unsatisfactory because it was a thinly veiled plan to move the skilled labour force away from all manner of factories and toward the War Office List firms, leaving behind them empty and useless workshops. Such a plan might, in the long run, prove successful; however, what was needed was an immediate increase in munitions sources and consequently in output. He remained convinced that only putting more of the industrial capacity of the nation to work on munitions production would remedy the situation.

On 7 April 1915 Booth met Lloyd George and the newly organized Treasury Committee. The Chancellor of the Exchequer encouraged his efforts at local organization and offered his unqualified support. Booth wrote to him the following day to amplify his own position on the importance of local organization and to remind the Chancellor that the War Office munitions authorities were not totally convinced that he was on the proper track:

This method already exemplified in Leicester involves much preparation. Groups of manufacturers are invited to co-operate for production. I shall be able to do a lot of the preliminary work myself but when help may be required from (a) the Arsenal [at Woolwich] (b) the Director of Artillery or the M.G.O. himself, I understand that I can count absolutely on support from you in any measure of pressure I may find it necessary to exert to secure co-operation and prevent obstruction.[5]

George Macaulay Booth never lost his affection and his admiration for Lord Kitchener; on the other hand, he was never truly an admirer of Lloyd George. However, he could sense the rightness of the Chancellor's views of the matter of munitions production. Lloyd George, by this time, had gained considerable experience at putting pressure on the Master General and the Ordnance Department. From April 1915 he and Booth were allied in this struggle, and both benefited from that experience.

Taking the Leicester Munitions Committee of businessmen as a model, Booth, at the Armaments Committee, and Lloyd George, through his Treasury Committee, encouraged the formation of such groups throughout the country. By the end of May, such committees existed at Leeds, Birmingham, Huddersfield and Keighley, as well as Leicester, and others were being planned each day. As the enthusiasm of the industrial community was channelled into these committees, the War Office was finally compelled to put such energy to service.

On 22 April 1915 Lord Kitchener requested Sir Percy Girouard to give up his managing-directorship of the Armstrong Whitworth factory at Elswick and come to advise the War Office on munitions supply matters. From that time until the close of the brief lifespan of the Armaments Output Committee, the work of that group became a two-man effort.[6] At the insistence of Lord Kitchener, on 26 April Girouard became an additional War Office representative on the Treasury Committee; on that same day he presented the first of several alternative schemes for increasing munitions manufacture.

His first plan, written on 23 April and presented to the Treasury Committee at its 26 April meeting, called for a modification of the 'A' and 'B' area scheme.[7] Girouard appreciated the desire of civilian engineering firms to manufacture shells, but he felt they could only do effective work if supervised by managers from the established armaments makers. He felt the development of munitions production capacity in the 'B' areas could become productive and expand only very slowly and that, once this had occurred, it would eventually lead to greater competition for labour and resources with the Royal Arsenals and the War Office List firms.

Girouard's memorandum called for the conscription into State service for the War period of the managers of the great private armaments works, thus ensuring their cooperation with the policies of the Government for increasing output. He envisaged a coordinating body of some kind to secure the maximum benefit from the mutual development of the two orders of sources: 'A' and 'B' areas.

However, at the very meeting where he read his proposal, Sir Percy Girouard indicated that his thinking had changed in the few days since his memorandum was written. The quickest and most productive way in which the engineering resources and manpower supply of the nation could be brought to bear on the munitions shortage was for the State to undertake the construction of new publicly-owned arms factories.[8] Sir Percy saw them as extensions of the extant armaments works, built in what had been termed 'B' areas.

The National Factories which were constructed and administered by the Ministry of Munitions did not exactly fit the plan which Sir Percy envisaged. However, his case before the Treasury Committee favouring the building of new State factories was the beginning of what was to become a vast network of such workshops which eventually covered the industrial landscape of the nation. It was, perhaps, Sir Percy's greatest contribution to the munitions effort.

The Treasury Committee concluded at this meeting that George Macaulay Booth and Sir Percy Girouard should press forward with the plan to build the new factories as well as encourage the proliferation of local munitions committees. It was decided, however, that the appointment to take up their new work would be most effective if it came from the War Office, for that Department remained officially responsible for munitions production.[9] Lord Kitchener therefore issued the following Notice on 28 April:

> The scheme for increasing the output of ammunition submitted by Sir P. Girouard to the Chancellor of the Exchequer's Committee on Munitions has been accepted by the Government, and the Secretary of State for War has appointed Sir P. Girouard and Mr. G. M. Booth to carry that scheme into effect, so far as may be found practicable and subject to modifications of details as may be found necessary and expedient from time to time. In matters covered by the scheme, Sir P. Girouard and Mr. G. M. Booth are authorized to act without further reference to the Secretary of State. They will maintain cooperation with all Government departments concerned with the supply of munitions of war or of labour for producing such munitions and, in event of any difference arising between them and any departments which cannot be mutually adjusted, the instructions of the Treasury Committee on Munitions of War are to be followed.[10]

This announcement was significant for at least two reasons: in the first place, it was a strong step towards the creation of an independent munitions department. In the second place, it was a sound defeat for the policy, long defended by the Ordnance Department of the War Office, of restricting armaments manufacture to the Royal Arsenals and the firms of the War Office List.

The Armaments Output Committee, like the Treasury Committee, had one more month of effective life before it was absorbed into the new Ministry of Munitions. Lloyd George had long supported the distribution of munitions contracts throughout the country; he had supported the work of George Booth (and later of Sir Percy Girouard) and the Armaments Output Committee; he had supported the foundation of local munitions committees of manufacturers in industrial districts; finally, he had supported the plan to build new State munitions factories. After 26 May 1915 he brought these men and these ideas together under his control at the Ministry of Munitions.

When Lloyd George assembled his staff of department heads in June 1915, someone had to be found to turn these plans into reality overnight. Lloyd George said to George Booth about the Directorship of Area Organization, at this time: 'what is really needed is someone of your push and go type—a great salesman.'[11] The man he found for this difficult task was James Stevenson, who left the managing-directorship of the famous distilling firm of John Walker and Company and was reputed to have given up an annual salary of £14,000 to join the Ministry of Munitions.[12] Faced, on the one hand, by the obvious enthusiasm of the industrial community in Great Britain to aid in the munitions effort and, on the other, with the lack of anything more than the mere rudiments of a coherent scheme of organization, Stevenson immediately set to work to harness engineering labour, management and capital to the task assigned his department: the manufacture of artillery shells.

On his first day in his new post, the Director of Area Organization called for a map of the British Isles in order that he might survey the geographical relationship of the nation's industrial centres. Curiously enough, there seemed to be none available at Whitehall Gardens, so a boy was sent out to purchase one. Stevenson, once he had his map, divided the nation into ten districts, which he called Munitions Areas (England and Wales had seven, Scotland, two, and Ireland, one) and the Department immediately set to work to organize them.[13]

There had been no uniformity in the formation of the first local committees who sought to manufacture munitions. The committees were spontaneously organized, of course, and were called together by the local Chamber of Commerce, or the Lord Mayor, or the local association of engineering firms. In the case of small towns, sometimes the Lord Lieutenant of the county acted as catalyst. In other cases, large manufacturers summoned their smaller brethren together for the initial meeting of a committee. There was equal diversity in regard to the membership of the committees, to their size and to their authority.

The Department of Area Organization, at least initially, favoured a tripartite committee system in the local districts: one committee was to represent all manufacturers, another, all local labour organizations and a third and smaller executive committee was to be made up of representatives of the two former groups. It was soon discovered that this was an unwieldy and overly complicated system and it was soon changed.[14]

Instead, the various local committees were instructed by the Department to choose, not necessarily from among their own members, another committee—typically of five members—to be selected from the manufacturers of the district. The names of those chosen were to be submitted for approval to the Ministry and, once this new smaller panel was nominated, the larger original committees were to revert to a purely 'advisory' capacity. These new Boards of Management, as they were called, were then ordered to gather all pertinent information about the industrial capacity in their districts and submit it to the Ministry in order that a plan might be worked out to put each district to work on munitions production. The members of the Boards received no remuneration, save reimbursement for expenses incurred in pursuit of Board business. With a few exceptions—most notably in Swansea, Cardiff, and Birmingham—the labour representatives on the initial local committees took no part in the Boards of Management. Usually Labour Advisory Boards of munitions workers were formed in each district to act as a link between the Ministry and the shop-floor.[15]

Within a matter of weeks after the creation of the Boards of Management, the original Local Munitions Committees ceased to exercise any significant function. By the same token, the Labour Advisory Boards seldom took the place of the trade unions as a sympathetic ear for workmen's complaints.

The passing of the Munitions Committees and the installation of the Boards of Management ended any debate between adherents of central control or local autonomy in regard to Area Organization. While the Ministry announced that the ungainly size of the old groups (this reason was not entirely unfounded) and the potential friction between labour and management representatives on the various committees were the major reasons for the restructuring of the local committees, these were not the only factors considered by Stevenson's Department in ordering the change.[16]

The Boards of Management served at the behest of the Minister of Munitions. The Munitions Committees, on the other hand, were autonomous and, at least at the outset, spontaneous; their authority was drawn from the public spirit of their members. The members of the new Boards, however, acted as the unpaid servants of the Ministry of Munitions—nominated by the local manufacturers, but actually appointed by Lloyd George—and, as we shall see, were given clear guidelines upon which to act.

Secondly, the Boards of Management acted for the Ministry in their home districts only as Whitehall Gardens ordered. They manufactured what they were told to make, not necessarily what they wished. Furthermore, if a supply department felt it could better procure certain shells or components at a given time by dealing directly with local manufacturers, it simply bypassed the Board without the time-consuming bother of having to negotiate with an autonomous local organization.

The policies of the Department of Area Organization not only served to increase the manufacturing base for munitions in the nation, they also constituted another victory for the advocates of a policy of State control and centralization. The same thinking had inspired the various Defence of the Realm Acts; now it was about to produce munitions where formerly had been manufactured children's toys, ladies' clothing and gentlemen's motorcars.

IV

The dearth of concrete statistical information in regard to munitions supply had required great efforts on the part of Dr. Addison and the new Statistics Department of the Ministry to assemble a composite of the armaments needs of the Army. A similar problem confronted James Stevenson and the Department of Area Organization. There was no complete and up-to-date quantitative or qualitative analysis of the industrial capacity of Great Britain.

To formulate the best possible programme of industrial organization, Stevenson's department instituted a survey of the nation's factory districts. Between 19 and 26 June 1915, questionnaires were sent to 65,000 different manufacturing workshops throughout the United Kingdom, enquiring exactly what machinery the shops possessed, how many hours per day it was working, what manner of contracts the firm was fulfilling, &c. By mid-July 45,000 answers had already been received by the Ministry.[17]

With significant information pouring in to the staff at Armament Buildings, and with the obvious desire for involvement in munitions production of private manufacturers, the Department of Area Organization laid its plans to harness this potential. In the end a compromise plan was formulated by James Stevenson which stood midway between the suggestions already made: Booth's desire for contract spreading and Girouard's plan for State factories controlled by the large armaments firms. Once the Boards of Management were organized in the various Munitions Areas, they were given a choice of three alternative schemes for shell production.[18]

The first, the so-called National Shell Factory scheme, was commended to Boards in districts where circumstances allowed the easy concentration of men and machines under one roof, either in a hastily constructed new facility or an available vacant building. The Board of Management was allowed autonomy to conduct the day-to-day affairs of the National Factory, but was subject, of course, to the general policies of the Area Organization Department. Financial decisions were made by the Ministry, as all capital for building the factories and all salaries paid the staffs were provided by Whitehall Gardens. Plant and equipment purchased by the Boards in charge of the factories required Ministry approval and became the property of the State. Each Board was allowed to engage a local banker and a chartered accountant for the factory; but, once chosen, these firms became responsible to the Ministry in London, rather than to the local Board of Management. Of the forty-seven Boards which functioned during the War, fifteen chose the National Shell Factory scheme of production, called 'Class A' work by the Ministry.

The second option available to local Boards was the so-called Cooperative Scheme, which was applicable where circumstances made it impossible to concentrate productive effort in the district in one factory. The characteristic feature of this plan was that the Board contracted with the Ministry to deliver a stipulated number of shells (like those produced by the National Shell Factories, these were generally of 8-inch and smaller calibre) and arranged for the manufacture of the necessary components with local engineering firms. The Board provided premises for the assembly and inspection of the completed empty shells and guaranteed their delivery to Ministry specifications. These Cooperative Schemes were conducted, in Ministry terms, either as 'assisted' or 'Class B' efforts, in which the State provided the initial capital to begin manufacture, or 'unassisted' or 'Class C' plans, under which capital was raised locally. Boards working under these arrangements received the same assistance in regard to obtaining raw materials, machinery and labour extended by the Ministry to National Shell Factories. A total of eleven Boards of Management operated under the 'Class B' method, while seven chose 'Class C' plans.

The third option available to local Boards was essentially a combination of the 'A' and 'B' schemes. Under this plan, Boards which operated National Shell Factories in districts particularly rich in industrial capacity were frequently allowed to place contracts for additional shell components with local manufacturers. These elements of artillery shells were then assembled either on the grounds of the factory or in other premises provided by the Board. In certain cases, in Grimsby and Manchester for example, separate Boards of Management were organized within the same district to operate National Shell Factories and Cooperative Schemes side by side. Twelve districts adopted this so-called 'A and B' method of manufacture.

By December 1915 all Boards of Management had been formed and each had begun to act on one of these Department of Area Organization schemes.

To ensure that close communication with, as well as tight control over the Munitions Areas was maintained, the Ministry established a branch in each. These Area Offices, as they were called, made certain that current Ministry policies were known to Boards of Management and Government contractors and were on hand to see that they were obeyed. In addition, they were active as information-gathering agencies, concerning themselves with labour supply matters, production techniques, raw materials supply and a myriad other factors which affected manufacturing programs. If consultation, advice or information was needed by local Boards, for example, the Area Office provided a source readily to hand and often prevented unnecessary delays brought about through unnecessary communication with the Ministry in London.

The Area Office staff typically consisted of a Superintending Engineer, with his assistants, charged with acquainting himself with the manufacturing 'possibilities' of his Area. He advised Boards of Management and local contractors on their realistic capabilities in regard to munitions production and kept them well aware of their progress toward this goal. The Engineer, for all practical purposes, was to act as the eyes and ears of the Minister of Munitions and the Director of Area Organization in regard to all the many technical aspects of munitions production in his Area.

A representative of the Inspection Department at Woolwich was placed in each Area Office and given authority to approve or reject munitions produced under the various schemes in each Area.

An agent of the Admiralty was assigned to each Area Office to deal with naval contractors in the various districts and to prevent competition for workshops and labour between Ministry and Admiralty manufacturers.[19]

The daily conduct of correspondence, staffing and maintenance of each Office was placed in the hands of an Area Office Secretary.

A separate division of each Area Office existed solely for labour matters. The task of the Labour Officers was to attempt to mediate in labour-management disputes and to keep abreast of time-keeping and productivity among the workforce in the Area. The important labour sections of the various Munitions of War Acts also came within their competence. As we shall see in future chapters, this was perhaps the most arduous work carried on not merely in the Area Offices, but within the Ministry of Munitions as a whole.

The National Shell Factories and the various Cooperative Schemes produced, by the end of the War, approximately 25 per cent of the shells fired by the British Army; and, as we have observed, they were confined largely to the production of shells of light and medium calibres. They proved conclusively that engineering shops of all types and sizes were possessed of the expertise and, in many cases, even of the equipment to aid the War effort in a very direct fashion: through the production of warlike stores for the British Army. Their success vindicated, in the most eloquent terms possible, the faith which Lloyd George, George Macaulay Booth and many others had in them. Likewise, it disproved once and for all the belief held by the War Office that only the Arsenals and the established armament manufacturers could make munitions.

V

The National Shell Factories were not the only new production facilities constructed under the auspices of the Ministry of Munitions. The War had, by mid-1915, already resolved itself into a series of great artillery battles, followed by massive infantry attacks meant to dislodge the enemy from a heavily entrenched position. Such warfare required enormous amounts of large calibre shells, and the established armament shops were virtually the only source of such supplies before the organization of the Ministry of Munitions.

Lloyd George called the representatives of the greatest of these armaments firms to Whitehall Gardens on 13 July 1915.[20] Heavy shells, projectiles above 8-inch in calibre, were more difficult to manufacture than their smaller counterparts; on this point all agreed. Therefore, since the policy of extending the workshops of the munitions makers had not succeeded in producing a sufficient supply of such ammunition, the Minister of Munitions proposed to the War Office List firms that new factories be built in areas with a favourable potential labour supply. He suggested further that these firms supply the managers and technical experts for the new shops, which were to be called National Projectile Factories.[21]

While the representatives of the armaments firms were unenthusiastic about the prospect of the new factories, they agreed to the proposal. The firms were to receive a management fee for their services, based upon percentages of the expenditure by the State to construct and equip the new workshops.[22] In addition, they received payment on a per-shell basis, once production had begun.

These factories, built entirely with public moneys, remained the property of the State, as did the National Shell Factories. The managers loaned by Vickers, Armstrong Whitworth, Cammell Laird, and the other armaments makers, became servants of the Ministry of Munitions and were subject, for the duration of their service, to the commands of the Deputy Director General for Munitions Supply in charge of shell production.

In 1915 and 1916 fifteen National Projectile Factories were built; later in the War, five National Shell Factories were transferred to the programme and converted for the production of larger shells.

Generally, the Cooperative Schemes and National Shell and Projectile Factories produced empty shells, ready to be filled and capped. The products of these various shops were bound to far outstrip the already over-taxed shell-filling facilities at the Royal Arsenal at Woolwich. Therefore, at the same conference in which the decision was made to construct the National Projectile Factories, it was also decided to build a series of National Filling Factories to ease the pressure on the Arsenal.

Three types of factory were constructed: four were equipped to fill Q.F. (quick firing) and breech-loading shells; these were shells of light and medium calibre, often produced by the Cooperative Schemes and National Shell Factories. Five factories were equipped for filling heavy shells for large artillery pieces. The third group of six factories was meant to assemble and fill exploding shell components such as fuses, which ignited the main charge, and gaines, which contained a small charge to set off the fuse.

Each of the National Filling Factories was managed under one of three different schemes. Some were administered directly by the Ministry through a manager appointed by Whitehall Gardens. Others were managed by the great armaments firms under contract arrangements similar to those of the National Projectile Factories. The final method was to place the Filling Factory under the authority of a local Board of Management, like the Shell Factories and Cooperative Schemes. Three additional Trench Warfare Filling Factories were later built as part of this programme solely for the filling of grenades and mortar shells.

Due to the rapid increase in demands for rifle ammunition,

the Ministry of Munitions chose to augment the already over-worked Royal Small Arms Factory at Enfield and private contractors by building four new National Cartridge Factories. One was constructed near Woolwich and was operated by the Royal Arsenal, which itself came under Ministry authority in late 1915. Three other such factories were built and managed by contractors, who were rewarded on a contract commission basis.

Save for the manufacture of explosives, which we shall examine in a future chapter, these various kinds of National Factories and Cooperative Schemes encompassed the State manufacture of armaments during the first year of the Ministry's brief lifespan. In the more than two years which followed Lloyd George's period as Minister, however, the Department either came directly to manufacture or arranged to have manufactured heavy artillery, gauges, optical glass, shell steel, lumber products, anti-personnel chemicals and a myriad other warlike stores. The Ministry, in 1917, also converted several of its factories expressly for the repair and refurbishing of guns and other munitions. In each case, the mode of manufacture owed much to the pioneering efforts of the Department of Area Organization and the Munitions Supply Department in hastily creating the first new National Factories.

Lloyd George, since late 1914, had championed both national organization and strong Government control of resources for munitions production. The National Factories and Cooperative schemes were the fruits of those policies. Through the participation of several hundred engineering firms of all sizes, all under the firm direction of the Ministry of Munitions, the shells were made and filled and supplied to the British Army. After Lloyd George had left the Ministry, when other munitions were needed, their manufacture was organized by employing these pioneering arrangements as models.

Six

LABOUR SUPPLY AND CONTROL (i)

I

In May 1915 the new Ministry of Munitions was faced with a staggering array of challenges: the nation's factories had to be knit together into a coherent programme for production of warlike stores; machinery, raw materials and buildings had to be found or created; emergency measures had to be taken to get armaments into the field while long range production plans were laid. Each task required immediate attention and, upon examination, each clearly seemed to many to be the 'most important' problem. However, during the first year of its life the Ministry faced no greater difficulty than the shortage of skilled labour in the munitions trades. By late 1914 the supply of engineers, lathe operators, electricians, explosives craftsmen and virtually all other skilled mechanics, for reasons we shall see, seemed to be shrinking. Despite their other disagreements, after ten months of war the magnitude of the labour crisis was one phenomenon upon which politician and general, Ministry and War Office agreed.

At the outset of the First World War, however, no man in public life anticipated such a problem. On the contrary, in the first weeks of hostilities the Government, the trade unions and much of the public expected a wholly different sort of crisis. It was anticipated that even a brief war would precipitate serious unemployment in Britain due to the inevitable dislocation of trade. Therefore the Government created a Cabinet Committee on the Prevention and Relief of Distress, which encouraged local authorities to prepare to take steps to relieve the suffering of the unemployed. The Local

Government Board created a special section to seek ways to lessen unemployment. Private charity mobilized its forces by raising two great appeals for contributions, sponsored by the Queen and the Prince of Wales respectively, which raised thousands of pounds to aid the unemployed.[1]

The Labour Exchange Department of the Board of Trade notified its local officers on 8 August 1914 to cooperate with mayors and provosts throughout the country in their efforts to alleviate unemployment.[2] On 7 September local officers in the Exchanges were issued instructions to aid in the inauguration of public works projects to ease the anticipated unemployment crisis.[3] Only one week thereafter, however, the first signs appeared that the wartime labour crisis in Britain would not concern unemployment: on 14 September 1914 the Labour Exchange C.O. Circular sent to local officers recognized that strong new demands for 'fresh' labour were being received from the private armaments manufacturers, the Royal factories and other employers of skilled labour.[4]

There was no unemployment crisis among British workmen in the autumn of 1914 because, as the nation soon learned, the World War required seemingly endless quantities of manufactured goods for the Forces. In fact, before the end of 1914, it was becoming clear that there was a severe shortage of skilled men, which was made worse by the splendid response of the nation's young men to Lord Kitchener's call for recruits. Well represented among the volunteers was the cream of the British labour force: the skilled craftsmen so often called in the past the Aristocracy of Labour. The indiscriminate recruitment practices of the War Office worked terrible mischief on the labour supply of the most significant munitions industries. According to the *Report on the State of Employment in the United Kingdom,* issued by the Board of Trade in mid-1915, by May of that year recruitment had taken these percentages of 'the total occupied male population employed in each trade': mining, 21.8 per cent; iron and steel, 18.8 per cent; engineering, 19.5 per cent; electrical engineering, 23.7 per cent; shipbuilding, 16.5 per cent; small arms manufacture, 16 per cent; chemical and explosives, 23.8 per cent.[5] Indeed, before the close of 1914, the fear of widespread unemployment was replaced by an even more serious alarm that the war effort would bog down for the want of skilled hands to manufacture munitions. To understand the Labour policies of the Ministry of Munitions, it would be well to examine the efforts of the Treasury, the Board of Trade, and the various relevant committees put forth before May 1915, to overcome the shortage of skilled workmen.

II

Before World War I no Department of State in Great Britain had such direct dealings with working men as the Board of Trade. Arrangements had been made between that Department and the War Office and Admiralty to supply additional labour to aid in the mobilization of the Expeditionary Force and the Navy. These secret arrangements called for the transfer of men in necessary trades to War Office employ at Aldershot or Admiralty work in the Royal dockyards. A brief war was anticipated and the service departments undertook to pay not only for the transport and to provide a subsistence allowance in addition to salary to the men, but also to provide to their regular employers 'a weekly sum for keeping the places of the men open'.[6] Sir William Beveridge, then in charge of these operations, recalled in his memoirs that:

> Saddlers, blacksmiths, bakers and others were marked down in Midland and Western towns, to be sent converging on Aldershot on receipt of the starting telegrams . . . The scheme of labour for the Expeditionary Force went through like clockwork. . . .[7]

The satisfaction derived from the success of this operation was, however, short-lived, for the Board of Trade soon discovered that the demands for labour exceeded their ability to supply it.

Though the Labour Exchanges were able to secure more than 18,000 additional workmen for the Woolwich Arsenal and the War Office List firms in the final five months of 1914, there remained at the close of the year an unsatisfied demand for 6,000 workers. As the armaments makers all anticipated increasing the capacity of their factories, this shortage appeared destined to grow worse. Furthermore, by December 1914 the Royal Dockyards and private shipyards showed an unsatisfied demand for 8,000 men.[8] Therefore, the Cabinet Committee on Munitions, Lloyd George's Shells

Committee, called upon the Board of Trade to take 'instant measures' to meet these labour demands as quickly as possible. Few in Britain knew at that time what a difficult task that would prove to be.

In response to this call, a meeting was held at the Board of Trade on 30 December 1914 between its representatives and agents of the Army Council, the Royal Arsenal at Woolwich and the largest private munitions manufacturers. Agreement was reached that the Board and its Labour Exchanges were to concentrate their efforts towards supplying workers to these principal sources of armaments and that labour was to be drawn from the following sources: first, from among unemployed British engineers registered with the Exchanges; second, from among skilled Belgian refugees in Britain or in Holland; and third, from the vast number of skilled workmen in Britain employed on non-Government work. In addition to these sources of 'reinforcement' labour, the trade unions were to be induced to suspend their traditional restrictive practices to allow their members already employed on Government work to be used 'more economically and productively'. This latter policy was termed 'relaxation' of trade union rules.[9]

As we have seen above, the policy of the Government in regard to munitions production at this time was still attuned to the War Office design of concentrating armaments contracts within the small circle of Royal Factories and major munitions makers. Therefore, increases in labour supply were directed toward these shops and, for the first three months of 1915, the Board of Trade pursued its two-fold policy of 'reinforcement' and 'relaxation'. By 15 March 1915, however, it was clear that these methods were failing to overcome the growing labour shortage. In a report of that date, the Secretary of the Board of Trade, Sir Hubert Llewellyn Smith, indicated that, while several thousands of skilled workers had been placed since January, the number discovered since mid-February demonstrated 'clearly the progressive drying up of the sources of recruitment'. In brief, the earliest plan to overcome the labour shortage, the recruitment of outside labour—unemployed men, refugee workers and engineers released from private work by patriotic employers—had failed to supply the needs of the munitions shops. It was clear by March 1915, that there simply did not appear to be many more 'free' engineers to place in the munitions shops.

There were two major reasons which brought about the failure of these efforts of the Board of Trade. In the first place, while the Labour Exchanges attempted to put every possible skilled man at the disposal of the munitions shops, the War Office continued to recruit men engaged in the most important skilled trades. Recruitment remained virtually unchecked until mid-1915 and the compelling drives of patriotism, courage, desire for adventure and social pressure which constrained young men to enter the Army or Navy were very often too strong for the Labour Exchange officers to combat. In the second place, the policy of the War Office of concentrating munitions production with the Royal Factories and a small handful of established armaments makers made it almost impossible to utilize fully those workers—both skilled and un-skilled—who might have been transferred from private to munitions work, but who were many miles from the centres of munitions manufacture.

By March 1915 the shortage of munitions for the British Army was a stark reality that confronted and troubled the Government. We have seen that it led to an important meeting on 5 March 1915, at which the Master General of the Ordnance explained that the dearth of shells and guns was due to the fact that there simply were not enough skilled hands to make them.[10] Lord Kitchener's counter-blast against the crisis was the appoint-ment of George Macaulay Booth's Armaments Output Com-mittee later in the month. From this time, and virtually until the end of the War, the necessity to maintain an adequate labour supply in the munitions factories was recognized as one of the greatest challenges to the nation—a test equal, perhaps, to raising and training the greatest army in British history. Failure to meet either, it was becoming clear in 1915, could result in defeat in the Great War.

III

As early as September 1914 the great armaments manufacturer Vickers Ltd. had suggested to the Government the creation of a war service badge to signify that their workers were serving the national interest by labouring in the armaments factories. In addition, such a sign of the State's recognition of his service would, it was hoped, satisfy the skilled worker's patriotism as well as protect him from the onslaughts both of super-patriotic ex-suffragettes who passed out white feathers of cowardice to young men in civilian dress and of over-zealous recruiting sergeants who enrolled any able man, regardless of his trade.[11] The first real action of any sort in this direction, however, came from the First Lord of the Admiralty, Winston Churchill. In late October, he canvassed Admiralty contractors to discover the degree of damage done to their production by unrestricted recruitment. Satisfied that action was necessary to halt further attrition within the ranks of skilled men, he requested Government approval of a scheme to distribute Admiralty Service Badges to workers in the Royal Dockyards and in the shops of Admiralty contractors. While there was some delay in receiving Cabinet approval, it was finally granted on 26 December 1914 and the first Admiralty badges were issued to the Royal Yards and Admiralty contractors soon afterwards.[12]

Since the badging scheme set in train by the First Lord was largely to protect workers *against* Army recruiting officers, the Army Council and the War Office exhibited less enthusiasm for devices to impede enlistment. However, by March 1915 the Master General of the Ordnance had explained that the labour shortage was the single greatest cause, in his estimation, of the delays in deliveries of munitions and the War Office was under pressure to demonstrate its goodwill in overcoming the problem. In March, therefore, the War Office began the distribution to the Royal Factories and the armaments manufacturers of its own badges for circulation among workers in the most skilled trades. Under the authority of the Master General, however, War Office badges were issued with much greater restraint than those of Admiralty. In June 1915, when the administration of the two badging programmes was handed over to the Ministry of Munitions, there were 400,000 workmen wearing Admiralty badges, while only 80,000 men had been issued War Office badges.[13] The vast majority of these badged War Office workers were employed in the Royal Factories—most at the Royal Arsenal, Woolwich—

where the need was least, as there was already an aura of national service about the Woolwich man.

A temporary palliative at best, the badging systems of the Admiralty and the War Office were not sufficient to solve the labour shortage and curb the flow of skilled men into the forces. Men could not legally be prevented from enlisting, nor did recruiting officers always respect the purpose of the badge, which was, after all, to keep a valuable man in the place where he contributed most to victory. Likewise, the public often overlooked the badge when they inquired about the patriotism of a healthy young man who was not in uniform.

The appointment of Booth's committee by Lord Kitchener brought an additional policy into the field in March 1915. Booth suggested that badges were clearly not the best deterrent to recruitment abuses. He advised, therefore, that the necessary munitions trades ought to be singled out and orders issued to recruiting officers to refuse enlistment to men within those specific trades. With the aid of Llewellyn Smith of the Board of Trade and with the loyal support of his friend Kitchener, Booth succeeded in thrusting his policy upon an unwilling War Office. Accordingly, on 12 May 1915 the War Office issued a *Circular Memorandum to all Recruiting Officers and Secretaries of Territorial Associations,* advising these officers that workers within certain skilled trades, due to the serious shortage of such men, were thereafter 'off limits' to recruitment. Attached were lists of Admiralty and War Office contractors, whose skilled workers were not to be recruited at all.[14]

While the *Memorandum* was certainly a step in the proper direction, the list of occupations was incomplete to protect men of all skills important to munitions manufacture—workers in the steel producing trades were omitted for example—and, perhaps more important, recruiters who had ignored the war service badges were inclined to do the same with the lists of restricted occupations and continue to enlist invaluable mechanics.[15]

IV

While these efforts were being made to reinforce the labour supply and restrain the recruitment of skilled men into the Army, parallel efforts were being made to induce the trade unions to withdraw their traditional workshop rules which, in the crisis of wartime, restricted the output of munitions. This was, of course, the relaxation policy decided upon by the Board of Trade early in 1915.

The first steps in this direction were taken, however, without the assistance of any Government department. In November 1914 a labour dispute seemed imminent at the Crayford works of Vickers, the nation's greatest private armourer. While theoretically labour and management still clasped hands in the industrial truce declared at the outset of the War, the engineering trade unions at Crayford announced their adamant refusal to cooperate with the company's plan to dilute the skilled workforce with unskilled and non-union female employees. A conference was hastily called and, on 26 November 1914, the first important agreement leading toward what came universally to be known as Dilution was signed by the representatives of the trade unions and management. The compromise called for the employers to restrict the use of dilutees, in this case unskilled women, to the operation of fully automatic machines and to prohibit their participation in any process which required the 'setting up' or adjustment of machine tools. The trade unionists, under these conditions, agreed to accept the dilutees into the shops and work with them.[16]

The so-called Crayford Agreement applied only to one factory of one manufacturer; and while it was looked upon as a hopeful sign at the time in some quarters — as had been the vague industrial truce, for that matter — little came of it.

The next step in these attempts of engineering capital and labour to arrive at an agreement for the lowering of trade union restrictions was a joint conference of the representatives of both sides which met in early December 1914. The employers called upon the unions to surrender for the duration of the War their traditional regulations regarding the employment of non-union labour, the strict maintenance of separation between crafts and among workers of varying degrees of skill and the limitations on overtime work.[17] The proposals of the employers were nothing less than an invitation to acquiesce to full-scale Dilution.

A week thereafter the trade unions' reply to the engineering employers' demands was announced. These suggestions called for the spreading of Government contracts among non-munitions engineering firms, the release of skilled workmen from the colours, the transfer of skilled men from private to Government work and the importation of skilled labour from the Empire. As the suggestions of the employers were unacceptable to them, the proposals of the trade unions were equally objectionable to the employers. After a brief and rather recriminatory correspondence, the attempt at compromise was broken off.

At the prompting of the War Office and the Admiralty, a further attempt was made to bring the two sides of industry together that they might reach agreement without State intervention. The results were as unsuccessful as those of the previous month, and a brief meeting was adjourned without success. It was at this point that the Government entered the negotiations over trade union practices in the munitions shops: on 4 February 1915 the Prime Minister appointed a committee under the chairmanship of the most successful labour negotiator in the country, Sir George Askwith, of the Board of Trade. This Committee on Production in Engineering and Shipbuilding Establishments Engaged on Government Work, as it was rather expansively called, was instructed:

> To enquire and report forthwith after consultation with the representatives of employers and workmen, as to the best steps to be taken to ensure that the productive power of the employees in engineering and shipbuilding establishments working for Government purposes shall be made fully available, so as to meet the needs of the nation in the present emergency.[18]

A conference of the two sides with the Committee on Production was hastily called, but the results were not unlike those of the meeting held without Askwith's celebrated powers of conciliation. The Committee, thereafter, offered its own views on the labour situation at that time—views which, months later, came to greatly influence the labour policies of the Ministry of Munitions.

Four reports were issued by the Committee between 17 February and 4 March 1915 and they called upon the trade unionists in the munitions-related industries to accept both male and female dilutees where necessary, to suspend the traditional right to strike and accept compulsory arbitration through the agency of the State, and to suspend all other practices which might restrict in any way the output of warlike stores during the period of the War. The employers, according to the Committee, were to reciprocate by promising to maintain wage levels (particularly under the piece-work payment system) regardless of increased output, to accept the same compulsory arbitration and to have their profits monitored by the State in order to prevent war profiteering.[19]

At this same time there was one final attempt by employers and workmen to reach a national agreement on the matter of workshop procedures in wartime. On 4 March 1915, the same day the final report of the Committee on Production was made, the so-called Shells and Fuses Agreement was signed by the Engineering Employers Federation and the major engineering trade unions. While it covered only the processes of manufacture of these specific munitions, the Agreement did provide for the admission, under the careful scrutiny of the trade unions, of male and female dilutees into the munitions factories. The Agreement also called for the limitation of these extraordinary circumstances to the period of the War and, once the emergency was past, for the discharge of the dilutees and the return to normal shop practices.[20]

While the Shells and Fuses Agreement was a welcome sign in 1915, it was too limited in scope to satisfy either the Committee on Production—which had suggested in its reports that the various Defence of the Realm Acts had given the State coercive powers to compel cooperation from all elements in industry—or the Chancellor of the Exchequer. Lloyd George saw the increased production of warlike stores as a major factor in hastening the end of a terrible war, and he saw bringing the engineering employers and trade unions to agree on extraordinary labour practices in the munitions shops as the quickest way to increase that production. On 17 March 1915 Lloyd George, whose own powers of persuasion were not unrecognized, called representatives of the principal trade unions to the Treasury to secure their agreement to the proposals of the Askwith Committee.[21]

The Treasury Conference, as it came always to be called, consisted of the Chancellor, representing the Government, and agents of the various trade unions in the fields which contributed to the manufacture of munitions of war: engineering, shipbuilding, iron and steel, the metal trades, mining and many others. The meeting was not without drama: the Miners' Federation withdrew after the first session over opposition to compulsory arbitration and the Amalgamated Society of Engineers refused to sign any agreement without greater guarantees than the Government seemed willing to offer.

In the main, however, the conference proceeded smoothly, and the representatives of the State and of most of the major industrial trade unions placed their signatures on a document which essentially encompassed the recommendations of the Committee on Production. The trade unionists agreed to compulsory arbitration and suspension of the right to strike. Equally important was their agreement to suspend their traditional workshop regulations, thereby opening the factory door to Dilution. The Government undertook to guarantee that all such concessions by the trade unions would be limited to the period of the War only, that wage rates would be maintained despite the changes in shop procedures and that consultation with the workmen's representatives would precede any actual changes in shop procedures in these industries. The signatures of Lloyd George and Walter Runciman, for the State, and Arthur Henderson and William Mosses, for the trade unions, were affixed to the Treasury Agreement on 19 March 1915.

On 25 March, a week later, a supplementary meeting was held between the Chancellor and representatives of the Amalgamated Society of Engineers, without whose cooperation any attempt to introduce Dilution into the munitions shops would have surely failed. The A.S.E. demanded and received guarantees that the profits of Government contractors would be restricted by the State and that the Agreement would apply only to workers employed on Government contracts. Their representatives then signed the agreement. Immediately afterwards Lloyd George created the National Labour Advisory Committee under the chairmanship of the leader of the Labour Party, Arthur Henderson, to counsel the Government in making the undertaking productive.[23]

The Treasury Agreement appeared to be a step toward State control of the various munitions industries, and so it was. However, within a very few months it proved itself to be too small and even too timid a step. While labour had agreed to suspend several of its most cherished privileges, it had done so only on the promise of Government to require similar sacrifices of the employers. There was no State machinery to compel such cooperation. The Defence of the Realm (Amendment) Act of 1915 had technically vested a great degree of control over industry in the War Office and the Admiralty, yet neither Department had the staff, the administrative machinery or the expertise to bring such theoretical controls to bear. In March 1915 no other branch of Government had the power to compel cooperation from capital and labour in a State-controlled programme of industrial production.

Encouraging though they were, the clauses of the Treasury Agreement were valueless without a Department of State—endowed with suitable powers to compel obedience—expressly created to enforce them. The State had officially recognized the problem, but recognition was not enough to bring about a solution. Cutting through the Gordian knot of labour supply and control problems was left to the men who created the Ministry of Munitions.[24]

V

With the advent of the Ministry of Munitions, Lloyd George and his aides found themselves at the centre of the attentions of a number of opposing forces. Dr Addison recalled of those early days at Whitehall Gardens:

> Employers watching, trade unions watching, the Army clamouring for supplies, the Adjutant-General crying out for men—no man or woman who had to do with these things could satisfy all parties. It was a thankless, tedious, almost heart-breaking job. . . .[25]

Difficult though the task seemed, the men of the new Department thought it possible to arbitrate among opposing forces. The weapon which they meant to use to elicit cooperation from labour and capital was the Munitions of War Act, introduced by the Minister of Munitions on 23 June 1915.

Lloyd George saw the Act as the only viable alternative to

industrial conscription in Great Britain, and his speech in support of the bill in the House indicated as much.[26] Despite accusations of 'Prussianism' from the Labour benches, he clearly stated that even a 'perfectly democratic state ... has the right to commandeer every resource, every power, life, limb, wealth and everything else for the interest of the state.'[27] In the eyes of the newly appointed Minister of Munitions, the failure of the various agreements of late 1914 and early 1915 had all indicated that only State Control could guarantee that an adequate supply of munitions would be manufactured for the British Army and Navy. In his speaking tour of the industrial districts of the nation in the days immediately following his appointment, he spoke of a sort of industrial compulsion, though 'not necessarily conscription in any ordinary sense'.

Yet the reaction of the industrial classes to these political kites was not favourable. Though military conscription came to Britain as a result of the needs of the World War, industrial conscription did not. Dr. Addison, who opposed the whole idea of industrial conscription, recalled, years later, of this period:

The case against [industrial] compulsion was that ... even in a time of danger, the people would not tolerate a proposal that involved forced labour unless an overwhelming case could be made in favour of it. No such case could be made out.[28]

The almost unregulated voluntary system which had dominated the war effort in the military and industrial fronts until mid-1915, had helped to bring about the political crisis which the nation's leaders faced at this time. Clearly, it could not be continued. However, as Lloyd George learned, neither would British workers — upon whom rested all hopes of overcoming the *matériel* shortage — tolerate true industrial conscription. Hence, a compromise between the two poles was necessary, and it was at making such compromises that the Minister of Munitions excelled. The product of mixing together the spirit of voluntary sacrifice of the Treasury Agreement with the direction of the State, enforced by the power of statute, was the Munitions of War Act 1915.

The theme of the Act was that each invaluable skilled man — after the suspension of trade union practices which in any way restricted output and the introduction into the shops of unskilled dilutees—was to work at his maximum productivity and that the State, through the Ministry of Munitions, was to administer the entire productive process of the manufacture of munitions. Lloyd George would have preferred pure industrial conscription; under the Munitions of War Acts workers and industries were controlled under regulatory powers short of actual conscription, though critics of the Act and the Ministry saw it as little short, indeed.

The Munitions of War Act 1915 was based upon the assumption that, to overcome the munitions crisis, work in the various armament industries had to be continuous. Under the Act, therefore, strikes and lockouts were made illegal. Industrial disputes in the munitions industries were to be submitted to the Board of Trade for arbitration and Sir George Askwith's Committee on Production became the major arbitration panel for the duration of the War. Section 1 (4) of the Act declared: 'The award of any such settlement shall be binding both on employers and employed and may be retrospective; and if any employer, or person employed, thereafter acts in contravention of, or fails to comply with the award, he shall be guilty of an offence under this Act.'

To ensure that trade union practices did not interfere with the production of munitions, the Act further declared in Section 4 (3):

Any rule, practice or custom not having the force of law which tends to restrict production or employment shall be suspended in the [munitions] establishment, and if any person induces or attempts to induce any other person . . . to comply, or continue to comply, with such a rule, practice or custom, that person shall be guilty of an offence under this act.

In theory, then, the prerogatives of the trade unions—those concessions in shop practice wrung so slowly from their employers over years of struggle—were swept away by Act of Parliament. Yet, as the second Treasury Conference between the Chancellor and the Amalgamated Society of Engineers indicated, many trade unionists demanded equally unprecedented sacrifices from factory owners. Sir Hubert Llewellyn Smith, the Secretary of the Ministry of Munitions, wrote in early June 1915 as the Munitions of War Act was being drafted:

The difficulty . . . is that the workmen, though engaged in armament work, still feel themselves to be working essentially for
private employers, with whom they have only a 'cash nexus',
and that in the present circumstances a 'cash nexus' is quite inadequate to secure control. . . .

So long as contractors' profits are not brought under control,
the workmen feel that any sacrifice they make of their rules and
restrictions will directly increase the profits of private persons,
and their unwillingness to make the sacrifice is made almost
insuperable by this suspicion.[29]

Given the broad definition of what constituted the munitions
industries in 1915 and despite the fact that the various Defence of
the Realm Acts theoretically vested such powers in the War Office
and the Admiralty, complete State control of the arms industries
in 1915 would have been an unrealistic proposal. However, given
the failure of the old contracting system to provide a sufficient
supply of armaments and the need to prove to skilled workmen
that they were not alone being asked to make sacrifices in the
factories, a compromise form of State direction of private industry
had to be found. This *via media* might be found, it was hoped, in
the nine sections of Part II of the Munitions of War Act, which
created the controlled establishment in British industry.

The essence of these sections was this: the Minister of Munitions
could declare any factory felt to be necessary to the production of
warlike stores to be under the control of the Ministry. Controlled factories were required to display prominently the Ministry's
Rules for Controlled Establishments, which required good time-
keeping and good shop behaviour of all employees. Likewise, any
further shop rules which the Minister of Munitions found it
necessary to declare in future were, thereafter, binding in these
factories.

While the matter of wages will be dealt with more completely
in another chapter, it should be noted here that the 'cash nexus'
which bound employer and workman together was at least officially
severed under the Act. The profits of controlled establishments
were limited to only one-fifth in excess of the average profit of
the two fiscal years previous to the War. Provision was made

within the excess profits regulations, however, for the Minister to make allowances for expenditure on and depreciation of capital goods used for war production.[30] While these provisions surely did not wipe away the suspicion among many workers that their employers were amassing huge fortunes out of the War, the declaration of Ministry control over factories did help to allay these anxieties.[31]

In its earliest days, the Controlled Establishments Branch of the Ministry, created to oversee these provisions, found its presence most unpopular with many factory owners and managers. By December 1915, however, the Labour Department of the Ministry reported: 'Now they often ask for this,'[32] because the effect of declaring a firm controlled so often led to a great lessening of tensions within the factory. The memorandum continued:

> The Admiralty representative in London had volunteered the statement that, generally speaking, he found that labour difficulties ceased as soon as the establishment was controlled, and that a still further step in improvement was taken when the union jack [provided by the Ministry to all controlled establishments] was hoisted over the establishment, as the workmen then felt themselves unquestionably to be working for the State. . . .

The designation of a factory as a controlled establishment was, as we shall see, no guarantee of complete immunity from labour disputes—despite the fact that the Munitions of War Act disallowed strikes and lockouts. Yet it is not inaccurate to say that such disputes would have been far more frequent and long-lived had there not been this element of direct Ministry authority in the shops. The creation of the status of controlled establishment began with these controls over profits, workshop procedures, alterations in wages and compulsory arbitration. As we shall see, eventually it lead to greater controls over wages and unprecedented steps in the realm of social welfare programmes for employees which, without the crisis of the War, would have been quite impossible in 1915 and 1916.

The major area in which the Ministry of Munitions did not intend to interfere with the controlled establishments was in the day-to-day management of the factories. So long as they complied with the rules of the Controlled Establishments Branch, the shop managers and foremen were allowed to continue to conduct the factories as they wished. By the end of the War, the decision to implement this type of limited State Control was looked upon as one of the most significant and successful precedents laid down by the founders of the Ministry of Munitions.[33]

To understand the most contentious section of the Munitions of War Act, the notorious Clause 7 which virtually bound workers to their jobs, it should be remembered that the four or five years immediately before the outbreak of the World War had been difficult ones, both for labour and management.[34] Strikes and lock-outs had been frequent, inflation had severely depleted the buying power of both wages and profits and tension, bitterness and distrust had seldom been greater between employer and workman. With the flurry of activity which the War brought to the work-shops of Great Britain, particularly as the shortage of skilled workers manifested itself in the late autumn of 1914, workers and factory owners both saw an opportunity to recoup some of the losses of the pre-war years of the so-called Labour Unrest. There-fore, a period of labour movement began as skilled men were lured from factory to factory by the promise of ever-higher wages. The increase in numbers of munitions sub-contractors brought about by the contract-spreading policies of the Shells Committee worsened the competition. With the creation of the Ministry of Munitions, with its controlled establishments and its ambitious programme for the creation of National Factories, such a transient labour supply was intolerable.

Clause 7 was meant to curb this phenomenon. Under this section of the Act, it became illegal to engage a workman who had been employed on Government contract work unless he possessed a Leaving Certificate, which signified that his services were no longer required by his previous employer. Failure to secure the Certificate, according to the Munitions of War Act, rendered the worker legally unemployable for a period of six weeks.[35] Without the Leaving Certificate, the six-week wait became one of enforced inactivity — without pay — in a time when jobs were plentiful and wages generous. Equally intolerable to the workman was the fact that the actual form of the Certificate was unspecified by the

Act and, therefore, it was frequently used by employers to comment on the reasons for the severance of workers from their jobs—the Certificate, then, was used as a sort of negative character reference.

To the trade unions, Clause 7 of the Act seemed to bind their members in a sort of Government-sanctioned bond servitude to their employers—freedom from which could be purchased only by a six-week period of unemployment, after which time the worker was bound anew when he took a new job. To factory owners and managers it was often a baulk to hiring much-needed skilled men to bolster their perpetually understaffed production lines. While it is easy to see why Clause 7 was included in the Munitions Act, given the potentially disastrous labour shortage in mid-1915, it is equally easy to understand why it was so unpopular with many workmen and employers.

There was one alternative to the unhappy worker or employer: the munitions tribunal. These were small informal courts provided for in the Act, and it was hoped by Lloyd George, Dr. Addison and Sir Hubert Llewellyn Smith that the provision of these bodies might help to prevent problems in the factories arising out of disagreements over this and other sections of the Munitions Code.[36]

The Act created tribunals of two classes: first-class, which were empowered to deal with all disputes under the Act, and second-class, which dealt only with minor disputes which grew from disagreements over the work rules in the munitions shops—including the provision of Leaving Certificates. The tribunals were alike in that they consisted of a chairman, invariably a barrister or solicitor, and two assessors, chosen respectively by the workers and the employers in the district. The first-class tribunal could levy fines and, in certain serious circumstances, order brief terms of incarceration for violation of the Munitions Code. The second-class tribunal was limited to the collection of fines, usually not exceeding three pounds.

While the munitions tribunals did much to alleviate tension within the hard-pressed munitions factories, they did not succeed in making the troublesome Clause 7 more palatable to British workers. The Munitions of War (Amendment) Act of January 1916 did lessen somewhat the sense of outrage among working men in that it forbade employers to comment upon the character of employees holding the Certificate.[37] Likewise, the point was made clear in the Amendment Act that the Certificate was simply a statement that a workman was available to accept employment rather than a proof that the worker had been granted his employer's permission to seek other employment. Thirdly, the amended Code provided that employers were required, subject to fines before a munitions tribunal, to provide a Certificate to any workman discharged from his job, as well as to employees suspended without pay from their jobs for more than two working days. Finally, the worker subject to the Leaving Certificate was guaranteed by the Amendment Act one week's notice, or wages in lieu thereof, in cases of dismissal from his position.

The amended Clause 7 did lessen the harshest aspects of this contentious section of the original Munitions of War Act. Yet, the trade unions were not to be satisfied until the Clause was totally expunged from the Munitions Code. This was finally done with the passage of the Munitions of War (Amendment) Act, Number 2, 1917, passed during the Ministry of Winston Churchill.

The first Munitions of War Act was the first clear statement of policy laid down by the new department and far from the least extraordinary of all its clauses were those which dealt with labour supply and control. In mid-1915 Lloyd George and his small staff could only hope that it was sufficient armament to overcome the crisis in labour supply which plagued the British war effort in those months.

Seven

LABOUR SUPPLY AND CONTROL (ii)

I

When it became responsible for labour supply to the armaments factories in Great Britain, the Ministry of Munitions, as the Board of Trade had done, sought to move every possible skilled mechanic into these factories. Before British labour would accept a full-scale Dilution policy, each of the sources of skilled men not then employed on munitions work would have to be uncovered and, if possible, moved to Government work.

The Board of Trade had indicated in December 1914 that engineering factories then doing non-Government work might be a productive source of armament labour. The trade unions, in mid-1915, still believed that was the case. The Ministry of Munitions, soon after its creation, set out to uncover any available skilled mechanics who might be moved from private to Government work. This policy led to one of the most interesting experiments in labour supply and control of the entire period of the War, the War Munitions Volunteer Scheme. The idea originated with Captain R. C. Kelly, who, in April 1915, had returned from his battalion in France to direct the newly organized Northeast Coast Armaments Committee, with headquarters in Newcastle. Among the first of the local armaments committees, the Newcastle group had been organized with the advice of Sir Percy Girouard, who was then still managing Vickers' Elswick works and acting as adviser to Lord Kitchener. Captain Kelly was not long at his new post before he realized that the committee of businessmen and trade unionists faced a serious difficulty which was all too common in those days: 'I found,' he wrote, 'that the initial problem to be solved was that of labour.'[1] Kelly turned first to local engineering firms to release surplus skilled men for munitions work, but his experiment in voluntarism led only to failure. Kelly next conceived a 'flying column' of skilled engineers, a 'King's Squad' he called it, who, upon signing an undertaking with the Committee, agreed to place their skills at the disposal of Government contractors in the district. The Squad volunteers were to go where they were needed, when their particular skills were required. The idea met with enthusiasm among local workmen for, in the six-week period ending on 30 June 1915, approximately 6,000 men in the Newcastle area had signed the agreement.[2] A similar committee of businessmen organized on Clydeside followed the Newcastle King's Squad plan and gathered in more than 9,000 signatures of skilled mechanics. The King's Squad idea, like the two munitions committees, was noticed and absorbed into the new Ministry of Munitions.

As the first Munitions of War Act was being drafted, Lloyd George considered expanding the Newcastle scheme as a possible answer to the difficulties inherent in moving skilled men from civilian to Government work. No employer, regardless of whether he manufactured bombs or bowler hats, was unaware of the scarcity of skilled workmen and few were enthusiastic about losing more. Kelly's scheme, with the pledges of both the workman and the committee satisfying the fundamental requirements both of voluntarism and legal contract, showed possibilities of spiking the guns of employers unwilling to surrender valuable skilled men. The Minister of Munitions favoured a scheme in which the volunteer was expected to submit to a semi-military code of discipline. When he met the Labour Advisory Committee on 8 June 1915, they expressed their doubts about Lloyd George's plan—to them, any hint of military discipline seemed to step toward labour conscription. They suggested a compromise which they felt would be acceptable to the trade unions and to the Minister of Munitions.[3] It was accepted by both sides and, as the War Munitions Volunteer programme, the Henderson Committee's variation of the scheme was included in the first Munitions of War Act as Clause 6.

The War Munitions Volunteers, like the Newcastle King's Squad, agreed to leave their regular employment and place themselves at the disposal of Government contractors. Once in the hands of the Ministry, of course, these local arrangements became a national scheme, and the major recipients of Volunteers' skills were to be the controlled establishments. Those who joined were asked to sign the following pledge:

> In accordance with the arrangements which have been made with the Minister of Munitions by the National Advisory Committee, acting on behalf of the Trade Unions, I undertake with the Minister of Munitions to accept employment in making munitions of war in such controlled establishments as may be named by him, and to remain in such employment during the War for as long as required (not exceeding six months in all), subject to the conditions set out on this form.[4]

The terms of the agreement guaranteed to the Volunteer that he would be paid either the wage he received in his home district or the wage prevalent for his craft in the area to which he was transferred, whichever happened to be higher. He was also guaranteed, if transferred to a factory beyond a reasonable day's travelling distance, railway fare to and from his new job. Furthermore, if transferred in this way, the Volunteer was to receive a subsistence allowance of 2s. 6d. per day, for the length of his term of employment. If the job to which he was transferred could be reached from his home each day, the Volunteer was to receive the cost of his train ticket and, if his daily travelling time exceeded thirty minutes, an additional thirty minutes' wages per day computed at the rate of time and one half.

Lastly, the War Munitions Volunteer agreed to submit his workshop disagreements to the munitions tribunals and to abide by their decisions. As the terms of the Volunteer scheme were set out in the Munitions of War Act, workers who signed the undertaking were bound by the force of law. By the same token, employers who discouraged their employees from signing up or interfered with the transfer of Volunteers from their shops became subject to the jurisdiction of the tribunals.

Enrolment of the War Munitions Volunteers was carried out

both in normal Labour Exchanges and in specially created War Munitions Bureaux, many of which were set up in municipal halls and other public buildings.[5] The reaction of British working men to the announcement of the scheme was gratifying to the National Advisory Committee, who had sponsored the programme in this form, and to the Labour Department of the Ministry, and thousands of willing and presumably skilled men voluntarily signed the undertaking. Between 24 June and 24 November 1915 more than 107,000 workers joined the Volunteers.[6] In the end, however, the elation in Whitehall Gardens at these enormous figures was short-lived: during this same four-month period, only 5,600 of these Volunteers were actually transferred from private to Government work. By the close of Lloyd George's tenure at the Munitions Office there were more than 120,000 names on the rolls and yet the total number transferred to munitions work was only about 12,000 men. In brief, the War Munitions Volunteer scheme had failed to live up to the expectations of its creators.

The major reason why so few Volunteers were transferred early in the life of the scheme was that the vast majority were already at work on Government contracts, in munitions-related industries or in indispensable civilian employment. To prevent the accidental transfer of such men, the employers of Volunteers were allowed to submit official protests after being notified of the possible loss of their workmen. Before the end of 1915, more than 60,000 such objections had poured into the Ministry of Munitions. In addition to the thousands of mechanics who could not be transferred, there were thousands more who, it was discovered, did not possess the sufficient level of skill to warrant transfer to controlled establishments.

The War Munitions Volunteer scheme had not been a complete failure, however. In the first place, it laid to rest the theory that the absolute shortage of skilled men in Great Britain could be overcome by shifting workers from one shop to another. This especially strengthened the hand of the Minister of Munitions in his dealings with the trade unions as he turned toward the ultimate solution to the labour shortage, the dilution of skilled labour. The Volunteer programme had been, as the Ministry itself pointed out, a sort of 'Derby Scheme for labour'—that is, a last gasp for the voluntary principle. In a meeting of the senior staff of the Ministry with the National Labour Advisory Committee on 13 September 1915, Lloyd George informed his listeners that the scheme had failed. Thereafter, while the War Munitions Volunteers would remain a part of the labour strategy of the Ministry and workmen would be transferred from their employers to controlled establishments whenever possible, the Department must concentrate, he said, 'on getting men away from work which unskilled persons can do just as well, and concentrating those skilled persons on work of an expert character. That is a problem of removing restrictions which have been imposed by custom and usage of the past, and I shall want to advise you as to the best method of approaching that problem.'[7] In short, the failure of the Volunteer scheme to provide the needed skilled labour for munitions production was the best possible argument for Dilution.

There was a further service performed by the scheme. Securing signatures of willing workmen was no hardship and thousands continued to enrol. Once their names were on the Volunteer lists, under the 1915 Munitions of War Act, it was a violation of the Act for their employers to interfere with the transfer of the men. Hence the mere threat of transfer of much needed skilled men was used by the Ministry to bring to heel troublesome employers.[8]

Wide-scale transfer of War Munitions Volunteers was not possible until the Dilution programme of the Ministry of Munitions rendered highly skilled men more mobile. Before the end of the War more than 80,000 transfers were carried out under the scheme. Though it was supported by many trade unionists as an alternative to Dilution, the War Munitions Volunteer scheme, quite to the contrary, proved effective only after the introduction into the armaments factories of many tens of thousands of unskilled workers.

II

A second source from which the Ministry of Munitions hoped to draw reinforcements for the skilled labour force in the armaments factories was the British Army itself. As we have seen, efforts had been made since early 1915 to restrain the movement into the Forces of skilled men—efforts which had met with only limited success. When the Ministry of Munitions became responsible for labour policy, they meant not merely to cut off this flow but also to gain the return of as many of those skilled recruits as possible.

As early as January 1915, due to the protests of certain War Office contractors who had lost valuable skilled men to the Army, Lord Kitchener had allowed the release from their battalions of a small number of such men. In April 1915, after the creation of the Armaments Output Committee, a small department was formed within the War Office to oversee the release from the Army of needed workmen. These efforts, however, were pursued on a very small scale: while the Army had absorbed thousands of skilled mechanics, only approximately 3,000 such men were released for service in the munitions factories before the creation of the Ministry of Munitions.[9]

Soon after Lloyd George moved from the Treasury to Whitehall Gardens, a Release from the Colours Department, under the authority of Major F. J. Scott, was created to secure the return of as many skilled recruits as possible. Major Scott discovered that the task would not be an easy one. The Army, of course, was reluctant to give up each man, and the recruits themselves were often less than enthusiastic about leaving their comrades and returning to civilian life. In addition, locating the right men—men with the needed industrial skills and experience—was no mean task. Finally, two parallel methods were employed to overcome these problems and secure the return of many needed mechanics.

Under the first method the Ministry Release from the Colours Department called upon munitions manufacturers to submit the names and regiments of their former skilled employees known to have enlisted. While more than 41,000 names were submitted to the Department under this Individual Release scheme within the first year of the programme, only those thought suitable, those who possessed the needed skills and experience, were requested by Major Scott's Department. Once closely examined by them, the names were sent to the War Office for action. If the Adjutant General's office was satisfied that each man in question was sufficiently skilled to warrant release, and if he was still in Britain and had not yet undergone advanced training for imminent service abroad, then the man was released from active service. If the workman, who remained a soldier even if released, desired to return to industrial life, he was thereafter placed in a controlled establishment. During Lloyd George's period at the Ministry, almost 20,000 recommendations for release were forwarded by Major Scott's department to the War Office and more than 14,000 men actually returned to work.[10]

The second method by which skilled recruits were secured for the factories was the so-called Bulk scheme, employed first during July and August 1915. Unlike the Individual Release method, the Bulk scheme consisted of a call by the Ministry to all skilled men within 'non-barred units'—that is, units which had not undergone advanced training or which did not require the skilled men—to offer themselves for interview by Ministry inspectors and possible transfer to controlled establishments. Under the first Bulk Release programme, almost 7,000 men were interviewed and 2,100 were found suitable for transfer.

The second Bulk scheme of September to November 1915 was considerably more ambitious as more than 1,500,000 men were paraded before and addressed by Ministry inspectors. Approximately 103,000 men volunteered their skills for munitions work and 40,000 were recommended for transfer by the Release from the Colours Department.

During December 1915 and January 1916, the Ministry's inspectors were allowed by the War Office to address certain units of the British Army in France. This third or B.E.F. bulk scheme had been approved by Sir John French under the condition that only 2,000 men might be returned, and 1,996 were provisionally recommended for transfer to munitions shops. To ensure that only the most skilled men were selected for release, tests were given at Le Havre to measure the proficiency of these soldiers. Finally, 1,732 men were recommended for release for munitions work.[11]

During Lloyd George's ministry, the Release from the Colours Department recommended the return of more than 19,000 men under the individual release procedure and more than 43,000 under the bulk schemes. In the end, 14,130 and 29,101, respectively, were actually placed with controlled establishments. This ended the Release from the Colours programme for, with the exception of small bulk returns of men with specific skills for which there were immediate and serious needs, most men returned from the Army after this period were invalided out in the usual fashion. Beginning in the autumn of 1916, a programme called the Reserve Army Munitions Workers was begun to place men in the munitions shops who had been classified as suitable for Home service only.[12]

Under the provisions of the Release from the Colours scheme, and unlike the various programmes which followed it, the skilled mechanics who returned to the factories remained soldiers. Their command was transferred to the Ministry of Munitions, but they remained subject to military discipline—they could, in short, be moved about where they were needed without the concern and problems inherent in attempting the same procedures with civilian trade unionists. The released man, however, received the wage prevailing in the area to which he was transferred, or his Army pay and allowances, whichever happened to be higher. If transferred to a district away from his home, the returned soldier's family was also entitled to receive a separation allowance. Such arrangements were expensive, and all allowances or military pay were supplied from War Office funds, which made the Release from the Colours procedure even more unpopular with the military than it already was. However, the fact that these highly skilled men constituted a mobile corps of experienced engineers made them far more valuable than their numbers indicated. The feeling at Whitehall Gardens was that the Ministry had laboured hard to secure each release. Lloyd George told the National Labour Advisory Committee and his senior staff in late 1915:

> We have had to get them by a process of extracting teeth. We have had to use forceps to get every turner and fitter back from any division or any platoon.[13]

Major Scott's department later estimated that these workers, drawn from 4,136 different units of the Army and distributed to more than 3,800 different employers, played a highly significant role in the Dilution campaign. Such a policy could succeed only if skilled and unskilled labour were closely coordinated, and Scott's estimate that each of these returned mechanics—placed where the Ministry felt them most necessary—created jobs for ten unskilled dilutees, was probably not far from the mark.[14]

III

A further source of labour supply considered by the Board of Trade, by the various munitions committees, and, finally, by the Ministry of Munitions was the importation of skilled men from the Dominions and from foreign nations. As early as December 1914 the Board of Trade had received communications from Canada indicating that there was a surplus of such labour which could be brought to Britain for munitions work. The original Shells Committee and, later, the Treasury Committee had considered the possibility of importing Canadian labour. Each time the idea was examined, however, plans were scuttled due to several serious problems: Dominion labour generally received a higher wage than British workers and, if higher pay were guaranteed Canadians in British shops, ill-feeling among British workers would have been inevitable. Likewise, it was feared that British trade unionists would not work side by side with imported labour while their own shopmates were being recruited for service in the trenches. A third factor which proved to be a problem in importing Canadian labour was the hostility of Dominion employers, who preferred that the Imperial Government in London place contracts with them, rather than remove their labour to Britain.[15]

Finally, in mid-1915, a Board of Trade mission, including the Labour M.P., George Barnes, sailed for Canada to ascertain if indeed there were skilled men available for work in British munitions shops.[16] They encountered not only the hostility of Canadian industrialists but also the surprising fact that there were not great numbers of unemployed skilled men, as they had expected. In the end, the mission arranged the importation of approximately 1,000 men; and, before the close of the War, an additional 1,000 Canadians came to Britain to work in the munitions factories.

Offers of skilled workers came to Britain from South Africa, New Zealand, and Australia in 1914 and 1915. While only a trickle of skilled men entered Britain from these Dominions during Lloyd George's time at the Munitions Office, before the Armistice approximately 5,000 men arrived in the British munitions factories.[17] In the end, the problems created by the difficulty of measuring the skills of men in distant lands, along with the expense of bringing them to Britain, as well as the hostility of Dominion employers and British trade unionists doomed any large-scale migration of Dominion workers into the controlled establishments and National Factories of Great Britain.

The last attempt to supplement the supply of skilled labour was by no means the least interesting; it was the importation of foreign labour into Britain. While there were workmen of many nationalities in the munitions-related trades in Great Britain during the War, with the exception of a number of Danes recruited to work in the timber industry, the vast majority of foreign nationals who worked on British munitions were Belgians.[18]

Within a matter of weeks after the beginning of the War more than 100,000 Belgian refugees had flooded into Britain, their own nation occupied by the German conqueror. The Board of Trade sought to recruit skilled men from among these unhappy masses almost immediately. By early December 1914 the Labour Exchange Department had begun to assemble a 'live register' of potential skilled workers—that is, a list of men who both possessed the necessary skills and who wished to find employment in Britain.[19] Soon thereafter, the Board of Trade sent agents to Holland to seek further skilled men from among Belgians who had sought refuge there. Before May 1915, approximately 4,100 Belgians had been given employment in British armaments factories.[20]

With the advent of the Ministry of Munitions Labour Department, the active recruitment of skilled mechanics within units of the Belgian Army in unoccupied territory was begun. Though Belgian military authorities were at first difficult to persuade of the wisdom of such a policy, their objections were finally overcome and the release from the colours of these highly skilled men was begun.

It was soon discovered that attempts to integrate Belgian workers into British shops were not generally successful—the fears expressed at the prospect of bringing Dominion workers into British shops were shown to be too true in the case of the Belgians. The language difference, of course, made cooperation even more difficult. More significant was the fact that the Belgian workers were accustomed to a totally different factory-routine from their British counterparts. Many British workers made no secret of their preference for their old shopmates, many of whom were by then in the trenches, rather than the Belgian refugees.[21] The solution to this problem was to gather together as many Belgians as possible in order to establish separate departments, manned exclusively by refugee labour, within the factories.

By late 1915 representatives of two Belgian firms were invited to establish and administer small factories staffed by their own countrymen on British soil.[22] However, the most colourful result of this policy of allowing Belgian workmen to function autonomously within the armament production programme of the Ministry was the creation of a complete Belgian factory community near the village of Birtley in Durham.[23]

Under the authority of the Munitions Office, both a National Factory and an entire village (called Elizabethville in honour of the Belgian Queen), were constructed. It was a curious mixture of traditional Belgian and contemporary 'garden city' thinking in layout, and in it the Ministry constructed several large dining halls, a number of shops to supply the needs of the populace, and even the Church of St Michael. Since the overwhelming majority of the residents of Elizabethville had fled their homes and belongings at a moment's notice, the Ministry supplied with each dwelling furnishings, cooking utensils and other necessities of life.

The overwhelming majority of Belgian workers in the local National Factory at Birtley, overseen by Armstrong's Ltd, were soldiers released from the colours. Totalling more than 4,000, most of these men were skilled mechanics. Under the direct authority of a resident Belgian general manager, M Debauche, who acted under the supervision of Maurice S. Gibb of the Ministry of Munitions, the rather unprecedented experiment of creating a foreign industrial enterprise on British soil was quite successful. Every effort was made to make the Belgians feel at home: Belgian police enforced Belgian law, French language road-signs and newspapers were seen in the street and even a typically Belgian café, the *Cheval Blanc,* was provided. Like so many other compromises worked by the Ministry, the building of Elizabethville proved to be a considerable success by the end of the War.

IV

By the late summer and early autumn of 1915, it was becoming apparent to the Minister of Munitions and his advisers on labour supply matters that the various programmes meant to supplement the skilled workforce in the munitions shops—the policy generally called reinforcement—would not overcome the shortage of such men. At this time the Army was moving quickly toward the conclusion that it would require 1,500,000 men for the 1916 Campaign, and each day the new National Factories and the extensions to the assembly lines of the armament manufacturers were that much closer to completion. These factors all pointed in the same direction: the only possible solution to the labour problem was a cooperative policy of labour, management and the State to maximize the effectiveness of each skilled worker. In short, the initial four or five months of the lifespan of the Ministry of Munitions had proved that only a vigorous policy of Dilution of skilled labour was Britain's last best hope for armaments production in the War.

An unorthodox and, to those who feared each step toward State control, a rather worrying step was taken by the Government at about this same time. In mid-July a National Registration Act was passed into law and Sunday, 15 August 1915 was set aside as Registration Day. This was, in fact, another step on the path toward Dilution, toward the more efficient distribution of labour. On the appointed day, each man and woman in the nation between the ages of fifteen and sixty-five was required to reveal to canvassers his name, occupation, skills, employer and other vital data to provide a detailed picture of the size and talents of the maximum possible workforce in Great Britain.[24]

A policy committee, under the chairmanship of Walter Long, the President of the Local Government Board, was created to advise on the best use to be made of the Registration.[25] Their most significant suggestion was that a permanent committee was needed to employ the Registration to correlate the manpower needs of industry and the military. This led, in October, to the creation of the Reserved Occupations Committee, which began to work in this direction. When the results of the Registration were tabulated by the Committee, the forms of males of military age who were in occupations necessary to the war effort were abstracted and black stars were put on them. They numbered approximately 1,500,000 out of a total in this age and sex division of about 5,000,000.

What did the Ministry of Munitions learn from this exercise? In the first place, the Registration proved that no more men in the highest categories of skilled labour could be lost to enlistment. Next, it demonstrated that, even allowing for a certain degree of error in the figures obtained by the Registration, in no circumstances could Britain expect to continue to attempt to produce munitions with male labour while maintaining an army of continental size. The Ministry estimated that on the basis of these figures, after subtracting men necessary to the production of munitions, necessities of life or export-goods, it would be impossible to raise the 1,500,000 men for the 1916 campaign without diluting the male workforce.[26]

The implementation of Dilution had not been far from the minds of the Minister of Munitions and his labour advisers since the creation of the new Department. It had been at the root of the Shells and Fuses Agreement and the Treasury Conference, before that time, and it had influenced the Munitions of War Act. The failure of the War Munitions Volunteers and of Release from the Colours schemes to produce enough men had made it inevitable. Finally the National Registration indicated that the time had arrived for a full-scale campaign of intensified use of skilled labour.

Lloyd George chose to take his case directly to the only men in the nation who could make Dilution work: the skilled workmen themselves. On 9 September 1915, he addressed their representatives at the Trades Union Congress at Bristol. He called on them to throw aside their restrictive practices which, he reminded them, they had already agreed to do at the Treasury

Conference months before. Reassuring his audience that their traditional relations with their employers would be restored when the War was over, he promised them that they would be asked to submit to State direction only as the owners, shareholders and managers of the factories had already been required to accept under the excess profits regulations of the Munitions Act. He chided them for placing their own interests before those of the nation and reminded them that the World War could be won only with their complete cooperation.[27]

A week later, on 16 and 17 September, Henderson's National Labour Advisory Committee organized a conference of the executives of the most important engineering trade unions at the Wesleyan Hall in Westminster. Lloyd George addressed the meeting and heard the complaints and apprehensions of the labour leaders about Dilution. They feared the use of female and un-skilled male labour as 'blacklegs' to break the power of the unions. They insisted upon assurances from the Minister that agreement to a Dilution scheme would not see trade unionists delivered bound and gagged into the hands of the factory owners. The Minister of Munitions gave exactly these assurances, but he reminded his listeners that, since all other expedients had failed, only the success of Dilution could prevent some form of labour conscription—or the destruction of the nation.[28]

To assure that labour's interests were safeguarded as the Dilution campaign was planned, Lloyd George suggested the appointment of a joint committee of representatives of the trade unions, the engineering employers and the labour and supply departments of the Ministry of Munitions to aid in creating and implementing the new scheme. The idea was enthusiastically received and the Central Munitions Labour Supply Committee was appointed with Arthur Henderson serving as chairman. On 22 September 1915 the Committee held its first meeting and dutifully advised Lloyd George that Dilution was indeed the sole expedient which could overcome the labour shortage. Over the signature of the Minister of Munitions, a circular, known as C.E. 1, was issued by the Munitions Office to all controlled establishments instructing them:

to take immediate steps to replace skilled men wherever possible by less skilled labour, either men or women, and to employ the skilled men so released in establishing night shifts or upon machinery hitherto standing idle in their shops, and surplus which might exist being available of course for transfer else-where.[29]

C.E. I, issued on 13 October 1915, was the first official announcement of what came to be called the October Programme of Dilution.

The philosophy and goals of the Dilution scheme begun in October 1915 may be summarized under several heads: the most significant principle was that no worker in the munitions shops was to be employed at any task which required skill of a lesser degree than he possessed. Secondly, the Dilution programme required that in any trade in which there was a shortage of man-power, the deficiency was to be made good through the introduction of soldiers invalided home, of those men physically unfit or over age for military service, and of women and juveniles. Thirdly, the substitution of unskilled dilutees for skilled men was to be effected through the subdivision of skilled tasks into their simplest processes, through the introduction of automatic machines which required little skill to operate and through the constant process of training and 'upgrading' of dilutees.[30]

Under the authority delegated it by the Ministry of Munitions, the Central Munitions Labour Supply Committee issued a series of recommendations to controlled establishments concerning the October Programme of Dilution known as the L Circulars. The most famous, L2 and L3, dealt with wages policies and will be treated in detail in the next chapter. However, circulars L5 and L6 laid down general policies in regard to the implementation of Dilution in controlled establishments.[31] In particular, they recommended that the institution of Dilution in a controlled establishment be preceded by consultation with representatives of the workers and a clear explanation by management of the details of the alterations in workshop procedure. L5 and L6 reiterated the guarantees Lloyd George had made to trade unionists as inducements to cooperate with the Dilution programme. While they were not binding on all controlled shops, these circulars had the support of the Minister and were generally observed in diluted factories.

In order to fulfil its pledge to keep the representatives of the workmen informed of any contemplated changes in controlled establishments, the Ministry Labour Department relied first upon the Labour Advisory Boards in each industrial district to act as agents between the Ministry and the trade unionists. It was hoped that these representative committees might help to speed the beginning of new Dilution schemes. In addition, executive control of the entire October Programme was vested in a Director General of Munitions Labour Supply. Before the end of Lloyd George's tenure at the Munitions Office, however, a different executive structure for the implementation of Dilution was developed.

The Ministry of Munitions, as it so often did under Lloyd George's leadership, impatiently turned to a policy of Central Control when local autonomy proved inefficient or slow. The office of Director General of Munitions Labour Supply was that of a kind of arbitrator, who watched over the Dilution arrangements made by factory manager and trade union representatives and made certain the Ministry's policies were not violated. This machinery was replaced in 1916 by a Dilution Section of the Labour Department, based in London, which operated through a staff of inspectors who visited hundreds of factories each week. With the Dilution objectives of the October Programme in mind, this department either closely advised factory owners and trade unionists or actually provided Dilution plans for each shop. In 1915, before the executive machinery of Dilution was fully developed, only 700 works were visited; in 1916, when the Dilution Section was organized, Ministry Dilution Inspectors visited almost 6,500 different factories and revisited virtually all those examined in the previous year.[32] The creation of the Dilution Section, like all the other efforts made by the Minister of Munitions and his staff in 1915 and 1916, were only as effective as the cooperation of British labour would allow them to be. Factory owners could be coerced relatively easily; Lloyd George and his successors at the Munitions Office discovered that the millions of workers who actually manufactured munitions could be more difficult.

Strikes and lockouts had, of course, been outlawed by the Munitions of War Act, 1915. Despite the law, however, stoppages occurred from time to time. Less than a fortnight after the passage of the Act a great, though brief, strike broke out in the South Wales coalfields. Of greater import to the Ministry of Munitions was a bitter strike which occurred at the Fairfield Shipyards on Clydeside in September 1915: the Welsh coal stoppage had concerned wages, while the shipbuilders struck over opposition to the hated Section 7 of the Munitions Act. Though the Clydesiders were brought back to work and the Act was more or less victorious, this affair was an ominous herald of future problems in the North. Indeed, a short time after the Fairfield strike, 'Red Clydeside' came to dominate the attentions of the Ministry of Munitions as it became the first great test of the ability of the new Department to implement the October Programme of Dilution. [33]

In the autumn of 1915, the Ministry announced plans to introduce female dilutees into the machine shops of John Lang Ltd., of Johnstone. The experiment had proceeded according to the Dilution guidelines of the Central Munitions Labour Supply Committee; after conferences with both the national and local representatives of the Amalgamated Society of Engineers executive, nineteen women were put to work in late October. The shop stewards on Clydeside, well aware that the machine tool trade was perhaps the most skilled of all the engineering trades, chose to make a struggle of it. [34] They announced that a strike would be called if the Dilution plan were continued and no one, on Clydeside or in Whitehall, considered the threat an empty bluff.

In an attempt to head off a crash, Lloyd George chose to turn his own personal magnetism to the task of composing the disagreement on Clydeside—he had, after all, settled the South Wales miners' strike of May in short order by being lavish indeed with the money of the coal-owners. He could not, however, afford to solve the Lang strike by giving in to the men, for that would mean the sacrifice of the principle of Dilution. Lloyd George had faced many hostile audiences in his career. During his pro-Boer days he had more than once risked life and limb to tell an assembly exactly what it did not wish to hear. The crisis dragged on through November. Finally, on Christmas morning, Lloyd George addressed the assembled trade unionists of the district at St. Andrew's Hall in Glasgow. He received a hostile reception unlike any he had faced since those days at the turn of the century when he spoke against a different war. A conference with the local shop stewards was no more successful at composing the differences between Ministry and men than was the general address.[35]

On 22 January 1916 the Government announced the appointment of a Commission to Effect Dilution of Labour to solve the problems impeding the October Programme on Clydeside. Chaired by the well-known barrister, Lynden Macassey, and including Sir Thomas Munro and Sir Isaac Mitchell, the Commission worked tirelessly to bring employers, workmen, and the Ministry of Munitions into a common viewpoint on implementing Dilution. Despite the impatience of many owners and the constant suspicion of the shop stewards, and with an eye always on the terrible need to hasten munitions production, the Macassey Commission succeeded in employing a slow and patient application of the accepted Dilution procedures of the Henderson Labour Supply Committee. The beginning of a new Dilution scheme in each shop was preceded by discussions of all parties under the eye of the Commission. In the end, they were quite successful.[36] Before the Macassey Commission was dissolved in August 1916 and Dilution procedures of the sensitive Clyde region were returned to the Dilution Section of the Ministry, more than 14,000 female dilutees were at work in the district. Dilution was, of course, never popular among British workmen, yet they had accepted it as an inconvenience of wartime. It was only through this acceptance that the policy was successful.

V

The decision to implement Dilution on a wide scale, the conversion or defeat of its enemies and the raising of many thousands of dilutees did not end the responsibilities of the Ministry of Munitions in the realm of labour supply. No doubt many Britons assumed that unskilled men and women were collected through the various appeals for War workers and sent into the engineering shops to make armaments. This was not the case at all, of course, for the Ministry found itself in the business of training dilutees to be useful in their new occupations.[37]

The London County Council in 1914 had taken the lead in the movement to train new volunteers for munitions work during the early days of the War. 'The early classes,' the Ministry reported later, 'aimed principally at providing simple training to fit the unskilled worker to take his or her place usefully and quickly in a factory.[38] Shortly thereafter, under the aegis of Mrs Fawcett's National Union of Women's Suffrage Societies, a scheme was financed to convert a workshop maintained by a lady silversmith into a training facility for female oxy-acetylene welders for the aircraft industry.[39] These are, of course, only examples of many such efforts.

With the creation of the Ministry and its October Programme, the training of novice munitions workers ceased to be a sporadic local or private movement and became part of the policy of a Department of State. Arrangements were made by the Labour Department under which the Board of Education placed its expertise and its facilities at the disposal of the Munitions Office. The task was no small one, for Great Britain had not led the nations of Europe in technical or industrial education. Hence, many training shops had to be built and many private Government contractors, as well as the new National Factories, established such shops under their roofs to train their own dilutees. Shortly after Lloyd George had left Munitions to move to the War Office, the Ministry completed the construction of several factories devoted almost exclusively to the training of dilutees.

The Director of the Training Department of the Ministry, T. M. Taylor, reported in August 1916:

The result has been that 21,700 students have completed a course of instruction in the 65 training classes that have been held in various centres, a great majority of these have been known to have been placed on munitions work . . . .
Additional facilities for obtaining up-to-date machinery have enabled the Ministry to undertake on a fairly extensive scale the

training of men and women for more highly specialised lines. The result has been that over 500 men have been trained as Toolsetters on one special type of machine and placed in Munitions Factories, nearly 200 plumbers have been trained as Lead-burners for the Explosives Factories and 130 jewellers have already been trained and placed as gauge makers.

It is anticipated that in the coming year in view of the increasing difficulty of meeting the demand for skilled labour in Aero-engine works and other Munitions Factories a considerable extension of training on specialized lines will be necessary.[40]

In addition to the training or retraining of men, women and juvenile dilutees, there was a further effort by the Ministry to allow patriotic Britons to 'do their bit' for the War effort. Two official vehicles were created to this end: the Volunteer Munitions Brigade and the Women Munitions Workers. The former organization enrolled approximately 15,000 men, almost entirely from the non-industrial population. By June 1916 approximately half of the Brigade—city men, tradesmen, university dons and many others—had been temporarily employed to allow regular munitions workers recuperative time away from their machines. The latter group consisted of ladies of the 'educated classes' and was constituted of approximately 2,000 such women who were employed from time to time in munitions-related industries to relieve over-burdened factory women in London area munitions shops.

'In addition,' the Labour Department of the Ministry reported, 'there were large numbers of male and female volunteer workers throughout the country for which there were no reliable statistics.'[41] While employers and workers were often decidedly hostile to such dilettante munitions workers at the outset of these programmes, within a few months of the beginning of wide-scale Dilution these men and women came to be appreciated as the terrible results of overwork appeared among full-time dilutees.[42]

There are, of course, no reliable figures of the results of the training of regular and part-time munitions workers, as most took whatever training was easily available to them. What is more interesting is the result of the entire Dilution Programme: the maximum training course given by the Ministry or the National

Factories was 144 hours. Yet the quality of their products remained high, despite the ever-growing demands for shells and guns.

In assessing the policies of the Ministry of Munitions during 1915 and 1916 there are several things we must notice. In the first place, of all the problems which confronted the new Department in May 1915, the matter of labour supply was the most difficult. The Ministry was faced, on the one hand, by a serious shortage of skilled workers and the prospect that, with the completion of the new National Factories and the increases in capacity of the older State and private shops, the requirement for labour would only grow larger. On the other hand, they knew that the traditionally strong trade unions were extremely reluctant to abandon the complicated system of shop privileges they had built up over many years. They were also acutely aware that the labouring classes were deeply hostile towards any suggestion of labour conscription. In short, the labour problem took on mammoth proportions when seen in conjunction with these realities.

To overcome the challenge, the Minister of Munitions uncovered relatively few skilled men who were not already on Government work. As in the cases of the new National Factories and Cooperative Schemes, the men of Whitehall Gardens turned to a policy of combining conciliation with State Control to overcome the problem. The ideas behind release from the colours, the relaxation of trade union rules, even of Dilution itself were not new when taken up by the Ministry. However, Lloyd George, Addison, Llewellyn Smith, Beveridge and the others who made the labour policy of the Ministry took these ideas, and the new powers granted their Department, and made them more effective than they had ever been before. Armed with the knowledge that the vast majority of Britons were willing to make unprecedented sacrifices and to expect them of their fellow citizens, the first Minister of Munitions and his staff imposed upon industrial life in Great Britain the greatest degree of State control and centralized management ever seen in that nation to that time.

Lastly, it should be noted that at no point could the labour problem be considered thoroughly solved during the duration of the War. While the most pressing problem in 1915 and 1916 was the shortage of men for munitions work, in 1917 and 1918 the most significant need was to maintain armaments production while releasing more men for military service. The Dilution policy of the Ministry of Munitions and the hard work of British labour met those needs.[43]

Eight

'THE WOMEN'S PART'

I

To the popular mind in Britain, Dilution meant women. And, for all practical purposes, it did. The lives of millions of women in Britain were for ever altered by the munitions crusade; many discovered they could do productive and useful things which they had never before been allowed to attempt. In the discovery they for ever changed not only their own lives, but the lives of all Britons from that time on.

Hard work was nothing new for many British women, however. Out of a total female population in Great Britain of approximately 24 million, about one in four was employed on the eve of the War.[1] The largest single source of women's employment was domestic service, which accounted for almost 1,700,000 jobs. More than 800,000 women worked in the textile industry and another 600,000 laboured in the clothing trades, two basic industries in which they outnumbered their male work-mates, while half a million were employed in commerce. National and local government accounted for an additional 262,000 positions, and this included the many women employed as teachers.[2] With the coming of the War and the advent of the Ministry of Munitions, perhaps Britain's most significant industries were metalworking and engineering; these trades employed more than 1,600,000 males on the eve of the War, but only 170,000 females. These women worked in what were termed the minor metal trades and only in specified aspects of production which forbade their direct competition with skilled men.[3]

While the 1909 Trades Boards Act had alleviated many of the worst aspects of the sweating of female labour, in 1914 women were still the drudges of factory life; their tasks were usually uninteresting and often unpleasant and their wages averaged no more than one-half of that of male workers.[4] With the happy exceptions of the few who had begun to open the traditional professions to females, the economic future for working women in Britain in 1914 was not encouraging.

When the World War began, as we have seen, the great economic dislocation expected by many in Government and business did not occur and there was no general increase in unemployment. Among women, however, there was a short-lived growth in numbers of unemployed as industry shifted from a peacetime to a wartime footing. In September 1914 the total reported contraction in women's employment was 190,000; it fell to 139,000 in October and to 75,000 in December, then to only 35,000 in February 1915.[5] The Board of Trade estimated that even in March 1915 36 per cent of women workers were employed on short time.[6]

Concern for the plight of unemployed women was shared by the State and private charity. In August 1914 a Central Committee on Women's Employment was appointed by the Government to examine ways in which work could be found for unemployed females. The Committee hoped that through such expedients as a shortened working week, public works projects by local government and the institution of a minimum wage, serious distress could be alleviated and available work spread around among the female work force.[7] Though the War was, at this time, still expected to be brief, there was considerable concern that women might become not only cold and hungry, but also dependent upon the State.

At about this same time Queen Mary formed the Queen's Work for Women Fund to create jobs for unemployed females 'in the firm belief that prevention of distress is better than its relief and employment better than charity.' £20,000, reportedly, was subscribed for the Fund within twelve hours of its creation.[8] Within a year, however, all these concerns about women's unemployment would be forgotten.

When the War Office List firms began to report shortages of

labour in the autumn of 1914, the Board of Trade did make efforts to place women in their shops. Approximately 2,000 women were found places in private munitions factories before March 1915, though most of these were placed before the end of 1914.[9] Undeterred, the Labour Exchange Department announced on 16 March 1915 that it intended to gather a *War Register* of women who wished to find employment in the munitions shops for the duration of the War.[10] Posters were displayed at the Labour Exchanges encouraging women to sign up if they wished to aid the War effort and announcements to the same effect were printed in the newspapers. Public meetings were held and the Prime Minister himself was pressed into service. On 4 May Asquith spoke extolling the virtues of the employment of women on 'men's work' in order that men might be released to do their duty in the Army.[11]

The *War Register* was rather an unprecedented experiment and the entire effort became cloaked in rumour and misinformation. Some felt that it was the beginning of the conscription of women into the services; others were certain that it had some connection with the prohibition by the State of strong drink. As though overcoming such notions was not trouble enough, registrars at the Labour Exchanges reported that many women changed their minds about signing up when they discovered that volunteering required revealing their ages.[12]

The initial purpose of the *Register* was to collect the names of those women who wished to do munitions work, and to that limited end it was a great success. By 22 May 1915 more than 1,500 women had enrolled; by 4 June 1915, after the *Register* had become nationally known, approximately 79,000 women had signed.[13]

There was little success beyond the collecting of names, however, for of that vast number, only 1,816 were actually found munitions-related employment.[14]. The majority of Government contractors had no desire to take women into their shops, for even females with factory experience were invariably unskilled and, thus, required training and close supervision. In addition, alterations in the plant buildings would be required for their convenience which would, in the end, be wasted investment. Therefore most employers were uncooperative with the Board of Trade campaign. The patriotic sentiments of these women were welcome to the

Government, but it mattered little, finally, whether 80,000 or 800,000 signed the *Register* if places could not be found for them.

II

For women who wished to take an active part in the War this was a frustrating period. The War Office, for example, had rejected the efforts of would-be Florence Nightingales and these women doctors and nurses were thrown on their own resources. The results were nothing less than heroic. British women set up, staffed and conducted military hospitals in Serbia and France and Poland —often financed by suffragist and feminist societies—before the British War Office sanctioned their serving their own country-men.[15] While a handful of like-minded women were given the opportunity during the early months of the War to serve as tram conductresses or tube station attendants at home, this period saw few women labouring at what was generally termed 'men's work'.[16]

Women were advised to continue to do what women had done before the War, albeit more thriftily and with an air of patriotism; and if they were still dissatisfied they were expected to expend their frustrations on their knitting needles. The articles in newspapers and magazines variously titled 'What Women May Do' or 'The Women's Part' or something of the sort, generally advised them of the great value of knitting or sewing 'comforts' for the troops, or making War puddings and, of course, the nursing of wounded soldiers returned from the Front. Mrs Peel recalled that 'in those first years of War those who sold knitting needles and wool must have amassed fortunes'.[17] For many women, however, it was not enough.

The years immediately before the War, it will be recalled, had seen the greatest women's rights movement of the century. After August 1914 the majority of the most extreme believers in the movement, the Suffragettes, had thrown themselves enthusiastically into the campaign for patriotism and sacrifice. When the creation of the Ministry of Munitions promised a more advanced and en-lightened management of armaments production, the leader of the late wars for the vote, Mrs Emmeline Pankhurst, moved to test the intentions of the chief of the new Department. This remarkable woman, who had once been sentenced to penal servitude for conspiracy to bomb Lloyd George's Walton Heath home, on 17 July 1915 led a demonstration of 30,000 women to wait upon the Minister of Munitions. While this time she came unarmed, she arrived no less determined; Mrs. Pankhurst came to demand not the vote, but the 'Right to Serve'.

Accompanied by a small deputation, Mrs. Pankhurst was interviewed by the Minister: 'The women in this procession to-day,' she said, 'have taken part in it because they wished to demonstrate their desire to serve in any and every capacity in which they may be of use.' Turning to the employment of women in armaments shops, she added: 'We do urge that wherever a woman is engaged to do work previously done by a man, if she does it exactly like a man, she should be paid the same rate of wages, whether she is doing piecework or she is engaged in what is called time work.'[18] Lloyd George assured her that he would tolerate no exploitation of women's work.

Accompanied by the deputation, the Minister walked the short distance from Whitehall Gardens to the Victoria Embankment where the huge crowd of demonstrators had waited patiently in the rainy July afternoon.

> The Government [he told them] will see that there is no sweated labour. For some time women will be unskilled and untrained, and they cannot turn out as much work as men who have been at it for some time. Therefore, we cannot give the full rate of wages. Mrs. Pankhurst is quite right in insisting that whatever these wages are, they should be fair, and there should be a fixed minimum, and we should not utilize the services of women to get cheaper labour.[19]

Within a matter of two or three months following this meeting, the Ministry of Munitions was to embark on its Dilution campaign. Once that decision was made, Lloyd George's pledge to the Women's Procession in July 1915 took on enormous significance.

During the weeks that the Board of Trade attempted to place women workers in the factories of Government contractors, it had been stipulated to all who would volunteer that they would be paid the same piecework rates as men who normally did those jobs. To many employers, such a promise was no great concession, for the chance of unskilled women really replacing skilled men—that is, actually doing the same job—was relatively small. Lloyd George, however, had promised that women would receive a fair wage while they learned industrial work and, as the Minister responsible for munitions production, he had pledged the Government to that position. He had no idea, in July 1915, that his guarantee of a 'fixed minimum' would require his new Department to set and enforce wage rates for millions of female and unskilled male dilutees for the entire War.

III

As we have seen, to many trade unionists each dilutee was a potential blackleg who provided factory owners with cheap, compliant labour and weakened the powers of the unions. If women, unskilled men and juveniles could be trained to operate factory machines and produce finished goods, all at low wage rates, the position of the 'aristocracy of labour' would be destroyed. If, however, the factory owners and managers could be required to maintain high wage rates for dilutees, that advantage of the employers would be lost—such was the reasoning of the trade unions.

In the late summer of 1915, as Dilution began to appear to be the only viable solution to the labour crisis in the munitions shops, the trade unions became very concerned with wages policies for dilutees. Spurred in part by the conviction of the National Federation of Women Workers that more than the promise of a minimum wage for dilutees was necessary, the Amalgamated Society of Engineers recommended the following proposal to the Minister of Munitions:

> Women over 18 when employed on any operation in connection with shells and fuses and all work in engineering establishments on munitions of war which necessitates machine operations for which tools and the setting up of machines is performed by skilled or semiskilled labour shall receive not less than £1 per week for a normal working week as recognized

prior to the War, except where such work prior to the War has
been recognized as women's work by the A.S.E. and the Allied
Trades in the district or districts concerned.[20]

On 24 August 1915 Lloyd George met with the A.S.E. leadership,
and wages policy was one of the topics of discussion at this conference. Labour hostility to the Munitions of War Act had begun
to build by this time—this meeting occurred as the Fairfield Ship-
yard strike loomed—and the Minister was well aware that Dilution
could not succeed without their cooperation.

The powers granted the Minister of Munitions over the wages
of armament workers were severely limited under the Munitions of
War Act of 1915—they were certainly inadequate to allow him to
satisfy the A.S.E. resolution. Under the 1915 Act, all anticipated
changes in wage rates in controlled establishments were required
to be submitted to the Minister for his approval. He could, in
turn, allow the change, veto it or refer the managers and workers
to compulsory arbitration. The purpose of this clause was, in
part, to prevent employers, faced with contract delivery deadlines
and scarce labour, from agreeing too readily to high wage demands
and thereby paying funds to workers which might otherwise find
their way into the Exchequer as excess profits duties. The Munitions
Act also forbade alterations in district piece-work rates for skilled
men due to the introduction of dilutees into the shops. This clause
was insurance against employers lowering piece work rates as
productivity increased.

Beyond these, and the 'fair wages' clause written into every
Government contract since 1909, which required only that district
rates should obtain for Government work, the Minister of
Munitions had no further powers over the wages to be paid
munitions workers. 'There was,' as the Labour Department later
reported, 'no provision at all for time rates to be paid to women
nor for the piece-rates if no customary rate obtained for the job,
owing to the alteration of the method of manufacture or to the
introduction of new processes.'[21]

Pressure on the Ministry increased as, at the suggestion of the
A.S.E., the engineering trade unions' representatives met in mid-
September; Lloyd George again faced the representatives of the

skilled mechanics and pledged to take action to remedy their grievances. Before the close of the month he had created the Central Munitions Labour Supply Committee, as we have seen, to consider the entire matter of Dilution. With the support of the Minister, they constituted a Sub-Committee on Wages, made up of Mary MacArthur of the National Federation of Women Workers, Allan Smith of the Engineering Employers Federation, and Glyn West and J. Kaylor of the Ministry of Munitions.

On 1 October 1915 the Sub-Committee presented its conclusions to the Henderson Committee and the Minister of Munitions. These findings were included in the series of L Circulars issued by the Ministry to controlled establishments for their guidance in labour matters. L1, the first of the series, was sent to the factories in November 1915, and it announced:

> that the Minister has decided to adopt the Committee's recommendations as regards munitions factories for which the Ministry is responsible, and also to commend them to the favourable consideration of other employers engaged on munitions work.[22]

Circulars L2 and L3 contained the Committee's and the Ministry's recommendations for wage policies for female and male dilutees, respectively, and were included with L1. The Wages Sub-Committee's instructions for women dilutees called for a guaranteed time rate of £1 per week for females eighteen years of age or older. L2 reiterated the policy of calling for the payment of skilled men's piece work rates to dilutees who actually replaced those mechanics. However, it exceeded that older pledge by calling for the payment to such women who took the places of skilled mechanics of similar time rates, premium bonus rates (this was a payment system under which a minimum time rate was combined with bonuses for output), and overtime, night shift and holiday allowances. To settle questions involving piece work rates for new operations—in cases where complex tasks were subdivided or wholly new processes begun—rates were to be agreed upon by the women and their employers, based upon the principle 'that on systems of payment by results equal payment shall be made to women as to the men for an equal amount of work done'.

L3 gave similar guarantees of the payment of a skilled man's wage to an unskilled or semi-skilled male dilutee who was able to perform the more difficult task. Recommended time wage rates were given for male dilutees in shops which did not normally produce shells and fuses.

In late autumn 1915, while wide-scale Dilution was delayed by controversy over wages policy, the Minister of Munitions hoped that the Henderson Committee and the L Circular recommendations would calm labour's anxieties. 'There should be a fixed minimum which would guarantee that we should not utilize the services of women merely in order to get cheap labour,' he had said. However, neither the recommendations nor the pledges settled the issue. Many Government contractors did adopt the recommendations of L2 (in the end, L3 proved to be virtually unneeded) but many did not. The very same month that the first circulars were issued, for example, the Midland Employers' Federation and the Workers' Union agreed upon a figure for female dilutees which provided a rate of 16s. for a fifty-three hour week.[23] At about the same time, Scottish female dilutees were being paid but 15s. per week, despite Circular L2.

The Ministry of Munitions had, by this time, begun to prepare an act amending the 1915 Munitions of War Act, and these circumstances required that greater controls over wages would be necessary to ensure the success of Dilution. To gauge personally the feelings of munitions workers, Lloyd George visited a number of munitions factories—G. D. H. Cole wryly remarked of this tour that on more than one occasion he received a 'warm reception' —and came away certain that female dilutees, who were virtually required to remain at their jobs by Clause 7 of the 1915 Act, needed more protection than the Ministry could then offer them. As the second Munitions of War Act was being drafted, the Minister offered to all sides in the controversy a mixture of compulsion and conciliation: employers would receive a greater and less disputatious labour force; skilled engineers would receive a greater guarantee that dilutees would not be used to break the power of the trade unions. Both, however, found that the price was greater control by the Ministry of Munitions.[24] Perhaps the greatest victors in the whole affair were the female dilutees themselves; they benefited not only in that their wages often were raised, but also, as we shall see, in regard to their welfare inside and outside the armament factories.

In January 1916 the Munitions of War (Amendment) Act was passed, giving the Minister statutory powers in several areas, including the authority to regulate the wages and working conditions of dilutees.[25] Circulars L2 and L3 were almost immediately made mandatory in controlled establishments and with other non-controlled Government contractors.[26]

In March 1916 the Minister exercised a further power granted him by the Amendment Act and appointed two Special Arbitration Tribunals to adjudicate differences over wage policies for male and female dilutees. Wage problems concerning male dilutees were relatively minor, as unskilled men became more likely to enter the Army than to replace skilled men. The board for men's wages disputes, therefore, was seldom overworked and normal arbitration procedures between employers and workmen usually made recourse to the tribunal unnecessary. The Special Tribunal for Women's Wages, on the other hand, was kept busy for the remainder of the War. Acting as both a court of arbitration (taking precedence, in most cases, in matters affecting women's wages over the Committee on Production) and an advisory panel to the Minister of Munitions, it played an important role in setting forth the Ministry's policies in regard to the matter of women's wages.

The decision to take control over the wages paid to all women subject to Clause 7 of the 1915 Munitions of War Act threw on the Ministry responsibility for a number of difficult judgements. For example, few women dilutees, as we have seen, actually did the same job as the skilled men they replaced—the subdivision of complex tasks and the introduction of automatic machinery divided the experienced mechanic's task into several simpler ones. In early 1916 the Ministry, the Special Tribunal for Women's Wages, the Central Munitions Labour Supply Committee, the Amalgamated Society of Engineers and the Federation of Women Workers found it necessary to compose their differing interpretations of this problem to settle it. Between February and December 1916 it was decided, in the first place, that a woman performing a portion of the work of a skilled mechanic was entitled to the full rate for the skilled man, less ten per cent for the expense of having her machine 'set up'. In the second place, it was decided that, beginning with the guaranteed rate of £1 per week, female dilutees were to advance to the adjusted skilled man's wage over a period of thirteen weeks.

These findings were summarized in Ministry Order 885, issued on 24 December 1916, which also ruled that the standard working week for female dilutees was to be forty-eight hours or less. Order 885 also referred questions concerning women on semi-skilled work to local arbitration, rather than attempt to set a single standard for the many and varied tasks collected under that description.

Once the first steps had been taken to control the wages of women on men's work, it was virtually inevitable that demands would be made that the Ministry define rates of pay for women on what, by pre-War definition, was considered women's work. Finally, in July 1916, the Minister of Munitions issued Order 447 which applied to adult women, for the most part, in the engineering trades. It guaranteed to them a rate of 4½d. per hour, if paid by time wages, and a minimum of 4d. per hour, if paid by piece work method. These women were also guaranteed an additional ½d. 'danger money' if their jobs were in particularly hazardous areas, such as explosives or chemical factories. These rates were scaled down at the rate of ½d. per year of age for girls seventeen to fifteen.[27]

These figures for remuneration of women working in munitions trades either on men's or women's work did not remain unaltered during the period of the War, as upward adjustments were made from time to time to account for increases in the cost of living. The results for working women were remarkable, despite the inflation which the wartime economy wrought on the pound. More than a million women were directly affected by the wages policies of the Ministry of Munitions between 1915 and 1918. These women, had they held jobs before the War, would have earned, on an average, about 10s. to 12s. per week. By the Armistice, they earned between 30s. and 35s. per week; those in the more skilled engineering trades and the explosives works exceeded even these averages by a further 10s.[28]

These decisions of the Ministry of Munitions were based upon several premises. In the first place, their ambitious armament production programmes could not succeed without a sufficient labour force and only Dilution could supply the needed workers. Furthermore, the complete cooperation of skilled men was conditional on guarantees that the sacrifices of their shop privileges would not be used to undermine their trade unions. In the second place, Lloyd George had, in his speeches before trade unionists and women's demonstrations in 1915, pledged that the Ministry of Munitions had no desire to exploit the women called to replace men in the factories. He offered a 'guaranteed minimum' and 'equal pay for equal work', and his audiences expected him to make good his promise. In the third place, the Minister and the men and women who advised him on labour policies came to the conclusion that these guarantees could be made good and the Dilution Programme could succeed only if the Munitions Office took unprecedented controls over the wages of hundreds of thousands of women dilutees. It would be wrong to suggest that these policies were part of a coherent scheme, revealed in mid-1915, with the creation of the Ministry. Rather, they developed out of need and were cautiously followed along untravelled paths. In 1916, when the first Minister of Munitions left that Department, the task was not complete. However, the general lines of policy laid down in that period remained largely unchanged through the terms of future Ministers of Munitions.

IV

The promise of high wages was not the only reason women entered factory life as dilutees. For some women, it was the desire to demonstrate their competence, their ability as productive members of society, which sent them to the Labour Exchanges or Munitions Labour Bureaux. No doubt for many it must have seemed exciting to rise early each morning and dress in the newly designed trouser suits or 'cover-alls' and go to the factory, there to control a huge machine producing shell casings or machine-gun barrels. For others, the drive of patriotism, perhaps coupled with the knowledge that there were few other ways in which women could so directly affect the battles at the Front, were the paramount factors in their decision to join 'Mr. Lloyd George's Munitions Girls'.[29]

The tales of the various backgrounds of the women who chose to become dilutees were well known and popular during the War. L. K. Yates, herself a welfare supervisor in the Ministry of Munitions, in her study of women's munitions work, wrote of the strange social mix in the armaments shops. Working-class girls shared the assembly line with the widow of the late Antarctic explorer, Sir Robert Falcon Scott; the daughter of the Duke of Abercorn, Lady Mary Hamilton; as well as an aristocrat of another sort—Stella Drummond, the daughter of the well-known 'General' Drummond of the Women's Social and Political Union. While the vast majority of 'Munitionettes' were themselves from the working-class, each factory seemed to have its favourite stories of the great and the near-great who served the Ministry of Munitions 'just like us'.[30]

There was, of course, a great deal of scepticism in Great Britain about the ability of these dilutees, whatever their class, actually to perform the tasks expected of them. The Dilution campaign did not take long to prove how misplaced were these suspicions. The Labour Department of the Ministry, as the new policy was getting under way, issued a series of Dilution progress reports beginning in the autumn of 1915. In the first of these memoranda, those tasks recorded as being successfully carried out by female hands were considered 'light': the earliest dilutees were essentially 'machine-minders', who operated screw-making machines or filled smaller calibres of shells. Few, if any, were charged with discretionary powers over their tasks. The Labour Department reported later: 'It is clear that employers at the date were diffident as to the possibilities of the policy [of Dilution], and the fact that it was seriously debated whether women could be employed on turning the copper bands of small shell, shows how little the possibilities of female labour had been appreciated.'[31]

Within a month, however, reports came to the Labour Department of increased demands for dilutees, as managers and foremen discovered the ingenuity and ability of their new workers. Women had begun to work as oxy-acetylene welders—a task which required both skill and courage—and to operate medium size lathes for the turning of bands for 4.5-inch shells. They had learned to operate drill presses, to manufacture helical gears on huge milling machines and to machine gaines, which detonated the fuses in artillery shells.[32]

In January 1916 the Ministry prepared and distributed to controlled establishments an illustrated booklet, *Notes on the Employment of Women on Munitions of War*, which listed and displayed photographs of the tasks women were successfully performing by that time. Shortly thereafter, the Minister again turned to personal diplomacy through a series of visits to controlled establishments to encourage workers, to call attention to successfully diluted programmes of munitions manufacture and to hasten Dilution in the shops of reluctant manufacturers. Managers and employers who were tardy in implementing Ministry policy in this regard received from the Munitions Office in February 1916, Circular L29, which informed them in no uncertain terms that they courted the displeasure of the Minister of Munitions:

> . . . I am [wrote the Secretary of the Ministry, Sir Hubert Llewellyn Smith] now to instruct you that the dilution of labour should be pressed forward in your works, in accordance with the procedure indicated herein, as extensively as possible and without delay.[33]

The procedure, of course, called for the replacement of skilled men on all but the most highly technical processes.

By 1 March 1916 the Labour Department reported that women were by then not only employed on most facets of the manufacture of implements of war, but also in the strongest bastion of the skilled worker, the manufacture of machine tools. By July 1916 they reported that women in previously diluted programmes were entering the factories in greater numbers and that, in newly developed areas of manufacture, such as optical munitions for example, female labour already constituted a majority. When Lloyd George left the Ministry in that month, there was no longer any question whether women were capable of performing the tasks of dilutees.

The number of women who took employment in industry in the years of World War I was remarkable. In the year July 1914 to July 1915, 382,000 entered factories; between July 1915 and July 1916, as the Dilution campaign got under way and the barriers in the path of this migration were overcome, an additional 563,000 women took industrial jobs. Between July 1916 and July 1917, 511,000 more women entered industry; and from July 1917 to July 1918, a further 203,000 were given factory jobs.[34]

Even more revealing of the success of Dilution is the following chart, which shows the percentage of women employed in the most important munitions industries:

PERCENTAGE OF WOMEN EMPLOYED IN MUNITIONS TRADES

Date	Metals	Chemicals	Textiles	Government Establishments
July 1914	9.4	20.1	58.0	2.6
July 1915	11.4	23.0	61.0	3.8
July 1916	17.8	33.0	64.6	26.5
July 1917	22.8	38.0	66.1	45.9
July 1918	24.6	39.0	66.8	46.7

If Dilution meant women, then clearly these figures indicate that the efforts of the Ministry of Munitions to bring about such a policy had been successful. Yet the true measure of the success of Dilution was the remarkable success with which women adjusted to their new posts and helped to produce the wide variety of warlike stores.

V

Under the powers granted him by the Munitions of War (Amendment) Act of 1916 the Minister of Munitions could direct not merely wages to be paid female dilutees, but their 'conditions of work' in the factories as well. This began a gigantic social welfare programme directed by the Ministry unlike any which preceded it in Britain. The condition of many factories after late 1914, and the advent of wide-scale Dilution, made such a policy not only possible, but necessary.

As armament makers clamoured for Government contracts and added to their workforces, factories became more crowded and even less sanitary than they had been before the War. With the beginning of sub-contracting and the engagement on munitions work of all manner of factories, this situation spread throughout much of the engineering industry of the nation. To make matters worse, efforts to meet delivery dates on contracts led to excessively long hours of labour and a general decline in the physical condition of many factory employees. Some women had, of course, entered factories soon after the Declaration of War and the Home Office did hold powers to regulate hours of work for women and youths. The pressure of War Office munitions requirements and pleas of patriotism, however, had forced Home Office inspectors to relent and allow excessive overtime work for these newcomers to the munitions industries. The Factory Acts gave the Home Office little control over the working conditions or hours of labour of men in the works. The result was that efficiency, productivity and the physical condition of munitions workers all declined in 1914 and 1915.

With the advent of the Ministry of Munitions and the development of the Dilution policy in 1915, Lloyd George saw the opportunity to change these terrible developments. The introduction of women offered the occasion for an effective social welfare policy: there was a long tradition of regulation of factory conditions for women in the nation—dating at least from the time of Shaftesbury in the nineteenth century—and such a programme would be based, therefore, upon long-respected precedent. It was not only necessary, but also politically feasible. Lloyd George recalled in his memoirs:

A singularly favourable opportunity thus presented itself for introducing into industry a great forward movement for improving the general conditions of the welfare of the workers—an opportunity of which as Minister of Munitions I proceeded forthwith to take full advantage.[35]

In September 1915 Lloyd George had appointed a Health of Munitions Workers Committee, under the chairmanship of Sir George Newman, the Chief Medical Officer of the Board of Education.[36] Created 'to consider and advise on questions of industrial fatigue, hours of labour, and other matters affecting the physical health and physical efficiency of workers in munitions factories and workshops', the Committee produced a series of recommendations which came to be the basis of Ministry welfare policy.

In its report on *The Employment of Women,* the Newman Com-

mittee set down five major concerns for the Minister: the prevention of excessive hours of labour, the provision of adequate
sanitary facilities and conditions, the protection of the physical
condition of dilutees and the provision of proper management
and supervision of women in munitions shops. The passage in
January 1916 of the Amendment Act gave the Minister sufficient
power to turn this advice into effective policy. He created the
Welfare Section of the Labour Department to execute the
Ministry's new authority and he appointed, to head the new office,
B. Seebohm Rowntree, the reform-minded industrialist and factory
owner.[37]

The first problem which the Welfare section attacked was that of
excessive hours of labour. Factory managers had, as we have seen
above, frequently opposed reducing hours in the mistaken belief
that longer shifts would lead to quicker delivery on Government
contracts. Workers themselves often rejected shorter hours of
labour, for they preferred the fatigue and tedium to the loss of
lucrative overtime pay bonuses. It was clear to the Welfare Section
(and the Home Office's Chief Inspector of Factories agreed) that
the efficiency of male workers declined sharply after approximately
sixty hours of work in a single week; the figure for women in
factories was lower.[38] While in 1915 some men remained at their
machines for seventy and sometimes as much as one hundred hours
per week, the Ministry was able to reduce such excesses until they
had virtually passed away by 1916. If managers or men would not
cooperate voluntarily in these efforts, the Ministry always had
recourse to its wider powers over female dilutees—without whom
the factories could not operate—or to the threat of transfer of men
who were War Munitions Volunteers.

The Ministry of Munitions did not initiate the movement to
provide sanitary canteens and dining-rooms in armaments factories.
Charitable and public-spirited organizations such as the Y.W.C.A. had
provided such facilities to pioneering employers who first brought
women into the factories. As well, the Central Control Board for
Liquor Traffic had appointed a sub-committee which encouraged
the building of factory canteens.[39] With the creation of the
Ministry Welfare Section, however, these canteens were brought
under the Minister's authority and were regulated by Rowntree's

office. Every effort was made to provide hot meals for workers and to give them a clean, well-lit, properly heated and satisfactorily ventilated area in which to take their meals and to rest during work breaks.

Within the year of Lloyd George's tenure at the Munitions Office, all controlled establishments were required to provide such canteens and the new National Factories also were so furnished. By the close of the War more than 700 factory canteens had been built in Great Britain. As in so many other cases of Ministry welfare policies, dilutees were not the only workers to benefit. Regular employees, of course, enjoyed use of the canteens and meal facilities; often, male workers were provided with separate canteens and dining rooms. In the non-munitions industries—particularly those which were also employing large numbers of women—employers often discovered that only the provision of a canteen or similar facility would satisfy the desires of their workers. The goal of Lloyd George, Rowntree and other supporters of the canteen movement was to prevent the return of the day when most factory workers took their meals beside the machine or, what was far worse in Lloyd George's eyes, retired to the local public-house at midday. In that regard, the Ministry's canteen policy was significant far beyond the needs of War production.[40]

The Welfare Section, again following the recommendations of the Newman Committee, intervened in the munitions factories to protect dilutees in 'danger areas'—that is, shops in which explosives or toxic materials were regularly handled. The substitution of trinitrotoluene (T.N.T., as it was popularly known) for the traditional lyddite as the charge for high explosive shells posed serious problems, for example. The substance caused frequent, severe illness among workers—mostly female dilutees—who were required to handle it. A medical committee was appointed to consider the problem and steps were taken to ensure adequate ventilation and even a special diet for explosives workers who came in contact with the chemical. Other perhaps less dramatic cases of the Welfare Section's intervention into particular health problems were numerous. Minor injuries were not overlooked, either, as the Section required first aid rooms in all controlled shops. In large factories, a full-time medical officer was required.[41]

The Welfare Section also came to require that proper clothing be made available to dilutees—and trouser suits and serviceable dresses came to replace previous finery as the typical attire of factory women.[42]

Well aware that engineering works were foreign enough to most dilutees without making a strange world more terrifying by providing only male authority, the Ministry welfare policy required the provision of female welfare supervisors in diluted factories. These 'mature ladies', as they were called, were generally chosen by the employer from a list of approved candidates provided by the Welfare Section. Their wages were paid by the factory, yet they remained subject finally to the authority of the Ministry of Munitions, not the factory management. Their tasks included the investigation of complaints by or against female dilutees, supervision of canteens, lavatories, and dining-rooms, overseeing the health of dilutees in the works and general supervision of female employees. In large factories welfare supervisors superintended recreation programmes within the factory and, at times, they oversaw housing and transport of women as well.[43]

In their earliest days in the factories, the women's welfare supervisors were often not welcomed by management, for they represented the rival authority within the works of the Ministry of Munitions. Within the first year of the welfare programme, however, these tireless and courageous ladies proved their worth again and again. Their popularity among dilutees varied—many young women, enjoying their first taste of such 'male' independence, often resented the management of the supervisors—but in times of small or large crisis they were generally acknowledged by most dilutees as very valuable indeed. To the Welfare Section of the Ministry, of course, they were invaluable, both as investigators of factory conditions and executives of welfare policy.

Rowntree's Section also employed 'outside' welfare supervisors to organize recreation for the munitionettes, as they were often called. In October 1915 the remarkable Maharaja of Gwalior provided the Minister of Munitions with a fund of £6,000 to be used for the benefit of munitions workers. These funds were used by the welfare supervisors to purchase innumerable pianos for canteens established in neighbourhoods housing dilutees; they built tennis courts, provided dancing instructors and paid for amateur theatrical productions.[44]

The outside welfare supervisors took on many other responsibilities as well. They organized nurseries, for example, for the children of many munitions workers who were mothers. The children of dilutees in National Factories and in controlled establishments were cared for, fed, educated and, in many cases, even clothed while their mothers worked. Costs, in most cases, of building the nurseries were borne by the State; the Ministry of Munitions provided three-quarters of the funding necessary to operate them and the remaining quarter, paid by the controlled establishment, could be deducted from excess profits.[45]

While not directly under Rowntree's Welfare Section, closely allied to its efforts to provide the healthiest possible life for munitions workers were the Ministry's efforts to provide suitable housing for thousands of dilutees. Just as no one had expected a great labour shortage early in the War, neither was a shortage of suitable working-class housing in industrial districts anticipated. Crowding soon became a problem in traditional munitions and engineering areas like Woolwich, Coventry and Birmingham. The new factories were located in districts where labour, raw materials and machine tools could be brought together, and these were seldom places where adequate housing existed.

The Ministry, in its zeal to restrict the use of building labour and materials to War-related projects, had employed powers delegated it under the Defence of the Realm Act Regulations to plan the construction of buildings of a cost of more than £500. Coupled with the inflation in building costs, this effectively stopped the construction of many houses and multi-family dwellings by private capital.

In the autumn of 1915 the Ministry attempted to encourage local authorities to take responsibility for building permanent working-class housing. Offering to absorb up to 30 per cent of the increases in construction costs over pre-War levels, the Munitions Office did succeed in persuading a number of town councils to begin building programmes. 600 houses were built in Coventry, for example, and 260 in Sheffield, but most local authorities feared that the post-War period would find them with unrented and unsaleable buildings.[46]

In some cases the Ministry made arrangements with the large armament manufacturers which employed dilutees to construct housing for their workers. The manufacturers were permitted to deduct a percentage of the difference in pre-War and current building costs from what would normally be paid into the Exchequer as excess profits. Several hundred houses were built under these terms, primarily by Vickers in Barrow and Weybridge. The manufacturers, however, considered it unprofitable, and the Ministry soon came to the conclusion that it was unsuitable for these firms to act in the dual capacity of employer and landlord to their workers.

The ultimate solution of the Ministry, made early in 1916, was that the Department itself should take the responsibility for building of housing for munitions workers. In the case of temporary housing, the Munitions Office bore the entire cost. If permanent structures were to be built, the Ministry absorbed the majority of the cost. If there were private armaments firms in the district who benefited from this increased capacity for the accommodation of workers, they made a small contribution, usually less than 10 per cent of cost. This became the customary method by which housing for munitions workers was constructed for the remainder of the War.

Thousands of female dilutees were housed in temporary hostels during their service in the armaments factories, under the watchful eye of a Ministry outside welfare supervisor. Yet by the end of the War, more than 11,000 permanent housing units had been contributed by the Ministry of Munitions toward lessening the shortage of working-class housing in Britain.[47]

The entire welfare programme of the Ministry of Munitions— the regulation of hours of work, the provision of welfare officers, the establishment of canteens, the building of housing and so on— was planned and carried out because it was absolutely necessary. The need was not so great simply because women had entered the munitions shops. The conditions in British factories in pre-War years were generally of a low standard and, for that reason, were both less productive than they might have been and injurious to the health and safety of their inmates. Walter Shaw Sparrow, in his chapter on welfare matters during the First World War in

G. A. B. Dewar's *The Great Munitions Feat,* quoted an unnamed 'statesman' on the welfare programme of the Ministry:

> 'The workers of to-day are the mothers of to-morrow. In a war of workshops the women of Britain were needed to save Britain; it was for Britain to protect them.' Obviously [Sparrow added]; but to state these truisms without any reference to the unpardonable blundering of pre-war times was to show a lack of penitence which historians will neither forget nor forgive.[48]

The coming of the War, however, and the creation of the Ministry of Munitions under Lloyd George supplied the opportunity and the authority to begin a reversal of this trend.

The effects of World War I on British women—perhaps even more than those wrought on men—were, in the end, almost incalculable. If it is overly dramatic to suggest one world died and another was born, it is not too extreme to say that many of the *mores* of their society were fundamentally altered. Women became more independent and self-reliant because they were required, or allowed, to be so; and few wished to return to the roles they had lived in the years before August 1914.

The Dilution programme of the Ministry of Munitions, of course, deserves no credit for these changes beyond the obvious fact that it gave women the opportunity to prove what many of them knew already: that they were capable of skill, endurance and responsibility far beyond what had usually been credited to them. Did their performance in the munitions shops earn for women the vote? 'In demonstrating their talents,' Arthur Marwick has written, 'women also demonstrated the gross national wastage implied in not exploiting these talents to the full, politically as well as economically.'[49] The munitions factories served, in this regard, simply as courts of public opinion in which women successfully proved their ability and their right to be equal citizens. The credit for righting a great national wrong justly belonged not to the Ministry nor to Lloyd George, nor to the politicians or newspapers or anti-suffrage women whose minds were changed. Rather, it rightfully belonged to the women—munitionettes and others—who served so well.

Nine

MUNITIONS TECHNOLOGY: THE BATTLE FOR WEAPONRY DESIGN

I

No one foresaw in June 1915, when the Ministry of Munitions was being organized, that the duties of that Department would extend beyond the production of munitions to War Office requirements. While there might have been reservations in the minds of some officials at Whitehall Gardens as to the wisdom of accepting too few powers over actual manufacturing facilities controlled by the War Office, there was no objection raised to the soldiers retaining authority over what was actually produced. Sir Hubert Llewellyn Smith acknowledged the Ordnance Department's pre-eminence in the field of armaments design on 5 June 1915, during the initial period of transfer of functions:

> The fixing of designs and specifications, and the tests to be applied [he wrote to the Army Council], will remain with the War Office, as well as research and experimental work.[1]

The sole important qualification in this arrangement between the two Departments in Lloyd George's view was that the Ordnance Department had to be willing to cooperate with the Ministry of Munitions in order that the production of armaments might be increased and hastened.

> On the other hand, [Llewellyn Smith concluded], it is essential that the whole technical resources and staff of the [Royal Ordnance] factories should be made fully and directly available to aid the development of the supply of munitions, not only within but outside the factories.

With the exception of the transfer of the responsibility for the inspection of munitions, made on 5 July 1915,[2] the War Office retained control over the Royal Factories at Woolwich, Enfield, Waltham and Farnborough, as well as final authority over the specifications and development of armaments. Under the authority of the Director of Artillery, Major-General Guthrie Smith, the War Office continued to control experiments on new munitions inventions as well as advanced developments of older designs. After it had satisfied itself through tests at the experimental grounds at Shoeburyness or Hythe, the Ordnance Board—an expert committee made up of serving Army officers—exercised its authority over setting specifications for armaments.

Once approval of a design had been granted, these standards and, usually, approved drawings and test gauges as well, were available only from the office of the Chief Superintendent of Ordnance Factories, at Woolwich. In short, at this early stage of transfer of functions from the War Office to the Ministry of Munitions, the Army was willing to allow the Ministry to provide labour for munitions shops and to deal with civilian contractors. It had no desire, however, to surrender authority over the designs of munitions being produced or the methods under which they were made. Within three months the arrangement had proved itself totally unacceptable to Lloyd George and the men of Whitehall Gardens.

The first step toward the increase of Ministry control over what had once been the inviolable domain of the Master General of the Ordnance and his subordinates was its capture of authority over the Royal Arsenals. Woolwich, before the completion of the National Filling Factories, was the greatest facility in Britain for the filling of artillery projectiles; more than three-quarters of all the shells fired by the Army at the Front had their explosive charges added at Woolwich. During June and July 1915, while the Munitions Supply Department made every effort to increase the production of shell components, it became clear that the officers in charge at Woolwich seemed to be able to do little to increase the shell-filling capacity of the Arsenal. Therefore, by August, the railway sidings around the great factory complex became clogged with shipments of empty shell casings, as they arrived at a rate of

100,000 per week in excess of the Arsenal's capacity to fill and complete them.[3] To the Minister of Munitions it was obvious that the productive capacity at Woolwich needed to be expanded, yet the War Office showed no signs of moving in that direction.

Perhaps more significant was the fact that the Master General and the Ordnance Board retained control over munitions design and specifications, all drawings and gauges would continue to come from the Royal Arsenal, Woolwich. Without those gauges and drawings, no new National Factory, inexperienced contractor or Cooperative Scheme could begin to produce the myriad components required for any armaments. To the Minister of Munitions, whose patience with these high-ranking soldiers had admittedly grown short, it appeared that, as the emergency grew more intense, the bureaucratic machine headed by the Chief Superintendent of Ordnance Factories moved more slowly.

The War Office rejected, of course, the suggestion of the transfer of the Arsenals to Ministry authority. Lloyd George, therefore, unable to secure what he wished through compromise with the War Office, turned to another approach: if the War Office would not give up the Factories, he would take them. The Minister of Munitions raised in Cabinet the matter of the unfinished transfer of functions to his Department. The Ministry, he said, controlled only the production of munitions among private contractors and not within the Arsenal; to complete its mission, the Royal Factories had to be transferred. His argument carried the day with the Prime Minister and on 19 August 1915 Asquith agreed to the removal of the great complex at Woolwich and the other Royal Factories to Ministry control. Four days later the transfer was effected.[4] Lloyd George wrote many years later:

> When I took over Woolwich I soon found why, in the words of M. Albert Thomas, it was *'une vieille boite'*. . . . [Those in charge] jostled each other, they were in each other's way, hindering but never hustling, and only acting together when there was any resistance to be offered to the political Hun. . . . My first duty was not exactly to lay these ghosts but to put them in their proper places; to see that each of them pushed his own trolley without running into anybody else's. I saw why we had been delayed in divers ways.[5]

Lloyd George discovered that the *vieille boite* needed a generous infusion of what he often termed 'push and go' methods. He found that there was no adequate statistical system by which a close watch could be maintained over raw materials, components and hourly production; he ensured that such a procedure was initiated.[6] As we have seen, the Ministry implemented an intensive Dilution programme to supplement the labour supply of the Arsenal. The filling capacity of the huge factory complex was hastily increased. In short, Lloyd George attempted to replace the traditionalist outlook of the masters of the Royal Arsenal with the more efficient 'businessman' standard fostered by the Ministry of Munitions.[7]

Formal control of the Royal Arsenals was vested in an executive committee, under the chairmanship of the Director General of Munitions Supplies, Sir Frederick Black.[8] In actual practice, however, the executive power over Woolwich and the other Royal Arsenals, was exercised by a branch, called CM7, of the department of the Deputy Director General for shell production, Eric Geddes. Before the close of 1915, the Minister of Munitions replaced the Chief Superintendent of Ordnance Factories, Sir Frederick Donaldson, with the Ministry's own appointee, Vincent Raven.[9] Raven had no experience in the armaments industry; in fact, like Geddes, he had been a railway executive. Lloyd George chose him for that important post because he had confidence in his ability to direct thousands of men and women on their important work, and because he knew Raven was not a part of the pre-War Woolwich system. The new Chief Superintendent would have to find new ways to accomplish difficult tasks in less time and with greater economy of labour than ever before. Raven proved to be one of Lloyd George's successful 'men of push and go'.

Securing control over the Royal Arsenals did not, by any means, solve all the Ministry's problems. While the shell production section of the Munitions Supply Department was better able to fill artillery projectiles, the Ministry of Munitions discovered that War Office control over munitions design continued to frustrate the Ministry's desires to produce not only more, but better armaments. Christopher Addison wrote in his memoirs:

The transfer of the factories, although it proved to be of immense help, by no means got us out of all our troubles. The delays and difficulties over designs, alterations in pattern and tests continued, with exacerbations now and then. . . .[10]

The exacerbations spoken of by Dr. Addison, at least in the realm of munitions design and development, generally began with the Master General, Sir Stanley von Donop. This single-minded and strong-willed officer came to embody for Lloyd George and his aides the traditional War Office view of munitions design. Before August 1914 it had generally been accepted that the development of munitions stopped once war was declared. New armaments were usually introduced in peacetime and, once hostilities began, they were put to use. The Master General, who maintained final authority over design at this time, came to be a roadblock in the path toward increased munitions supply and the development of new and better weapons.

The Ministry staff came to the conclusion that production and forward-looking research and development of armaments were inseparable. In short, they concluded that efficient production of warlike stores depended upon a 'nice balance' of three factors: in the first place, the supply authority needed to be constantly appraised of the needs of the military in the theatres of war. These requirements, of course, were to govern the nature and amount of munitions. Secondly, that supply authority had to carry on an active programme of research and development which would produce prototypes of new or improved armaments to meet the needs of the Army at the Front. Finally, the production authority had to monitor closely the factors of production: factory capacity, machine tools, raw materials, labour supply and so forth.[11]

Theoretically, all the necessary powers to accomplish this balance were vested in the Master General of the Ordnance before May 1915. Through its close relationship with the War Office List firms, its control over the Royal Arsenals, its close relationship with the Army command in the field and its increased powers gained with the passage of the Defence of the Realm Acts, the Ordnance Department had sufficient power and expertise to overcome the munitions shortage. The failure to do so resulted in the creation of the Ministry of Munitions, but it also brought about the severance of the unification of those three important factors. By the late summer of 1915, the Ministry was well on its way to controlling most of the elements of armaments production. It had gained control of the Royal Ordnance Factories; it was making every effort to discover and meet the requirements of the B.E.F. Yet, so long as the Ordnance Department continued to control munitions design, specifications and research, there would be no 'nice balance' under one authority.

One source of great frustration in this regard which irritated Lloyd George and his aides was the inability of the Ordnance Department to decide upon a new fuse for high explosive shells. The fuse pattern in use throughout 1914 and 1915 had proved itself unreliable; it frequently burst shells within their guns, with consequent death or destruction to men and artillery. Although this fact had been well known ever since the British Army had begun to rely upon high explosive shells in late 1914, no suitable substitute had been approved by the Master General of the Ordnance. Despite the fact that the private armaments firms, the Ordnance Board, the Royal Arsenals and the Ministry had all conducted experiments to overcome the problem, no final solution had been reached after a year of War. The Ministry of Munitions was required to provide the old pattern of fuse and was often criticized for producing a poor product. Yet, so long as the Master General retained control over munitions design, Lloyd George was helpless. However, about this same time he received unrequested aid.

Some months earlier, Sir John French had created an Experiments Committee at the Front to examine suggestions for new and improved weapons made by officers and ranks of the B.E.F. While the Commander-in-Chief will not be remembered as an innovator in the ways of war, even he was conscious of the limitations of the Ordnance Department. Presiding over this committee was Major-General Sir John DuCane. On 22 October 1915 DuCane wrote to his friend Colonel Arthur Lee, who had recently replaced Major-General Sir Ivor Philipps as Military Secretary to the Ministry of Munitions:

I am pretty sure that you will find that the system by which the War Office and the Ordnance Board retain responsibility for these [design] matters is your great stumbling block. The M.G.O.'s people seem to me to be mentally exhausted and the Ordnance Board and the Experimental Department at Shoebury to be hopelessly congested.

K's great argument for keeping control [of munitions design] was that he must be responsible for the safety of the troops. . . . He has failed hopelessly as regards safety, and the result of his control now is to prevent the causes of the trouble being definitely ascertained. . . .[12]

When the Minister of Munitions attacked the situation in the meetings of the Cabinet and the Dardanelles Committee, he was faced with the absolute refusal of Lord Kitchener to acquiesce to the transfer of munitions design to the civilian Ministry of Munitions. In early November, however, the Prime Minister intervened in the crisis by ordering the Secretary of State for War off on a fact-finding trip to the Eastern Theatre of War. Ostensibly, the purpose of the junket was to report on the status of the Dardanelles campaign. Equally important, however, was Asquith's desire to free the Government temporarily of the presence of the no-longer-welcome War Lord. It was accepted by many in the innermost circles of power that Kitchener was meant not to return at all.[13] On Wednesday, 4 November 1915, Kitchener sailed and Lloyd George prepared to attack the prerogatives of the Master General, in the absence of his protector. On the Friday, the Minister of Munitions called upon Dr. Addison and Sir Frederick Black to prepare the case of the Ministry for taking control of munitions design.[14]

Their memorandum, submitted to the Prime Minister, reviewed the situation: the separation of design from production led to delays and inefficiency. So long as the Ordnance Department maintained control over design, each question which touched upon any specification of any armament required submission to the Ordnance Board. The results were always the same—delay and the consequent slowing down of the production of munitions of war.

To illustrate their argument, Dr Addison and Sir Frederick Black pressed the sensitive case of the imperfect high explosive shell fuse. The French Ministry of Munitions and armaments manufacturers employed a simpler and more successful fuse; its use in British shells had been championed both by the Ministry's Munitions Supply Department and by Major-General DuCane, who had conducted investigations of alternative fuses through his Experiments Committee at the Front. Addison wrote:

> Illustrations in support of this point can be afforded if desired. The slow progress in deciding upon the adoption of the French fuse is a case in point. This fuse requires only about one-eighth of the brass needed for the British fuse with a corresponding saving in cost and amount of material; besides which it is more economical of labour and filling material. Our own fuse and gaine rest under grave suspicion of being dangerous to guns and gunners, and the point raised by the bursting of our guns eight weeks ago had not yet been settled. The French fuse, on the other hand, has proved during recent operations that it can be depended upon.

The memorandum concluded with a call for the transfer of the Ordnance Board and its entire research and development establishment from the control of the Master General to the Minister of Munitions.

The competition for control of munitions design, however, was not settled in early November. After two weeks' wait, Lloyd George again ordered Dr. Addison to prepare another memorandum restating the Ministry's case for the further transfer of authority.

This the Minister took to Asquith to demand final settlement of the question. The Prime Minister had been a masterful peacetime premier; he had managed to juggle the crises of the Labour Unrest, the Irish Home Rule struggle, the Suffragette campaign and the various political battles among his followers and still retain his own position and the supremacy of the Liberal Party. He was frequently criticized for his 'wait and see' policy, and yet waiting and seeing helped, in those difficult years, to prolong his rule. In wartime, however, the delays which resulted from such methods were intolerable to impatient men like Lloyd George. To the Minister of Munitions each day meant thousands of casualties and millions of pounds spent on violence which might have been better invested in other things. He had waited; he had seen—on 22 November 1915 he demanded the Prime Minister's approval of the transfer of the offending departments.

That same day, Asquith wrote to Mrs. Henley, the wife of his Military Private Secretary and one of his 'most valued and intimate correspondents':

> I went to the War Office where I had a succession of rather interesting (and exacting) interviews: . . . [among them, one] With Von Donop to whom I had to make the revelation that two or three of the remaining leaves of his attenuated artichoke are to be snapped off by Lloyd George. I handled him as well as I could, and I hope broke his fall.[15]

The fall, nonetheless, was almost complete, as Asquith had come down on the side of the Minister of Munitions. Sir Reginald Brade, the Secretary of the War Office, wrote to the Ministry his Department's understanding of the new 'Division of Functions between the War Office and the Ministry of Munitions in respect to Design etc.':

> The transfer to the Ministry of Munitions of the responsibility for designs, patterns, and specifications, for the testing of arms and ammunition, and for the examination of inventions bearing on such munitions, leaves the War Office the following functions only in regard to munitions of War, viz.:
>
> (1) The duty of fixing the requirements of the Army both as regards the general nature and amount of the munitions required, together with the duty of allocating such material.
>
> (2) The duty of receipt, custody and actual distribution of all such supplies. . . .[16]

Not present in the printed version of this memorandum was an additional paragraph which did appear in the copy which reached the Minister of Munitions:

The above was dictated to me by the Prime Minister with instructions to notify it as his decision arrived at after consideration of the relative positions of the War Office and the Ministry of Munitions in which each stands now that the transfer of duties, with which the correspondents in this paper deals, has been approved.[17]

This letter was undated but was probably written on 22 November, after Asquith's interview with von Donop. Four days later, the Director of Artillery informed the Ordnance Board that, effective 29 November, they, along with the Experimental Establishment at Shoeburyness and the War Office Inventions Branch, were to report to the Minister of Munitions.[18] Lloyd George's victory seemed complete; the War Office, however, and especially the Master General of the Ordnance, were not easy enemies to beat. There were other skirmishes to be fought after 22 November 1915.

Meanwhile, a Department of Munitions Design was constituted at the Ministry, and Major-General DuCane, an officer whose talents both the Munitions and War Offices respected, was recalled from France to become its first Director General. The Ordnance Board, made up, as we have seen, of military officers with a penchant for conservative and slow judgements, was dissolved five days after its transfer to Lloyd George's control. Replacing it was an Ordnance Committee under DuCane's presidency, made up both of military and civilian members. Major-General von Donop and his War Office colleagues seemed to have little left for comfort but the heart of their 'attenuated artichoke'.[19]

The War Office continued the offices of Master General and Director of Artillery, despite the transfers of authority. Likewise, the War Office managed to retain control of the School of Musketry at Hythe which, despite its name, was in reality a testing facility. Despite the Prime Minister's order of 22 November, these officers continued to conduct tests and experiments on various armaments at Hythe. They developed there a sort of *de facto* approval over design, as the War Office came to demand only those munitions approved by the staff at the School of Musketry. While this procedure ran contrary to Asquith's and Lloyd George's wishes, it was technically within the letter of the new arrangements.

Finding it difficult to contain his anger at this turn of events, DuCane wrote to Lloyd George on 14 December 1915:

> The difficult situation that it was hoped to avert, therefore, actually exists. There is still a rival technical department at the War Office, tenacious of its position. The officers of this department feel deep resentment at being deprived of their most important functions, and while they are the officers that should be in closest possible touch with my department, working harmoniously with my officers, the relations are so strained that they result in their avoiding one another as much as possible. The bad effects of this situation are already beginning to be felt, and if it is allowed to continue it will inevitably result in acute friction and loss of efficiency. . . .[20]

The War Office showed no desire to acquiesce to the transfer of the Hythe facility and the Minister of Munitions turned again to the Prime Minister and the War Committee. By 1 February 1916 the decision to transfer the School of Musketry was formally approved.

Furthermore, the War Office was reminded that there was, thereafter, no 'court of appeal' from the decisions of the Ministry of Munitions in regard to designs, specifications, and testing.[21]

Only nine months of strife between the respective champions of the War Office and the Ministry of Munitions finally brought about the release of munitions design from the restraints of the past. The delays caused by this inter-departmental warfare simply added to the burden of the Ministry to produce the best munitions, in the greatest quantities, in the shortest possible time.

II

Lloyd George, since late 1914, had repeatedly told the British people that the World War was as much a conflict of engineers and workshops as it was a battle between rival armies. His experience with the Treasury Committee and with the organization of the Ministry of Munitions convinced him that it was also a war of scientists, inventors and laboratories. He was equally certain that the directors of the War Office Ordnance Department were unwilling or unable to share that view. Hence, as in the case of the Arsenals or of munitions design authority, the stage was set for another of those battles fought between the two important agencies of wartime government. The prize, in this case, was control of munitions research and development.

As early as November 1914, the Royal Society began to mobilize the magnificent intellectual power of its membership for war purposes by creating a General War Committee to suggest and investigate new approaches to war technology. The Admiralty under Winston Churchill created its own Armaments Committee to work with the Royal Society as well as conduct researches of its own. The War Office maintained a small Inventions Branch, called A41, which served as a clearinghouse for suggestions of new and improved munitions. This small department, however, made little use of the help offered by the Society, save the investigations of the Chemical Sub-Committee, then engaged on poison gas research. A41 did not maintain its own experimental staff, nor was it delegated sufficient executive authority to make binding decisions upon the ideas submitted to it. Rather, it was empowered simply to send its recommendations to the Ordnance Board and the Master General, who retained the authority to commission actual experiments.[22]

In June 1915, as the Ministry of Munitions was being organized, the new First Lord of the Admiralty, A. J. Balfour, submitted a paper to his Cabinet colleagues calling for the creation of a joint 'inventions board' to coordinate efforts by all interested agencies to investigate and develop munitions invention ideas.[23] The project met with no enthusiasm from the War Office—without whose cooperation the project would be useless—so Balfour constituted an Admiralty Inventions and Research Committee under the chairmanship of the former First Sea Lord, Admiral of the Fleet Lord Fisher.

In July the Ministry of Munitions created its own Munitions Inventions Department, announced by the Minister in the House of Commons on the 28th. Chosen to head the new department was E. W. Moir, who left Eric Geddes' section of the Munitions Supply Department for the new post. To advise Moir, Lloyd George appointed a board of experts, taking members both from the military and from civilian life. The new Director of Munitions Inventions soon discovered, however, that the War Office considered his activities another Lloyd Georgian interference in the realm of professional soldiers.

On 6 August 1915 Sir Hubert Llewellyn Smith wrote to the War Office calling upon the Secretary of State to agree to place full responsibility for munitions inventions in the hands of Moir's department.[24] The letter was not received with pleasure: the War Office had no intention of surrendering control over this aspect of wartime technology.

Lloyd George met Kitchener about the matter and Moir interviewed the Master General of the Ordnance. Throughout August and September, however, the War Office seemed ready neither to cooperate with Moir nor to surrender munitions inventions to him. The situation was analogous to that posed by munitions design: the Master General's Department moved slowly and cautiously—too much so to satisfy Lloyd George. In addition, they refused the help offered by the new Ministry of Munitions. By mid-September Major-General von Donop had virtually forbidden Branch A41 to cooperate with Moir, save for the forwarding to his department of ideas already rejected by the War Office experts. Still smarting at this time from the loss of authority over the Royal Arsenals, the Ordnance Department, supported by Kitchener, met the aggressive new Ministry with an absolute refusal to cooperate.[25]

By mid-October the situation appeared to be reaching a crisis. Not only had communication between the rival inventions departments all but ceased, but the Master General had ordered the two War Office appointees on Moir's board of experts to leave that panel and return to full-time membership on the Ordnance Board. Though neither man seemed anxious to comply, they were given no choice—if they wished to remain members of the Ordnance Board.[26] On 14 October 1915 Moir again met von Donop in an attempt to solve the impasse between their departments. After the stormy interview, he wrote to his chief:

The whole matter seems to me to be a further indication, if any were necessary, of the spirit of objection to civil assistance by the military authorities, and I think that a good deal of the resistance comes from the gentleman with whom I had the interview. . . . Of course, we can get on without anybody, but there is, I think, an obvious effort to defeat the objects that you have set yourself out to attain, at least in some of your departments, on the part of the Military Authorities.[27]

Exactly one month later, 16 November 1915, Moir again wrote to Lloyd George. His message was unmistakable: the maintenance of two rival inventions offices was intolerable.[28] The Ministry of Munitions was responsible for the production of armaments for land warfare. If it failed in that task, the result would be not simply a setback for the political careers of its masters; rather it would be death and destruction to the British Army and, conceivably, defeat in the World War. The War Office Inventions Branch and the Master General of the Ordnance had proved themselves unable to master the tasks of research and development which the World War required of them; nor would they allow another Department to help them. Hence, the only solution was to strip those soldiers of the power they jealously guarded.

On 22 November 1915, as we have seen, the Prime Minister responded to Lloyd George's demands for the transfer from military to political control of munitions design. In addition, transferred at the same time was the authority over munitions inventions.

III

Lloyd George was himself the prototype of the man of push and go to millions of Britons. It was not at all surprising that many inventors and would-be inventors responded to his call for new and improved armaments through Ernest Moir's Munitions Inventions Department. The response was remarkable: before the end of 1915, that department had received more than 6,000 such suggestions.[29] By the time Lloyd George left the Ministry of Munitions to replace Kitchener at the War Office, an additional 14,000 ideas had been examined.[30]

There was clearly no shortage of imagination among those who sent their schemes to the Ministry. A Birkenhead man, for example, suggested that rubber tubes could be connected to soldiers' stockings in order that they might warm trench-chilled feet by exhaling their breath through the tubes. The same inventor suggested that bullets with lateral grooves cut into them could be employed by sharpshooters to tear down barbed wire defences. Other inventors suggested the filling of artillery shells not with high explosives or shrapnel, but with broken glass, red pepper, snuff and even bubonic plague germs.[31]

The Ministry of Munitions enjoyed more practical suggestions from inventors throughout the country, of course, and benefited from the development work of the experts within the private armaments firms. The Munitions Inventions and Trench Warfare Supply Departments conducted research on their own programmes and served to coordinate these other efforts to bring practical ideas to fruition. These departments played important roles in the development not only of new or improved guns, shells, fuses and the like, but also of protective devices such as helmets and bullet-proof waistcoats—important equipment in a conflict in which attack generally meant 'going over the top' into enemy fire. The two departments cooperated also in the development of flame-throwers, grenades and, as we shall see, one of the most significant weapons for trench warfare of the entire period of the World War, the Stokes mortar.[32]

These Ministry sections were not the only ones to advance the technology of warfare in response to the unprecedented demands of World War. The High Explosives Department under Lord Moulton did remarkable work in easing the dangerous shortage of both shell propellants and high explosives. Moulton's work, of course, began before the organization of the Ministry and Lloyd George developed a firm admiration for the jurist-scientist in the months before May 1915, as both attempted to help the War Office overcome munitions shortages.

While still chairman of the Treasury Committee, Lloyd George first encountered the work of another man of science, then an obscure professor of chemistry at Manchester University. He developed for Lloyd George's committee, and for the Ministry which followed it, a process whereby acetone could be produced artificially from maize. Acetone was an irreplaceable ingredient in the manufacture of cordite, the major propellant employed in all projectile manufacture in Britain—from bullets for the smallest handgun to shells for the greatest howitzer. When shipping losses, later in the War, shortened the supply of maize, the process was made to work using horse chestnuts.[33] The chemist was Professor Chaim Weizmann, the Zionist and indefatigable champion of a national homeland for the Jews. Lloyd George later credited the willing and unselfish cooperation of Weizmann as the real birth of what came later to be the Balfour Declaration, made during his premiership.

With the creation of the Ministry and the powers vested in its chief by the Munitions of War and Defence of the Realm Acts, Moulton's Department placed controls over the entire production of patent-distilled alcohol, that made from unmalted grain, to use in the production of acetone for cordite manufacture. This alcohol would, in normal times, have gone into the production of gin. Lloyd George was certainly not himself a teetotaller, yet he remained convinced in these days at the Ministry that what he simply termed 'drink' was as great an enemy of the British Empire as were the armies of the Central Powers. No doubt the employment by the Ministry of the substance which might otherwise have become gin gave him great pleasure.

Perhaps the most important technological innovation carried out by the Explosives Department was the development of methods to increase the production of high explosives. Shortly before the outbreak of the World War, the British Army had adopted trinitrotoluene as the replacement for lyddite and the principal high explosive for artillery shells. Moulton was aware that T.N.T., as it was called, could be diluted with other substances because of its quality to animate, that is to render explosive, these other chemicals. He was able to convince the artillery experts of the two services that such a process was not only successful, but absolutely necessary if Britain were to manufacture enough high explosives. While this agreement had been reached by April 1915, Moulton discovered that, two months later, Woolwich Arsenal continued to employ only the less effective lyddite or undiluted T.N.T. as the explosive charge in H.E. shells.[34]

This period corresponded with the organization of the Ministry of Munitions and Lord Moulton turned to Lloyd George for aid. The Minister championed the use of amatol, a mixture of T.N.T. and the more widely available ammonium nitrate, for use in shell-filling. This required the development of entirely new processes in order to employ T.N.T. in the most economical way, in a ratio of 80 per cent ammonium nitrate to 20 per cent T.N.T. Much of the credit in this development must go to Lord Chetwynd, another of Lloyd George's men of push and go. Chetwynd was called to the Ministry to construct and direct the new National Filling Factory at Chilwell, near Nottingham. Chetwynd defined the process of filling shells with the new and rather tricky substance; by the close of Lloyd George's Ministry, amatol had become the standard charge for high explosive shells. Without the cooperation of scientist, industrialist and politician, it might never have come about.

The Minister of Munitions prided himself on the recruitment by his Department of what were to him among Britain's greatest national resources: her intellectuals, and primarily her scientists. With the assistance of the Royal Society, a Scientific Advisory Committee was appointed. Made up of chemists, physicists, biologists and other specialists, the Committee was, in late 1915, attached to the Trench Warfare Department, under the authority of Brigadier-General Louis Jackson. Their work included research and development of poisonous and irritant gases, scientific instruments and optical glass, as well as many other products.[35]

IV

Lloyd George was neither an engineer nor a scientist, and he readily admitted that his experience as Minister of Munitions never made him a true expert on the technology of munitions design. He became Minister, in part, because of his ambition, his self-confidence that he alone was the man for the difficult job. Other character-assets from which wartime Britain benefited were his ruthless energy and drive and his ability to dispense with established procedures without looking back. He demanded of his men of push and go the same qualities: they were required to produce what was needed as quickly as possible and without regard for the suspended 'rules of the game'. There are perhaps no better case-studies of these attitudes at work than those of the two greatest developments in land warfare of the War: the Stokes mortar and the tank. The Ministry designed neither, but it ensured the survival of each because the men of Whitehall Gardens were willing to support and nurture unorthodox solutions to the munitions requirements of an unorthodox war.

Inspired by the suggestion of H. A. Gwynn, the editor of the *Morning Post,* that the British Army required a counter-blast to the 'frightfulness' of the German *minnenwerfer,* Wilfred Stokes, the chairman and managing director of Ramsomes & Rapier Ltd., developed in late 1914 a working model of a simple and efficient trench gun.[36] The need for trench weapons was well known by this time, but the War Office had already turned to Woolwich Arsenal and to Vickers to develop trench mortars.[37] Stokes was able to gain a trial of his weapon before the Ordnance Board Inspectors on 30 January 1915. After correcting defects in the mortar in line with their criticisms, he presented a modified gun for trial on 2 February. Within a fortnight, however, the Director of Artillery informed the inventor that his device was of no use to the War Office.[38]

Stokes, convinced that his 3-inch mortar was superior to older standard trench howitzers or any new trench guns, pressed the War Office for a further opportunity to demonstrate its merit. He was granted another viewing on 24 March 1915, which gained him only a further rejection from Major-General Guthrie Smith, who wrote five days later: 'in view of satisfactory trench howitzers now in France and the fact that this makes another form of ammunition it is not proposed to adopt the design.'[39]

The greatest virtues of the Stokes mortar were its simplicity both of manufacture and of operation. It consisted of an unrifled steel tube with neither breech nor triggering mechanism, and the weapon was activated by simply dropping the projectile down the bore. The simplicity of the gun was matched by its accuracy and speed of fire—three bombs could easily be put in the air at once, and, in the hands of an expert, twice as many bombs could be sent toward their targets at the same time.[40]

As Stokes continued doggedly to press his invention on the War Office, the Ordnance Board reported to the Director of Artillery that the uncomplex Stokes mortar would have the virtue of opening sources to the manufacture of trench armaments which could not conceivably make the far more complicated standard 3.7-inch trench gun. Their report also praised the accuracy of the weapon and surmised that it 'doubtless' could be made effective.[41] Despite this confidential evaluation, the Major-Generals in charge of weaponry design remained unconvinced.

On 4 June 1915, after six months of attempting to satisfy the Ordnance Board of the superiority of his invention, Stokes was conclusively informed that the War Office would not approve his weapon for manufacture. The reason stated was that it was un-desirable at that time to multiply the types of trench guns then being manufactured.[42] After his own arduous trial, Wilfred Stokes himself began to doubt the value of his revolutionary weapon:

> It was an absolute and definite turn down [he wrote in 1917] which, while I greatly regretted personally after all the trouble I had taken, made me wonder if the information I had received as to the shortcomings of the four service patterns of trench mortars could be true or not.[43]

Just as the creation of the Ministry of Munitions had occurred in time to ease the frustration of Lord Moulton, it corresponded also with Stokes' time of self-doubt: on 14 June 1915 Lieutenant-Colonel J. C. Matheson of the Ministry Trench Warfare Supply Department discovered the mortar with the Ordnance Board. Risking the anger of the Master General, Matheson's department obtained a sample of the gun from the inventor.[44] Initial trials were conducted at the Trench Warfare Experimental Ground at Wormwood Scrubs; among the observers was Lloyd George.[45] Impressed by the demonstration, the Minister of Munitions reques-ted the Ordnance Board to examine the Stokes mortar again. In July, though it yet had no official sanction from the War Office to begin production of the weapon, the Ministry ordered for testing twenty complete mortars, and 500 bombs from Ransomes & Rapier.

While Wilfred Stokes and the Trench Warfare Supply and Inventions Departments of the Ministry cooperated in testing and attempting to improve the mortar and bomb, Lloyd George concluded that actual production of the weapon could no longer be delayed. The Ordnance Board had withheld approval of the mortar and the War Office had not requested its production. Lloyd George, however, intended to order 1,000 mortars anyway. The weapon was unorthodox, and so was its source—a manufacturer of sluices and electric industrial cranes—so the Minister planned equally un-orthodox methods to bring it to production. Orders could not be officially made, and consequently paid for, without a War Office demand. Hence, on 12 August 1915, contracts were prepared for the manufacture of the initial 1,000 mortars, and funds to cover the cost were pledged from a special fund provided for the Minister for munitions purposes by a wealthy Indian maharajah.[46] Thereby production was begun and funds were provided in the event of the War Office continuing to refuse the new weapon. It was a procedure as appropriately unusual as the Stokes mortar itself.

Lloyd George's confidence in the mortar was soon vindicated. In August Sir Douglas Haig, soon afterwards to become Commander-in-Chief of the B.E.F., was shown samples of the Stokes mortar—over the objections of the Master General. On 22 August 1915 he wired to the War Office that the weapon was suitable and would be useful immediately for firing chemical smoke-screen shells. He wrote: 'as many Stokes Guns and smoke for them as can be made available are urgently required to be delivered to France by 1 September.'[47]

Presumably Haig was either unaware or uninterested in the fact that the mortar had been repeatedly rejected by the Ordnance Department of the War Office. Conditional approval of the gun by the Ordnance Board was not even granted until six days after his telegram, and final approval was given only on 18 September 1915. Then, further delays were caused as the master gauges for manufacture and inspection of the weapon were not immediately available from the one official source of these necessary testing tools, the Royal Arsenal, Woolwich. No Stokes mortars were delivered to France by 1 September, but they did begin to arrive in October. Approximately 200 were delivered to the Army in France before the end of 1915. The delay might have been greater had not the Ministry of Munitions begun the cycle of contract, to preparation, to manufacture, to delivery of finished products, as early as it did.[48]

The remainder of Lloyd George's initial 'unofficial' order was completed by mid-January 1916. By the time he left the Ministry six months later, production of the new weapon was in full swing, and more than 2,500 3-inch Stokes mortars had been manufactured; in addition, more than 600,000 bombs per month were being issued to G.H.Q. France.[49] During the last months of Lloyd George's Ministry, the Stokes mortar became the standard trench gun of the British Army, eclipsing all its rivals.[50]

The Ministry does not deserve the credit for the invention of the Stokes mortar. Yet without the energetic interference by Lloyd George in what was then the business of the Ordnance Department, the valuable weapon might have been long delayed or even doomed. This salvage operation, to save what might have been lost, was but one case study of many which helps to explain why the Minister of Munitions demanded and secured, one by one, the leaves of what Asquith had termed 'von Donop's attenuated artichoke'.

V

The most brilliant breakthrough in land warfare technology of the years 1914–1918 was the intervention of what was then variously termed the landship or machine-gun destroyer, but was finally christened the tank.[51] The Ministry of Munitions did not create the weapon; yet without the support of that young Department, it would surely not have appeared when it did. In fact, it might never have been fully developed at all. Several times in its development the idea was almost lost for lack of official support. When the brilliant infant was virtually orphaned, the Ministry became its foster parent and protected it, granting the opportunity to grow to its destructive maturity.

Two lines of development led to the creation of the tank: the first of these began with conversations in October 1914, between the Secretary of the Committee of Imperial Defence, Lieutenant-Colonel Maurice Hankey, his deputy, Lieutenant-Colonel Ernest Swinton, and a retired engineer officer, Captain T. G. Tulloch.[52]

All agreed that some revolutionary device was needed to break the trench- and machine-gun-imposed deadlock on the Western Front. Hankey submitted a memorandum on New Year's Eve 1915, to certain members of the War Council; his famous 'Boxing Day Memorandum', as it came to be called, envisaged:

> Numbers of large heavy rollers, themselves bullet proof, propelled from behind by motor engines, geared very low, the driving wheels fitted with 'caterpillar' driving gear to grip the ground, the driver's seat armoured, and with a Maxim gun fitted. The object of this device would be to roll down the barbed wire by sheer weight, to give some cover to men creeping up behind, and to support the advance with machine-gun fire. . . .[53]

Among those who took notice of the memorandum were the two figures who were then clearly emerging as the two most adventurous minds in the Council: the first, Lloyd George, had already chaired the Shells Committee by this time and was very interested in suggestions on how to break the deadlock on the Western Front. The second, Winston Churchill, shared the feelings of the Chancellor of the Exchequer. As First Lord of the Admiralty, Churchill had men, money and authority to conduct experiments in developing military hardware, and the next step in the tank story was his.

The First Lord had created the Armoured Car Division of the Royal Naval Air Service for the purpose of recovering British pilots downed behind or near enemy lines in France. It was certain of the officers of 20 Squadron R.N.A.S. who provided the second line of development by involving their chief in a tank project. In early February 1915, Major T. H. Hetherington, Commodore Murray Sueter, and Lieutenant Albert Stern, all enthusiasts for some sort of landship project, arranged a dinner at the home of the Duke of Westminster, the Commander of the Armoured Car Division. The purpose of the dinner was to interest the First Lord in sponsoring research into the development of such a vehicle.[54] The guest of honour, having read Hankey's memorandum, was entirely receptive to the idea.

On 20 February he called a meeting of interested parties and constituted a committee under the chairmanship of Sir Eustace

Tennyson-d'Eyncourt, the Director of Naval Construction, to look into the matter. Both caterpillar traction and giant wheel propulsion were to be considered as means of moving the landship. At this stage, inspired by the ideas of Major Hetherington, Churchill invisaged a huge land battleship, carrying 100 men on an armoured platform supported on fifteen-foot wheels. It was an awesome, if impractical, vision; its major service was that it served to interest deeply the First Lord in landship research and caused him to constitute the committee of believers who were destined actually to develop a workable tank.

The First Lord was aware that the War Office had been invited by Asquith to investigate the practicality of the ideas aired in Hankey's memorandum. It was, in fact, Churchill's support of the trench-destroyer foreseen in the paper which brought the Prime Minister to recommend to Kitchener researches toward this goal. Churchill, however, had no desire to involve his own committee with the War Office at this point:

> . . . . I knew [he wrote in *The World Crisis*] they would raise objections to my interference in this sphere, and I knew that the Department of the Master General of the Ordnance was not receptive to such ideas. . . .[55]

The First Lord, in this explanation, was perhaps more diplomatic than candid. He did not wish to see the chance of a technological breakthrough lost because of the deadening influence of the Master General and his colleagues at the Ordnance Department.

Churchill's instincts were proved quite right. In January, at the command of the Secretary of State who was himself acting at the bidding of the Prime Minister, the Master General of the Ordnance did appoint a committee to look into Hankey's idea of a trench destroyer; in the chair was Major-General G. K. Scott-Moncrieff, the Army's Director of Fortifications and Works. Investigations were made of the possibility of development of the Holt caterpillar, an American-made agricultural tractor, into such a weapon. Despite the urging of then Colonel Louis Jackson (later the Ministry's chief of trench warfare research) that development be continued, the experiments were declared failures. While Major-General von Donop was willing to allow further investigation into the matter if a satisfactory engineer could be found to direct them, quite remarkably the committee was unable to recommend one. By the close of February, then, the War Office abandoned research on landships.[56] At no time in these weeks did the Master General communicate with Hankey or Swinton or with the officers of the 20 Squadron R.N.A.S.—nor were they informed of the conclusions of the War Office committee. Until May 1915, when further examinations of a modified tractor originally designed for hauling huge guns met with a similar fate, Churchill wrote, 'the project was decently interred in the archives of the War Office.'[57]

The War Office had been given the opportunity to lead in the development of a revolutionary, perhaps a decisive, new weapon. The Ordnance Department and the Scott-Moncrieff Committee, after this brief examination, passed up the opportunity both to present the Army with a useful new weapon and to counter-attack against the critics of War Office control of munitions supply. They failed to do so, and the future Minister of Munitions observed the entire affair.

By May 1915 Tennyson-d'Eyncourt's Landships Committee had come to the conclusion that caterpillar traction was the only suitable method of propulsion for the new weapon. There was, however, little visible evidence of progress toward bringing the vehicle to life. It was at this time that the entire project came close to meeting its end: May 1915, of course, was the month in which the Government crisis removed Churchill from the Admiralty. The tank researchers saw their champion reduced to the Chancellorship of the Duchy of Lancaster, from which office he could no longer protect them.

Several events coincided in the weeks which followed to help save the work of the developers of the tank. In early June, Lieutenant-Colonel Swinton, who was then serving as the official newspaper correspondent with G.H.Q. under the pen-name 'Eyewitness', submitted a memorandum titled *The Necessity of Machine Gun Destroyers,* to Field Marshal Sir John French. Swinton, unaware of the developments in this regard at the Admiralty or War Office, reiterated his confidence in the usefulness of armoured mechanical traction vehicles for breaking through trench lines. French passed the paper along to the Chief Engineer at G.H.Q., Major General

G. H. Fowke and to the Chairman of the Inventions Committee, Major-General Sir John DuCane. On 22 June, 1915 the memorandum was forwarded to the War Office with French's recommendation that it should receive the proper attention.[58] French was not aware of the War Office's summary rejection of the idea five months earlier. Shortly before the paper was forwarded to London, Swinton himself returned to the capital to replace his former chief, Lieutenant-Colonel Hankey, as Secretary to the new Dardanelles Committee. Hankey was temporarily out of the country visiting the Dardanelles theatre of war.

More important, perhaps, than this development was the entry into the tank picture of Lloyd George and the Ministry of Munitions. On 30 June 1915 Commodore Sueter hastily set up a demonstration at Wormwood Scrubs of one of the Admiralty Landships Committee's research vehicles. The Killen-Strait agricultural tractor, shown that afternoon, resembled a large tricycle, with caterpillar tracks in place of wheels. The demonstration was significant in that it made a loyal supporter of tank research of the Minister of Munitions. Though A. J. Balfour, the First Lord of the Admiralty, was sympathetic to the tank experiments, the Sea Lords (except the Third Sea Lord, Admiral Sir Frederick Tudor), were not. Lloyd George, after the Wormwood Scrubs trials, offered to relieve the Navy of the tank research programme. The War Office, however, intervened and prevented the transfer.

Due in part to the interest shown in Swinton's 'Machine Gun Destroyers' paper by Field Marshal French and other high-ranking officers at the Front, the War Office was prompted to re-enter tank development, which it had earlier abandoned. At about the same time that the Wormwood Scrubs demonstration was being carried out, the War Office called upon Balfour to convert the Landships Committee into a joint services council by the addition of several Army officers. The enlarged committee was thereafter to be chaired by Major-General Scott-Moncrieff, who had directed the original War Office tank investigations. While the conversion of the group became official on the very afternoon of 30 June, and though Scott-Moncrieff and three other Army officers were added to it, the Tennyson-d'Eyncourt Committee essentially continued as it had done. The actual contribution of the new members was simply to lay down the Army's formal requirements for a practical and useful landship or tank. Lloyd George had not secured control of the research team, nor had he prevented the War Office from taking an influential position in its future. However, he had no intention of allowing the Ordnance Department of the War Office to secure control over the Tennyson-d'Eyncourt Committee or 20 Squadron

The critical period in the infancy of the tank continued through the months of July and August. Under considerable pressure from the Sea Lords, Balfour began to reconsider the value of retaining control over the Tennyson–d'Eyncourt Committee or 20 Squadron R.N.A.S. On 17 July, Lloyd George enthusiastically agreed to assume responsibility for all Admiralty land warfare research, though the Tennyson-d'Eyncourt Committee was excepted from the agreement. While ridding their service of most of these development responsibilities pleased the Sea Lords, they were not satisfied.[59] The Landships Committee was allowed to continue its work, in part because it had entered into contracts with engineering firms for prototypes of landships, but in late July 20 Squadron, never a favourite among the officers of the Board of Admiralty, was doomed. On 18 August 1915 its disbandment was ordered and its officers and ranks were ordered to prepare for posting to other units. Only intervention by Balfour's Naval Secretary, Commodore Charles de Bartolomé and, more important, by the Minister of Munitions, saved the squadron. The Armoured Car Squadron supplied virtually the entire working staff and equipment of the Landships Committee; without it, Tennyson-d'Eyncourt's group would have become an administrative unit without men to carry out its decisions—a mind without a body.

The Ministry provided other help at this time as well, as the Landships Committee moved from the overcrowded Admiralty and was provided with office space in the former Hotel Metropole, which had been taken over by the Munitions Department.[60] More important perhaps, 20 Squadron was installed at the Ministry of Munitions Trench Warfare Experimental Ground at Wormwood Scrubs. At this time, mid-August 1915, 20 Squadron, as well as the Landships Committee, were still officially part of the Navy. While their official parent was obviously uncomfortable at the fact, the Ministry of Munitions was already moving in the direction of providing a new home for the research team. By August 1915 the Ministry was already well aware of the limitations of the technological policies of the War Office. Lloyd George and his aides meant to prevent the fledgeling weapon from falling under the authority of the Master General of the Ordnance, once the Sea Lords succeeded in pushing it from the Admiralty nest.

On 28 August 1915 a meeting was held of representatives of these Departments in order to clarify the authority of each over the device which was rapidly reaching completion. The decisions of the meeting were several: in the first place, the Admiralty Landships Committee, in cooperation with E. W. Moir's Munitions Inventions Department, was to continue to direct the manufacture of tank prototypes already under construction. Secondly, when the prototype was complete and accepted by the War Office, the Ministry of Munitions was to become responsible for series manufacture of the vehicles.[61] These decisions were a further victory for the Ministry in its efforts to seize control of munitions technology for the Ordnance Department. They were an even greater victory for those who had worked so hard to make the tank a success. In regard to the attitude of the Master General of the Ordnance at this time, Sir Basil Liddell Hart has written:

> Having rejected the opportunity a year earlier to lead the way in developing the machine, that department now seemed to be aggrieved that the lead should have been up in other quarters. Its chief expressed his feelings in querulous complaints about procedures and a manifest attitude of non-co-operation.[62]

The first prototype tank, code-named 'Little Willie', actually clambered about under its own power in August 1915. While efforts continued to improve it, work was continued on a second generation model of improved design, which operated under its own power in January 1916. This second design, code-named first, 'Big Willie' and later, 'Mother Tank', became the model for the production vehicles which later were introduced on the Western Front.

On Christmas Eve 1915 a second inter-departmental conference was held to discuss further details of manufacture of the tanks. At this meeting the Ministry's representatives, unknown to

Lloyd George, came close to making a terrible mistake. Speaking for his Department, Captain T. G. Tulloch (who had joined the Ministry several months earlier) rejected the plan which called for the Ministry to take over production of the new weapons. It was decided, instead, that in order to keep the responsibility for the manufacture of tanks from the hands of the Master General of the Ordnance, a special production committee should be created to supply tanks to the War Office.[63]

Formal trials of the two prototypes were held at Hatfield Park on 2 February 1916 in the presence of representatives of the Admiralty, the War Office and the Ministry, as well as other dignitaries. 'Big Willie' was clearly the star performer and passed all the tests the War Office devised: it scaled heights, crossed trenches and crushed defensive obstructions effortlessly. The tank was a huge success. Sir Eustace Tennyson–d'Eyncourt wrote to his former chief, Winston Churchill, who was then on active service in France:

. . . in appearance it looks rather like a giant antediluvian monster especially when it comes out of boggy ground which it traverses well; I hope it will scare the Bosches.[64]

It did, indeed.

Despite Kitchener's personal scepticism about the future and usefulness of the tank, the Secretary of State for War requested that the Tank Supply Committee, the group authorized by the 24 December conference, be placed under the authority of the War Office. Lloyd George, however, had other ideas. Sweeping aside the reservations of Captain Tulloch and the conclusions of the 24 December conference, he was adamant that tank supply legitimately belonged under the wing of the Ministry. The idea of the production committee appealed to him, however. It was, in fact, a ready-made and experienced department, for the Chairman, Lieutenant Albert Stern, and the effective membership agreed upon at the conference, were veterans of service on the Tennyson–d'Eyncourt Committee.

With Balfour's approval, the Minister of Munitions ignored War Office objections and called Stern to the Ministry. The former banker, in Lloyd George's estimation, showed signs of being a man of push and go and, consequently, was judged suitable for Ministry service. Stern required a guarantee of autonomy for his new department and he produced a charter which he requested the Minister to initial as an act of good faith. Lloyd George, after asking Sir Samuel Hardman Lever to examine its financial clause, did so without further comment. The Tank Supply Committee soon lost its rather independent sounding name and became the Tank Supply Department, which produced the revolutionary weapons to War Office order for the remainder of the War.[65]

In regard to the field generals and military technology in World War I, Edward L. Katzenbach had written:

> The military generation which fought World War I never understood what technology had done to their profession. . . . The intellectual problem of the military is to translate the characteristics of a piece of hardware—a gun, a machine, a vehicle—into a doctrine for its use, that is, to relate technological possibility to space and time, to mass, and to human psychology. The military in World War I failed to do this.[66]

The same sort of blindness afflicted those generals who remained at home, charged with the responsibilities for munitions design, research and development. When challenged by those who could better solve these problems, they struck a defensive posture and fought to retain their powers, despite their inability to use them to the greatest good of their comrades in the trenches.

The conventional wisdom of the twentieth century dictates that technological development is the handmaiden of modern warfare. While it is perhaps comforting to believe that this variety of good always seems to develop naturally out of the horror of modern war, the experience of the Ministry of Munitions disproves that such technical advancements came quite so naturally, at least in World War I. Indeed, it was a monumental struggle.

Lloyd George, of course, was neither an engineer nor a scientist. Yet he did wish to exploit fully the technological resources of the country, as he was doing with her production facilities, to produce the most advanced as well as the most abundant munitions possible. His goal was to bring the War to an end as quickly as possible. He saw the securing of control over munitions design and research, as well as acting as foster-parent to the Stokes mortar and the tank, as steps toward achieving that goal. He was, in the end, proved right.

Despite the accolades of the crowds in 1918, neither Lloyd George nor any other one man won the War. In the light of these accomplishments in the development of armaments, however, it is easier to understand the extravagance of one of the tank pioneers who said of him in this period: 'as Minister of Munitions he saved this country from dire disaster.'[67]

Ten

DELIVERING THE GOODS

I

The tradition of the War Office for many years had been that munitions were supplied to the Army as the need of these armaments became known. The commanding generals notified the Secretary of State for War of their requirements; the Secretary of State passed the message along to the Master General of the Ordnance; the Master General, in turn, arranged for their delivery or, if the stores were unavailable, for their manufacture at the Royal Arsenals or the established arms firms. This procedure had armed the British force which pacified the Sudan and the Army which defeated the Boer commandos in South Africa. It would not, however, provide the munitions for a general war.

Britain's senior soldiers cannot be blamed for their surprise at the kind of warfare which developed on the Western Front in the autumn of 1914. By late in the year, however, Lord Kitchener had begun to think of fielding a force of continental proportions. There was, however, no systematic calculation made of the immediate and long-range needs of such an Army. No analysis had been made of the munitions production capacity of Great Britain or the Dominions, much less that of America. No information had been gathered in regard to how many guns, of what calibres and in what proportions, would ultimately be needed by the New Armies. No inquiry had been made in regard to the difficulties of providing ammunition for these guns. The War Office, while it retained control over munitions supply, continued to rely on the hand-to-mouth practices it knew best. This policy, even when modified under the pressure applied by Lloyd George and others, made the creation of the Ministry of Munitions virtually inevitable.

Soon after taking up the seals of his new office, the first Minister of Munitions crossed to France to confer with Field Marshal Sir John French about the munitions needs of his forces. French's advice came as no surprise to Lloyd George: in the massive artillery war of the Western Front, the greatest needs were for heavy guns and high explosive ammunition. Following this meeting, Lloyd George travelled to Boulogne to meet with the French Minister of Munitions, Albert Thomas, and representatives of the French War Office. The French generals urged that, in artillery warfare, heavy guns and howitzers were virtually all that mattered. Guns and howitzers of a minimum of 6-inch calibre were what was needed. Likewise, such guns needed a sufficient supply of shells: to equal the combined output of Germany and Austria, the French estimated, the Allies would have to produce at least 1,750,000 rounds per week.[1]

This advice was sobering to Lloyd George, for the British Army possessed at that time only sixty-one guns of 6-inch or greater bore. The production of shells had not begun to reach the proportions which the French generals saw as a minimum.

At Boulogne, the Minister of Munitions concluded that his worst fears of the previous ten months were quite true—the British Army was ill-equipped to carry out the awesome task which it had been assigned. With the advice of the French officials very much on his mind, and influenced by the impressions the Front had made upon him of the sort of warfare which lay ahead, Lloyd George questioned General Sir John DuCane, Field Marshal French's artillery expert, as to the artillery requirements of an army of 1,000,000 men. DuCane's answer is unrecorded, but the question reveals the direction in which the Minister's mind was turning: he anticipated that the British Army and the War itself were to grow larger before the fighting ended. This experience was the genesis of what came to be called the Boulogne Programme.[2]

On 22 June 1915, at the prompting of the Munitions Office, Lord Kitchener requested of Sir John French his assessment of the necessary increases in artillery supply. In response there arrived three days later the first coherent long-range projection of the heavy artillery requirements of the B.E.F. Calling attention to the practice of both his allies and his enemies, Sir John informed Lord Kitchener that his meagre artillery supply of only 1,487 guns of all calibres had to be increased if the British Army were to be effective in the near future. Basing his requests upon an army of an estimated fifty divisions, he required by March 1916 ('should the war continue so long'), an additional 400 60-pounder guns, 400 6-inch howitzers, 250 8-inch and 9.2-inch howitzers, and 40 12-inch and 15-inch howitzers.[3]

The armaments makers who were expected to produce many of the necessary parts and to assemble this vast new array of huge guns were warned, in the first week of June, of what the Ministry would be expecting of them. Plans were laid at Whitehall Gardens and, on 28 June 1915, they were disclosed to the War Office as *Programme B*. Basing their projections on a force estimated not at fifty but at seventy divisions, the Ministry hoped to increase the artillery supply of the B.E.F. and of reserves by June 1916 to:[4]

18-pounder guns	5,107
4.5-inch howitzers	1,618
60-pounder guns	800
6-inch howitzers	560
8-inch and 9.2-inch howitzers .	372
12-inch howitzers	48

To arrange for this lavish scale of armaments, the Ministry placed orders, in addition to those already made by the War Office and the Shells and Treasury Committees, in the following amounts:

18-pounder guns	582
4.5-inch howitzers	637
60-pounder guns	621
6-inch howitzers	458
8-inch howitzers	48
9.2-inch howitzers	156
12-inch howitzers	16

Without seeking the advice or the approval of the War Office, 'Mr. Lloyd George proposed placing additional orders for heavy guns in the hope that manufacturers would thus be enabled to accelerate deliveries on old as well as new orders.'[5] His reasoning was that the armaments makers would lay down further increases in their plants if they could depend upon large continuation orders for artillery. Furthermore, the Ministry agreed to provide additional financial aid in these increases, as well as help in securing machine tools and skilled and unskilled labour. In the end, the Minister was proved right.

On 27 August 1915 the Acting Director General of Munitions Supply, Major-General Sir Ivor Phillipps, submitted at Lloyd George's request a further estimate for the provision of artillery for a force even Kitchener had not yet contemplated: 100 divisions. The Minister had become convinced by this time that, before the War ended, a British Army of this size would most certainly be a necessity. He meant, also, to be ready to equip such a force when it was raised. Consequently, further orders were placed, for example, for an additional 320 6-inch howitzers, 208 8-inch and 9.2-inch howitzers, and 37 12-inch and 15-inch howitzers. Within a matter of days, inquiries were made as to the ability to provide such artillery of the Bethlehem and Midvale Steel Companies in America.[6] Positive responses from the United States were followed shortly by firm orders.

As a result of these further preparations, *Programme B* became obsolete rather quickly. A revised schedule of production, *Programme C,* called for, by December 1915, with the B.E.F. and in reserve:[7]

18-pounder guns	6,000
4.5-inch howitzers	1,920
60-pounder guns	920
6-inch howitzers	980
8-inch howitzers	462
9.2-inch howitzers	378
12-inch howitzers	85

On 14 September 1915 Lloyd George submitted these figures to the War Office, and they were received with intense displeasure. Lord Kitchener neither sought nor wished thrust upon him this vast amount of artillery; he felt it a wasteful programme and concluded that it would be an impossible task to supply enough trained

gunners to man these batteries when they did become operational.
The battle between the Ministers was carried into the Cabinet and
the Secretary of State for War circulated a memorandum to his
colleagues calling their attention to the extravagant production of
the Ministry of Munitions.[8] Lloyd George's counterblast was an
absolute refusal to cancel the new programme or, as Kitchener
suggested, to change the design of the guns to the Russian pattern
and give them to the Czar's armies, without the Cabinet assuming
responsibility for the decision he condemned. To compose the
latest 'royal row' between the two ministers, the Prime
Minister referred the case to a Cabinet Committee under the
chairmanship of the colleague whose judgement he valued above all
others; Lord Crewe, the Lord President of the Council.

The War Office case was presented by the Master General of
the Ordnance, Major-General von Donop. Lloyd George listened
and then made no reply.[9] Things appeared bleak for the ambitious
programme:

> 'I suppose sir,' said his Secretary J. T. Davies, as they walked
> away from the meeting, 'that means the end of your pro-
> gramme.'
> 'No,' said Lloyd George. 'It means the end of the Committee.'[10]

The Minister of Munitions was quite right. In the end, the
Committee upheld the Ministry and disappeared. The Secretary of
State for War was left to remonstrate in Cabinet and in correspondence with Lloyd George. *Programme C* stood as the Ministry had
planned it.[11]

The mass of figures and production plans which evolved into
Programme C represented the first attempt by Britain's leaders, either
military or civilian, to set down a plan of campaign by which the
shortages of guns and shells could be overcome. Of greatest importance was the Minister's decision, defended before Kitchener's
and von Donop's objections, to 'budget for surplus'—that is, to
produce greater quantities of munitions than the War Office sought,
in anticipation of both the British Army and the War itself growing
larger. Disregarding the opinions of the experts who exhorted
caution, the Munitions Supply Department was commanded to
bring plans to reality. The Labour Department was advised to

intensify its Dilution programmes and to concentrate skilled hands where they would be most useful. The Machine Tool Department was set to work to locate or to arrange for the production of the necessary lathes and milling machines for the manufacture of guns, shells and other warlike stores. Likewise, each of the other Ministry departments lent its strength to the common goal.

The confidence that the War itself would prove them right was realised in the most terrible fashion: before Lloyd George left the Ministry it was evident that the 'budget for surplus' policy was not the result of the prognostications of a group of woolly-minded amateurs. *Programme C* was vindicated before all of its critics because the surplus, and more besides, was needed.

The procedures of the Ministry employed to create these early gun programmes became standard practice in the supply of all *matériel*. In the first place, the needs of the Army were discovered. Then, the relevant supply department—for guns, shells, machine guns or other stores—was consulted in order to establish a figure for the greatest possible production of any particular item. Finally, as production plans were laid, that theoretical maximum was generally increased for good measure. What remained was to make every human effort to meet that difficult goal. To fail, and failure was not uncommon in the Ministry's Munitions Supply Department, meant encountering the wrath of the Minister and being advised that greater efforts were absolutely required. To succeed meant, usually, a compliment and the raising of requirements of production. It was a demanding process but, in the end, a successful one.

II

Artillery was in very short supply in June 1915. For several years before the War very few orders had been placed by the War Office due to the strict budget economies of the Liberal Government, the small size of the projected B.E.F. and the anticipation by the General Staff of the limited nature of any future land wars in which Britain might become involved. Many of the great armament firms remained solvent through orders placed by the Admiralty for the Dreadnought building programmes, or by manufacturing arms for foreign markets.

In the years 1902–1912, for example, the War Office took delivery of only nine 4.7-inch guns, twelve 60-pounders, four 5-inch guns, fifteen 6-inch guns, ninety-six 4-inch and 4.7-inch howitzers, and only a single 9.2-inch gun. The only sizeable accumulation of artillery of one calibre consisted of a total delivery of 657 18-pounder field guns. On the average, about seventy pieces per year had been received during the period, and the four months before the War saw the delivery of only one gun.[12] Subsequently, after 4 August 1914, with the exception of 18-pounder field guns, there was a serious lack of all natures of artillery.

As the Ministry's great ordnance programmes were being planned to overcome these shortages, several preliminary steps were taken to give them the best chance of success. For example, Walter Layton's Statistics Department was recreated as the Department of Munitions Requirements and Statistics. Thereafter, this section no longer merely acted as the repository of production, raw material or stock-on-hand figures; rather, all statistics of munitions requirements, whether demanded by the War Office or decreed by Whitehall Gardens, were immediately funnelled into it. Layton and his staff, therefore, were able to make daily comparisons between demands and deliveries, to forewarn of imminent dangers of shortages of raw materials or labour or components in the completion of a programme and, in general, to keep a finger on the pulse of the various manufacturing efforts of the Ministry. Such a practice allowed constant measurement of actual production against the ideal of such ambitious plans as *Programme C*. It seems, by contemporary standards, to be a logical and even simplistic step in any production organization; its importance is not entirely clear unless it is understood that almost a year of War had passed before a munitions authority was created which had the foresight to do it.[13]

While Layton's section kept the figures, money was provided on a lavish scale for the expansion of factories and production lines.[14] More than 2,500 machine tools were supplied to armaments makers and technical advice made available to all Ministry contractors, with special attention paid to those new to the production of munitions components.

Charles Ellis, the Deputy Director General of Munitions Supply charged with artillery production, laid down in 1915 that, while it was all but impossible to manufacture the huge barrels of heavy guns outside the established armaments shops—due to the shortage of the enormous lathes used in their production—contracts for their manufacture were to be at all times divided between two such manufacturers. His thinking was that if one manufacturer fell behind on delivery, perhaps the other would not. Ellis was well aware that arrears in delivery had been a terrible cause of slow production of guns before the creation of the Ministry. As the programmes progressed and expanded, eventually this policy was increased to cover four such contractors.

Such artillery pieces required hundreds of components of course, and Ellis' department worked to expedite the completion of the guns by judiciously spreading the contracts for production of such pieces among all manner of manufacturers. While the production lines of the arms makers were kept busy doing only what they could do, clockmakers manufactured springs, railway engine manufacturers made limbers and carriages and even a court jeweller made firing pins for artillery pieces.

The results of these policies demonstrated their effectiveness. The B.E.F. had taken with them to France: 897 18-pounder guns, 169 4.5-inch howitzers, 31 60-pounder guns, and 86 6-inch howitzers. Between August 1914 and June 1915, due to the efforts to the Master General of the Ordnance and the various Cabinet and War Office Committees who laboured to increase this supply, it was augmented by a further 723 18-pounder guns, 160 4.5-inch howitzers, 36 60-pounder guns, 23 8-inch howitzers, and 18 9.2-inch howitzers.[15]

While the Ministry of Munitions was unable to meet its own ambitious production schedules set forth in *Programmes B* and *C* in the time provided, it is equally clear that that artillery was produced and delivered in numbers and with a frequency never before seen by the War Office. In the six months following Lloyd George's appointment as Minister, the new Department produced more field guns and almost as many heavy guns as the British Army had possessed at the outset of hostilities and had received from the War Office before June 1915. In the first six months of 1916 the production figures for artillery were ever more impressive and, during the year June 1916 to June 1917, though Lloyd George had left the

Ministry to become Secretary of State for War, the production programmes of the Ministry laid down under his leadership began to mature. The result was that guns and howitzers, particularly of heavier calibres, at last were supplied in adequate numbers to meet the needs of the trench warfare of the Western Front.

During Lloyd George's tenure as Minister of Munitions the production capacity of the armaments firms and other industrial facilities in Great Britain which were involved in gun production were affected in the following way: for lighter calibres of guns, it was reduced by 28 per cent. The purpose of this action, of course, was to put machinery and labour and raw materials toward the manufacture of heavier artillery. The capacity for medium gun production, therefore, rose to 380 per cent of what it had been in May 1915; capacity for heavy gun manufacture grew to 1,200 per cent of the May 1915 figure.[16]

Much the same success story is told if figures of proportionate increases are used for comparison. If a standard of unity of artillery deliveries in June 1914 is employed, the proportionate increases were:

June 1915–June 1916 (monthly average)		*July 1916*
6½ times	18-pounder guns	17½ times
8 times	4.5-inch howitzers	27 times
7½ times	all medium calibre artillery	34½ times
22 times	all heavy calibre artillery	94 times

Guns and howitzers were of little use to the B.E.F. without ammunition. It was, after all, the shortage of shells which was instrumental in bringing to the attention of the politicians and the public the whole munitions crisis and, therefore, in bringing the Ministry of Munitions to life. The production of shells was the object of the earliest experiments in contract-spreading encouraged by the Shells Committee; it was the goal of the local Munitions Committees and the later Cooperative Schemes operated by the Management Boards; it was the purpose of the National Shell and National Projectile Factories. In the end, the output of artillery projectiles was one of the most brilliant successes of the Ministry of Munitions—equalling or outdistancing the production of guns and howitzers.

The index numbers for shell production make understandable this achievement. Using June 1915, as a base (base equals 100), the index number for production of light shell in June 1916, rose to 940, and for medium shell to 695. The most striking figure is the index for heavy shell production, which increased to 1,240.[17]

The Shells Section of the Munitions Department reported proudly to the Minister on 1 July 1916: 'A year's output of shell at the rate at which it was produced during the year [August] 1914-[August] 1915, can now be obtained in the following period—

18-pounder [gun]	3 weeks
4.5-inch [howitzer]	2 weeks
medium [up to 8-inch]	11 days
heavy [over 8-inch]	4 days[18]

The production of artillery ammunition, though demands were regularly raised after mid-1916, never again fell behind requirements as it had done throughout the first year of the War. There were no more Shell Scandals.

IV

Among the most glaring failures in the supply of *matériel* to the B.E.F. in the months before the Ministry of Munitions was organized was the inadequate provision of machine-guns. These twentieth century weapons had become invaluable in the trench warfare on the western Front and the War Department had failed to provide the Army with enough guns to meet even the modest requirement then thought adequate. Up to May 1915 only short term contracts had been placed for machine-guns, calling for 3,344 weapons, and only a portion of these agreements included continuation clauses for further production. Assuming that such continuations would have been arranged on all contracts and that the huge arrears in deliveries could have been overcome, by March 1916 the total number of machine-guns available to the British Army would have been 12,344.[19] Requirements by that time had already reached 14,000 weapons—a number which was itself wholly inadequate.[20]

In the summer of 1915 the Secretary of State for War was not alarmed by the situation. In an interview with Lord Kitchener on 26 July 1915 Eric Geddes, whose section of the Munitions Supply Department was charged with machine-gun production, was advised that two machine-guns per battalion were to be considered a minimum. Four guns per battalion were to be considered a maximum and anything over four, a luxury.[21]

Geddes had tried in vain for several weeks to secure from the Master General of the Ordnance, or any other War Office official, a figure of required machine-gun production for the B.E.F. This was the first such statistic he had learned and, as was his habit, he put it down in a hastily-produced holograph memorandum and requested that the Secretary of State initial it. Kitchener was infuriated at the suggestion and agreed to it only when Sir Percy Girouard interceded on Geddes' behalf. 'Geddes is like that,' Sir Percy advised, 'He won't act unless you sign a paper.'[22]

Lloyd George and his Deputy Director General of Munitions Supply considered the figure given them by Kitchener and immediately began to plan upon a 'luxury' supply of machine-guns. The Minister advised Geddes:

> Take Kitchener's maximum . . . square it, multiply that result by two; and when you are in sight of that, double it again for good luck.[23]

Disregarding the figures reported by War Office contractors as their 'maximum' capacities for the production of machine-guns, the Ministry took measures to provide these weapons on a scale previously unheard of in the British Army. The construction of a new factory for machine-gun production planned for Vickers' facility at Crayford was accelerated and equipped by the Ministry Machine Tool Department; another such factory was planned and built at Vickers' Erith works. In addition to these new shops, extant machine assembly-lines were expanded under Ministry authority using State funds. Plant extension begun at the B.S.A. works was diverted from rifle to machine-gun production. A new factory was erected at the Hotchkiss works at Coventry to increase the production of that French-designed gun. All this activity was carried on in addition to the regular Ministry practice of arranging for an increased flow of components through contract-spreading among non-armaments engineering shops.

Not long after these steps were taken, official recognition of the importance of these weapons and of the validity of the Ministry's estimates of the numbers required came in the form of a request by the newly appointed Chief of the Imperial General Staff, Sir William Robertson. The new C.I.G.S. called for an increase in the maximum number of guns supplied to each battalion to sixteen, a figure which neither shocked the Ministry nor found it unprepared.[24]

The results of the efforts of Geddes and E. W. Moir, who in the first months after the creation of the Munitions Supply Department was placed in charge of machine-gun manufacture by Geddes, were remarkable: in June 1915, for example, fewer than 1,000 Vickers guns were produced in Great Britain. By December of that year, however, more than two and a half times that number had been delivered.[25] Approximately 500 Lewis guns were in the hands of the Army in June 1915; by September, the monthly delivery of such weapons exceeded that number.

The British Army had begun the World War with only a handful of machine-guns and was slow to realise the great influence these weapons were to have in trench warfare. By the end of the conflict, they possessed more than a quarter-million of them. Once the provision for their manufacture had been completed by the Ministry, after June 1916, production kept pace with the ever-growing demands from the Front.

V

The final class of munitions supplied by the Ministry during Lloyd George's tenure was termed trench warfare supplies; that is, grenades, mortars and other lightweight weapons of particular effectiveness from the entrenched positions which characterized the Western Front.

Until the creation of the Ministry, trench warfare equipment was largely improvised on the field of battle, resulting in the ingenious 'jam-pot' and 'hairbrush' grenades which British soldiers constructed and then hurled at the enemy. The Trench Warfare Supply Department, created in July 1915, discovered that only a token quantity of grenades, mortars and mortar ammunition had been provided by the War Office. Neither did there appear to be sufficient War Office orders placed for the provision of these valuable munitions. It was estimated that, until late July 1915, the office of the Master General of the Ordnance had supplied less than 150,000 grenades of all types, of which less than 16,000 were of the most current design—the so-called Mills grenade. When asked, however, how many of these weapons were required in the summer of 1915, the generals replied that eventually a daily supply of 10,000 rifle grenades, 30,000 Mills grenades and sufficient numbers of all other types of grenade totalling approximately half a million per week were wanted. This was more than three times the absolute total supplied to that time.[26]

While the Trench Warfare Supply Department began immediately to arrange for a regular delivery of grenades, it was discovered that emergency measures had to be taken to produce simple but effective hand-bombs for use in the Dardanelles theatre of war. General Sir Ian Hamilton, the commander of that ill-fated expedition, wrote of the desperate need of his men for grenades: 'Anything made of iron and containing high explosive and detonator will be useful. I should be greatly relieved if a large supply could be sent . . . as the bomb question is growing increasingly urgent.'[27] This message reached the desk of the Director of Trench Warfare Supply, Alexander Roger, at 5:00 pm on 9 July 1915, and the Trench Warfare Supply Department was immediately notified of Hamilton's plight. That same night representatives were dispatched to Gathurst, to arrange for explosive, and to Manchester, with hastily designed plans for a simple cast-iron grenade body, to make provision for their rapid manufacture. Despite the fact that the contractors enthusiastically pressed into service for this project had no experience at all with such devices, within five days 25,000 grenades had been manufactured. Within seven days of the receipt of Hamilton's message, these weapons, along with sufficient fuses and detonators, had been 'loaded, packed, and dispatched to a steamer which was taking cargo for the Dardanelles. In addition, 10,000 pitcher grenades, 5,000 Phosphorous bombs, together with 330 Catapaults were provided in the same consignment.'[28]

This experience in providing grenades on such short notice became quite valuable later that same month. On 21 June 1915 Sir John French had requested of the Quartermaster General: 'hand grenades of any type available may be sent out in large quantities as possible to meet the urgent and growing demands received from the Front.'[29] This requirement did not come into the hands of the Ministry until 20 July, and it was discovered that little had been done by the War Office to overcome the need. Emergency measures of the same type as those used to meet Hamilton's demands were effected and 50,000 hand bombs were on the way to France within a fortnight. Two weeks after that shipment, regular consignments of 300,000 emergency grenades per week were being sent to French's headquarters.

The story of regularized grenade production is scarcely less remarkable than these emergency measures. At the time of the take-over of this responsibility by the Ministry, more than half of the small trickle of grenades came from the Royal Arsenal at Woolwich, which was already so terribly burdened with other duties. The Ministry Trench Warfare Supply Department immediately began a programme of contract-spreading and firms of all sorts were called upon to make fragmentation-grenade bodies, pins, levers, detonators, fuses and other components for hand bombs. Twenty-two so-called 'filling stations', in which explosives were added to completed grenade bodies, were established throughout the country. Within five months of the establishment of the Department, more than two hundred different contractors were involved in grenade production. Of great significance is the fact that the vast increases in production were arranged outside of Woolwich Arsenal, leaving that establishment free to perform functions which could only be carried out there.

The War Office and the Ministry of Munitions had together

delivered approximately 400,000 grenades during the first calendar year of the War.[30] By November 1915 the Trench Warfare Supply Department was producing 800,000 grenades of all types each week.

The other major weapon produced under the aegis of this section of the Ministry was the mortar. As we have seen above, the Stokes mortar, after much trial and irritation, was finally accepted by the War Office as the standard trench howitzer. Getting the weapon into production was difficult, due to the obstructionist tactics of the Master General of the Ordnance and the perfectionist proclivities of the inventor, who was wont continually to make changes in the design. These matters were eventually overcome and a valuable trench weapon was added to the arsenal of the B.E.F.

While in June 1915 there were but 300 mortars of all types in the field, within six months the total was increased fivefold.[31] In July 1915 a weekly total of 6,000 mortar bombs of all types were produced; by December, an average of 22,700 were manufactured each week. The 3-inch Stokes mortar became the standard trench mortar in the winter of 1915. In April of 1916 production of these weapons reached 250 per week and thereafter levelled off at between 100 and 200 per week. Total production of the mortar by June 1916 was 2,500; by December 1916 it had reached 3,500. By May 1916, production of bombs for the 3-inch Stokes gun reached more than 600,000 per month, thereafter levelling off at approximately 300,000 per month.[32]

As in the case of grenade production, the T.W.S. Department did not simply produce more mortars than the War Office; rather, they produced in great quantities a necessary weapon which the Ordnance Department had been almost unable to supply at all.

There was no doubt in the mind of the first Minister of Munitions that Sir John French's qualification of his artillery needs for 1916, 'should the War last so long', was short-sighted. Lloyd George was certain that the War would last a very long time and, like Lord Kitchener, he also felt that the British Army in the field in mid-1915 was but a shadow of the huge force which the nation would have to raise before the World War was ended.

It was this understanding of the size and scope of the World

War which led to the policy called 'budgeting for surplus'. The ambitious programmes for guns and shells which grew out of the Boulogne Conference in 1915 were, in most cases, not met by the target dates of June or December 1916. If this completion by the specified time is taken as a measure of success, then the Ministry surely failed. This is too narrow a context, however. The purpose of the great munitions programmes was, of course, to provide sufficient quantities of armaments for the B.E.F. as quickly as possible. However, of almost equal importance was the need to lay down long-range plans for the production of increasingly large stores of weapons in the knowledge that the Army was to grow larger in future. The programmes allowed for such planning; for shops, labour and raw material supplies were all gathered together with these huge plans in mind.

Perhaps the most important measure of the short-range success of the Ministry's munitions production efforts was the fact that in the case of each calibre of artillery and ammunition, as well as in the instances of the myriad other weapons used by the men in the trenches, the Ministry of Munitions brought about rapid and marked increases after it took over responsibility for the provision of such armaments.

The Ministry of Munitions under Lloyd George, despite the spiralling requirements for warlike stores on the Western Front and in the Dardanelles Campaign, did indeed deliver the goods as no agency had done before. After December 1916, when these arrangements reached their maturity, they remained virtually unchanged throughout the War, even though requirements continued to increase up to the very eve of the Armistice and through the Ministries of Montagu, Addison and Churchill.

Eleven

EPILOGUE

I

Lloyd George and the officials of the War Office seemed agreed on at least one fundamental point in May 1915: the Ministry of Munitions was to produce the abundance of guns and shells which the British Army had lacked until that time. Beyond this small area of agreement all was grey, blurred and a source of disagreement and makeshift compromise. In fact, no one knew, in these first days of the new Department, the breadth of power it was to possess and the huge number of tasks for which it was to become responsible. What had been termed 'the scope of the Department' continued to grow from mid-1915 until the end of the War. Lloyd George laid down the policy that if weak links in the chain of munitions production could be isolated, then it was the task of the Ministry to strengthen that weakness. More often than not, in 1915 and 1916, this resulted in the Ministry taking on additional duties.

Lloyd George left the Ministry in early July 1916 and his place was taken by Edwin Montagu, who retired from that office in December with the formation of the Lloyd George Coalition. Montagu was himself replaced by Dr. Addison, the former Parliamentary Secretary to the Ministry, who gave way, in July 1917, to the final wartime Minister of Munitions, Winston Churchill. The last Minister of Munitions was Lord Inverforth, who took Churchill's place in January 1919 and served until March 1921. Each of the Ministers who held that post throughout the period of the War continued Lloyd George's policy of adding to the duties of the Munitions Office. The result was that the Ministry continued to increase both in the size of its staff and in the diversity of its activities.

We have seen that under Lloyd George the Ministry, far from being only an assembler of shells and guns, became responsible for the design of munitions, for the supply of tanks, for munitions inventions, for the manufacture and distribution of machine tools and for a myriad other things. In 1916 and 1917 were added the responsibilities for the wartime development of mineral resources in Great Britain and for the import and allocation of petroleum supplies. In 1918 the Petroleum Production Act vested in the Minister of Munitions the power to grant all licences for the exploration for petroleum in the United Kingdom.[1]

In early 1917, due largely to the increased demand for engines for aircraft and tanks, the supply of all internal combustion engines for Government use became another of the Ministry's duties. The same period saw the Ministry become responsible for the provision of railway supplies and mechanical transport, which consisted largely of the manufacture of equipment to move the huge quantities of munitions already manufactured under the authority of the Ministry.[2] In mid-1917 the manufacture of agricultural machinery was added to the Ministry's burdens; before the close of that year, control over design and development of tanks was vested in the Minister of Munitions.

Perhaps the most important single duty which the Ministry gained in the post-Lloyd Georgian period was the manufacture of aircraft, which was transferred from the Services late in 1916. Authority over aircraft design was vested in the strengthened Air Board under Lord Curzon.[3] Demand was to remain with the 'user' Departments: the War Office and the Admiralty. Lloyd George, who became Prime Minister shortly before this development, decreed that cooperation among these four Ministries was to be ensured by housing the relevant sections of each in the same building—the Hotel Cecil was pressed into Government service for the purpose. Though this compromise worked reasonably well, in January 1918 all the occupants of the Hotel Cecil passed under the authority of the Ministry, as the entire power over design and production of aircraft was handed over to that Department.

The new Aeronautical Supply Department, formed early in 1917, followed proved Ministry techniques in laying down production plans for aircraft. The Machine Tool Department supplied heavy equipment for new National Aircraft Factories; the Labour Department arranged for a suitably 'diluted' labour supply; extant private aircraft manufacturers were declared Controlled Establishments and brought under Ministry authority; and, like shells and guns, aircraft were manufactured in greater numbers than had been believed possible in the years before the World War. In the first twelve months of the War, it was estimated that an average of fifty machines per month were constructed, almost entirely by private manufacturers. By the last full year of hostilities, more than 3,500 aircraft per month were being manufactured in National Factories and Controlled Establishments.[4]

These additional duties, each of which required its own department, added to the Ministry's great success, to its remarkable growth and to its awesome complexity. When Lloyd George handed over the Department to Montagu it had eighteen departments and a staff of approximately 5,000 employees. By the time Churchill became Minister a year later, the Munitions Office encompassed more than fifty separate departments and had almost tripled its staff.[5]

The Ministry of Munitions, as we have seen, was an emergency Department of State, created to serve one purpose—the organization of productive resources for munitions manufacture. Lloyd George had invested all his great energies in his year at Whitehall Gardens in that task and had succeeded beyond even his own estimates. He worked closely with each department head, giving them personal access to his office at all times, and delegated his own authority as Minister to his men of push and go. The result was that the initial goal of the new Department was achieved—the nation's factories, raw materials, and labour supply were put to work making munitions. However, there was little thought invested in creating even a semi-permanent departmental organization. The various sections of the Ministry constituted a confederation of separate units, tied together through the person of the Minister and his personal staff. It was a difficult job—perhaps unlike any performed by a Cabinet Minister in those years.

Both Montagu and Addison, in the year following Lloyd George's leave-taking, attempted to create a departmental scheme which would relieve the Minister of some of his ever-increasing duties. Edwin Montagu told a meeting of department heads soon after he became Minister:

> [The Minister of Munitions] cannot regard himself, as he does in an old established office, as a transitory fount, a telephone for communicating the activities of the department to the House of Commons. He has got to regard himself as a sort of epitome in himself of the permanent head of the department and the political head of the department, the sole focus of the co-ordination that exists. Well, I do not say it with a desire to shirk responsibility, but I do not think it is fair to him, and I do not think it is the best way of securing co-ordination between departments and the Ministry.[6]

Lloyd George's two immediate successors sought a reorganization of the Department which would relieve the Minister of some of these duties. Both men preferred a somewhat more normalized procedure, with 'proper channels' approximating to regular Government Departments. They were well aware, however, that the unorthodox senior staff of the Ministry would resist any attempt to restrict their jealously guarded privilege of direct access to the Minister.

In the end, while several expedients were tried, neither of these men governed the Ministry long enough to develop a satisfactory alternative organization scheme. This was left to Churchill, who instituted in August 1917, what was called at the time a 'group' scheme. Each department was classified according to general function and placed with similar branches in one of ten administrative divisions of the Ministry, each of which, in turn, took charge of one of the major spheres of the Department's work. Each of these divisions was placed under the authority of an experienced Ministry Officer, who was relieved of departmental responsibility. They collectively constituted the Munitions Council, which both supervised the routine of the various departments and advised the Minister.[7]

Churchill's reorganization served its purpose: a more coherent order was brought to the Ministry which had tripled in size since July 1916 and the Minister was relieved of the almost impossible task of acting as the major cohesive force in the Department. All this had been accomplished without stripping the Ministry of its push and go character. Section chiefs retained the privilege of personal access to the Minister, but what Churchill termed a 'more accessible minister', the Munitions Council Member for their Group, was readily available to manage many matters which formerly were passed along to the Minister. This system continued until the dissolution of the Department in 1921.

Winston Churchill, throughout his long career, was sometimes accused of appropriating credit for accomplishments which were not rightfully his own. Such a charge could not be brought against him in this case, for in his memoirs of the period he made very clear that his own work at the Ministry did not overshadow the major honour in the story of the Ministry of Munitions. He wrote:

> That belongs in the first instance to Mr. Lloyd George, who gathered together the great majority of these able men, and whose foresight in creating the national factories laid the foundations for subsequent production. It belongs also to the men who did the work, who quarried and shaped the stones, and to whose faithful, resourceful, untiring contrivance and exertion the Army and the nation owe a lasting debt.[8]

It is worthy of note that, though changes in the organization of the Ministry were necessitated by its continued growth, there was no such reorganization necessary in the philosophies and methods of munitions production laid down by Lloyd George in 1915 and 1916.

II

During the final days of World War I it appeared that the Ministry of Munitions, in somewhat altered form, would survive the Armistice and become a permanent department for the supply of warlike stores. In March 1921, however, the Department was disbanded. In these two years, conditions made the survival of the Munitions Office, in any form, impossible.[9] In the first place, the military Departments retrieved, one by one, many of the powers which had been taken from them by the Ministry. Arguing that the emergency which had made the transfers necessary in the first place was past, the War Office and the new Air Ministry were unenthusiastic about the continuation into peacetime of any department which had recently been such a threat to their authority.

In the second place, the amazing efficiency with which the Ministry of Munitions carried out its tasks found Great Britain in the winter of 1918–19 with huge stocks of warlike stores of all kinds. This situation, at a time when the Government was faced with returning the nation to a peacetime footing, reduced the question of creating a permanent war supply department to a very low priority.

Thirdly, the nation was exhausted in virtually every meaning of the word. Not least of all, she had used up her last ounce of enthusiasm for war. The idea of the permanent supply ministry simply could not generate much enthusiasm either in or outside Parliament.

Finally, the Government was preoccupied with two matters in these early post-World War years: the first was foreign affairs, which took much of the time and energy of the Prime Minister and Cabinet. The second was reconstruction, the ambitious programme to convert the exhausted nation into a 'home fit for heroes to live in'. The men who had made the Ministry, Lloyd George, Addison, Churchill, Geddes, Booth, Beveridge and the rest, were absorbed in one facet or another of these matters.

A bill creating a Supply Ministry was actually drafted in 1919. The proposed department was to possess only those powers given it by the Service Offices, and it surely would have been a pale shadow of the Ministry of Munitions. The bill never received even a first reading in the House, for fear that the obvious half-measure could not be defended against its attackers in Parliament. No further attempts of the kind were made, and the Ministry of Munitions, in the name of economy, was quietly disbanded. It was never resurrected.

The experience which necessitated the creation of the Ministry of Munitions, as well as the lessons taught by the Ministry itself, were not entirely forgotten in the inter-war years.[10] Throughout the 1920s, for example, there was greater cooperation between the three Services in regard to supply procedures than there had been between the Army and Navy before 1914. The Admiralty supplied the Army and Air Force with torpedoes and small craft; the Air Office supplied aircraft and air stores to the other Services; finally, the War Office supplied general stores and small arms to the Navy and Air Force.[11]

Late in the 1930s, when the European situation again appeared to be moving toward war, the precedents laid down by the Ministry of Munitions became valuable once again. After Munich, in 1938, for example, Britain's first peacetime conscription law was enacted. The needs of a huge new Army were not met this time by obsolete measures cloaked in secrecy, as in 1914–15. In fact, the Secretary of State for War, with full support from the Army chiefs, requested the immediate creation of a new Ministry of Supply to perform essentially the same functions as were carried out by the Ministry of Munitions in World War I. Like its predecessor, this new Ministry was meant initially to be a supply source for the Army. When it began operations in mid-1939, however, it exercised the powers over design and development of armaments for which the Munitions Office had to battle for months. Unlike the Ministry of Munitions, however, the Ministry of Supply was never empowered to provide stores for the Air Ministry.

In 1940 the Churchill Government set up a Ministry of Aircraft Production, under Lord Beaverbrook, which produced both planes and air stores for the Air Force for the remainder of the War. Again, the new supply department was granted full authority to design and develop, as well as manufacture, aircraft. Like the relations which finally evolved in World War I, the Service branch, in this case the Air Force, retained control only over requirements of aircraft and stores.[12]

The increased complexity of the problem of munitions production in World War II, due mainly to the fact that weapons were not only more numerous but far more complicated, made the creation of one Ministry of Munitions almost impossible.

Hence there were organized two new supply authorities in addition to the Admiralty, which continued, as it did in World War I, to manufacture its own ships and stores. In order to coordinate the efforts of the three departments, the Government created, in 1942, the Ministry of Production. This new Office did not actually administer many supply facilities; rather, it functioned to balance the programmes of the other manufacturing Departments of State. Its Minister held a seat in the War Cabinet, and he was close to the deliberations which shaped Allied strategy.[13] Hence, he was able to direct the relevant supply Department in laying down programmes which fitted the needs of the war planners. The Minister of Production also worked closely with Britain's Allies in production planning and enjoyed broad powers over imports, exports, allocation of raw materials, and over the organization of industries for armaments production.[14] It was this Minister who served virtually as a deputy Prime Minister for Production, exercising powers to rationalize strategy with armaments production, as even the Ministers of Munitions had been unable to do in World War I.

The second general war of the twentieth century did not witness an exact duplication of the armaments supply measures taken almost twenty-five years before. While it can fairly be argued that rearmament came too late in the 1930s, when it did come, it demonstrated that Britain was not required to relearn all the lessons of 1914 and 1915. The experiences and precedents of the Ministry of Munitions were invaluable when it became necessary to build a new munitions production organization in the period 1939–45.

III

The ultimate goal of Lloyd George and the men he called together at the Ministry of Munitions was not unlike that of all patriotic Britons: they wished to help win the War. The difference between these pioneers and so many of their contemporaries, however, was marked. They were willing and even keen to ignore all precedent—civil and military—in their efforts. Lloyd George, in effect, wished to fling from his window in Whitehall Gardens the burdensome weight of years of 'established practice' of the War

Office and the Civil Service. He chose to circumvent or, if that was impossible, simply to ignore that mass of procedures which he was fond of styling 'red tape'.

This commitment led the first Minister of Munitions to wager the nation's future on administrative talent, and businessmen, scientists, academicians and all manner of other men who passed his 'push and go' scrutiny were called to serve the Department. The civil servants who came to Whitehall Gardens and remained were those, like Beveridge, Llewellyn Smith and Black, who were able to adjust to the bizarre and hectic pace they found there. Lloyd George set out to mould a Department possessed of an élan which he felt was absent in the War Office; when he sensed the adventurousness, the spirit he admired in a man, he brought him into the orbit of the Ministry and pressed him for all he was worth.[15] If, as he admitted he did in some cases, he discovered that his judgement of a man was in error, that new face usually disappeared from Whitehall Gardens soon afterwards.[16]

The ability to lead other men and, as the Minister often put it, 'to get things done' came to be the sole criteria for success among the Ministry's senior staff. The risk was considerable, for such staffing practices were virtually unheard of. Critics were legion, but the rewards for success were great—and all other methods had failed. Like his disregarding of 'red tape' and established practice, Lloyd George's reliance on the talented outsiders, the men of push and go, proved to be successful.

The other major characteristic of Lloyd George's plan for 'delivering the goods' was his commitment to a policy of State Control of industrial production. He meant to direct the munitions effort through his Ministry, and this meant Government control of the factories, the labour force, the supply of raw materials, workers' wages and shareholders' profits and, finally, even of the electric power which lit and powered the munitions shops—all in an effort to produce armaments in the most efficient possible fashion.

To the Ministry staff, a munitions programme was nothing less than a coordinated assault upon a well-defended front; in this theatre of war, battlefields were production lines and victories were measured by numbers of shells or guns produced—yet it was a warrior's campaign just the same. The great conflict over State Control had seen skirmishes since the advent of the twentieth century. Never before had the Controllers won such a complete victory: by the end of the War, almost all Britons, grudgingly or not, had come to make their peace with what was often called 'War Socialism'. The advance force of that victory was the Ministry of Munitions, and its general staff was housed at 6 Whitehall Gardens.

What factors in this story can be attributed to the Minister himself? It is clear that this pioneering Department was not a one-man show. However, the Ministry of Munitions in 1915 and 1916 came closer to reflecting the personality of its founding chief than have most Departments of State in the twentieth century. That is because it drew its inspiration from one man, David Lloyd George. He infused in his subordinates a spirit, born of a great and frustrated urge to serve the war effort in an active fashion. It might be called an excitement, a dynamic energy which was harnessed simply to overwhelm and engulf the problems which confronted it. It was left to others to complete the construction of departmental machinery, that is true; however, there was an emergency in 1915, and nothing less than a munitions crusade could overcome it. Only after the emergency was past was there time to consider other things.

The wizardry which admirers and critics alike have seen in the works of the greatest war minister Britain had witnessed since the days of Chatham was not, of course, wizardry at all. With all the power and genius which had once made him the premier social reformer of his day, Lloyd George became what democracies require from time to time: the man of peace who went to war.

NOTES

1 Business as Usual

1 Lloyd George left the Treasury, temporarily at least in theory, and retained his residence at 11 Downing Street, the traditional home of the Chancellor of the Exchequer. Equally temporary was to be McKenna's tenure of his new office. The unusual arrangement did little to improve the already strained relations between the two colleagues; their mutual hostility, in fact, grew worse in the Coalition Cabinet.

2 A copy of this memorandum of 1 August 1914, may be found among the papers of the Ministry of Munitions, MUN 5/180/1300/57.

3 The Master General of the Ordnance, despite the obvious Teutonic flavour of his name, was spared the hysterical anti-German hatred which burst upon Prince Louis of Battenburg and Lord Haldane.

4 See Arthur Marwick, *The Deluge* (Harmondsworth, Middlesex, 1965), p. 30, and Sir Llewellyn Woodward, *Great Britain and the War of 1914-1918* (London, 1967), p. 456.

5 See Woodward, *Great Britain and the War,* p. 456.

6 Curiously enough, and probably much to the irritation of purist believers in *laissez faire*, both the railway takeover and the experiment in marine insurance showed a profit at the close of the War.

7 The popularization of the phrase is customarily accorded Winston Churchill. Arthur Marwick, however, has suggested that its first use in this context was by a London businessman. See *Deluge*, p. 39.

8 Lord Morley and Lord Beauchamp, as well as John Burns and John Simon, resigned over intervention, but only Morley, the last Gladstonian, and Burns, the first working-class minister, persisted in their resignations. Lord Lucas and Lord Emmott joined the Cabinet.

9 Lady Violet Bonham-Carter, *Winston Churchill As I Knew Him* (London, 1959), p. 257.

10   Sir Philip Magnus, *Kitchener: Portrait of an Imperialist* (New York, 1959), p. 284.

11   Woodward, *Great Britain and the War,* p. 36.

12   Lloyd George made the remark to George Macaulay Booth at the Kitchener memorial service in 1916. Duncan Crow, *A Man of Push and Go: The Life of George Macaulay Booth* (London 1965), p. 137.

13   See Magnus, Kitchener, pp. 284–287, and Woodward, *Great Britain and the War,* pp. 51–5.

14   Sir Edward Grey recorded hearing Kitchener make this remarkable statement 'more than once'. Grey of Fallodon, *Twenty-Five Years* (London, 1925) vol. II, p. 69.

15   Sir George Arthur, *The Life of Lord Kitchener* (London, 1920) vol. III, p. 265, n. 1.

16   Admiral Sir John Fisher to Lord Esher, *c* 7 November 1903. This letter, with its characteristic underscoring, is printed in *Fear God and Dread Nought: The Correspondence of Admiral of the Fleet Lord Fisher of Kilverstone* (edited by Arthur J. Marder: Cambridge, Mass., 1952), vol. I, p. 290.

17   Alfred Gollin, *Balfour's Burden: Arthur Balfour and Imperial Preference* (London, 1965), p. 4.

18   Balfour's Ministry was a particularly fecund one for commissions looking into military matters. Another such group, under the Duke of Norfolk, came out in favour of military conscription. Its recommendation drew support only from the small band of 'National Service' advocates gathered around Lord Roberts. See Eric William Sheppard, *A Short History of the British Army* (London, 1959, revised edition), p. 292. See also Correlli Barnett, *Britain and Her Army: 1509-1970* (New York, 1970), pp. 366–7, and Charles à Court Repington, *Vestigia* (London, 1919), pp. 256–7.

19   Roberts' admirers were especially displeased with the fashion of 'Bobs' retirement. See Repington, *Vestigia,* p. 258.

20   Cmd. 1932/1904, *Report of the War Office Reconstitution Committee, Part I: The Esher Committee.* See also J. D. Scott and Richard Hughes, *The Administration of War Production* in *The History of the Second World War.* Sir Keith Hancock, general editor. (London, 1955), Part I.

21   Woodward, *Great Britain and the War,* p. 462.

22   For the efforts of the various Conservative and Liberal Governments to improve the efficiency of the Royal Arsenals, see the Ministry of Munitions departmental memorandum titled 'Woolwich Ordnance Factories During the Thirty Years Before the

War,' MUN 5/152/1122.11/11. For the operation of the factories see *The History of the Ministry of Munitions* (London, 1922) vol. VIII, Part I, pp. 1–34.

23 For the position of the established armaments firms on the out-break of hostilities, see J. D. Scott, *Vickers: A History* (London, 1962), pp. 97–100.

24 The critic was the first Minister of Munitions. See *The War Memoirs of David Lloyd George* (Boston, 1933) Vol. I, p. 122.

25 Entry for 13 October 1914. *Lord Riddell's War Diary* (London, 1933), pp. 35–6.

2   The War in Whitehall

1 Arthur, *Life of Lord Kitchener* vol. III, p. 74.

2 *Ibid.*

3 Magnus, *Kitchener,* p. 331.

4 In October 1914, the peacetime Committee of Imperial Defence was transformed into a War Council, ostensibly to advise the Government on the higher strategy of the War. With the coming of the Coalition Cabinet in May 1915, this Council gave way to the Dardanelles Committee, another Cabinet Committee which concerned itself primarily with the Eastern Theatre of warfare. It was, in turn, replaced in October 1915, by the War Committee, which continued until the Cabinet itself was replaced in December 1916. See Lord Hankey, *The Supreme Command* (London, 1961) vol. I parts III & IV, vol. II part V, *passim.*

5 Magnus, *Kitchener,* p. 331.

6 Their interest came to be welcomed, however, at G.H.Q. in France. See Viscount French of Ypres, *1914* (London, 1919), p. 347.

7 Lloyd George's place as the pioneer of the new age of the 'cottage bred man' has been questioned in a recent biography. See John Grigg, *The Young Lloyd George* (London, 1973), p. 31. I am indebted to Mr. Grigg for insights into the character of the first Minister of Munitions, gained in conversation.

8 See Cameron Hazlehurst, *Politicians at War* (London, 1971), pp. 105–7.

9 See Grigg, *Young Lloyd George,* pp. 259–261.

10 For an excellent discussion of Lloyd George's position in August 1914, see Hazlehurst, *Politicians at War,* chapter 9.

11 'I think,' he told a deputation of the Association of Municipal

Corporations, 'cash is going to count much more than we can possibly imagine at the present moment.' See *The Times*, 9 September 1914.

12   Peter Lowe, 'The Rise of the Premiership,' in *Lloyd George: Twelve Essays* (edited by A. J. P. Taylor: London, 1971), p. 99.

13   See Lloyd George, *War Memoirs* vol. I, p. 120, and Woodward, *Britain and the War*, p. 463.

14   *Lord Riddell's War Diary*, p. 36.

15   French, *1914*, p. 348.

16   J. A. Spender and Cyril Asquith. *Life of Herbert Henry Asquith, Lord Oxford and Asquith* (London, 1932) vol. II, p. 136.

17   Frank Owen, *Tempestuous Journey: Lloyd George, His Life and Times* (London, 1955), p. 279.

18   See *History of the Ministry of Munitions,* vol. I, chapter IV, part 1, for the six meetings of the Shells Committee.

19   See *Lloyd George: A Diary by Frances Stevenson,* (edited by A. J. P. Taylor (London, 1971), p. 7, entry for 23 October 1914.

20   Dr. Christopher Addison, M.P., who was destined to become the first political secretary to the Ministry of Munitions and its third Minister suggested at about this time that the efficiency of the War Office might be increased by placing it under the command of the manager of Selfridge's. See Stevenson, *Lloyd George: A Diary*, p. 7, entry for 30 October 1914.

21   CAB 42/1/39. A copy of the memorandum may also be found among the papers of the Ministry of Munitions, where it is dated 25 February. MUN/5/6/170/23.

22   For the National Efficiency movement in Great Britain in the years before the First World War, see G. R. Searle, *The Quest for National Efficiency* (Oxford, 1971). To those in touch with Lloyd George's activities in this sphere, his attraction to 'men of push and go' after May 1915, was no surprise.

23   Balfour to Lloyd George, 5 March 1915, Lloyd George Papers, C/3/3/1.

24   The minutes of this meeting are preserved among the papers of the Ministry of Munitions, MUN 5/6/170/22.

25   Lloyd George to Balfour, 6 March 1915, Lloyd George Papers, C/3/3/2. This letter is printed in *War Memoirs of David Lloyd George* vol. I, p. 158.

26   Undated memorandum by Edwin Montagu, Lloyd George Papers, C/14/3/19.

27   See the Earl of Oxford and Asquith, *Memories and Reflections: 1852–1927* (London, 1928) vol. II, p. 79, entry for 18 March 1915.

Asquith's 'contemporary notes' were not, in fact, a diary. This entry, like many others so classified, was an extract from one of his many letters to Venetia Stanley.

28   Stevenson, *Lloyd George: A Diary*, p. 36.

29   MUN 5/126/1000/120. Dated 31 May 1915, this document is a report to the Cabinet by Lord Kitchener on the conduct of the War by the War Office. A copy may be found among the Cabinet Papers as CAB 37/128/30. For von Donop's arguments, see MUN 5/6/170/22, the minutes of the 5 March meeting.

30   The remainder of the Armaments Output Committee consisted of Major-General von Donop; Sir Herbert Walker, Chairman of the National Railway Executive Committee; Sir Algernon Firth, President of the Associated Chambers of Commerce; and Allan M. Smith, Secretary of the Engineering Employers Association.

31   See Crow, *Man of Push and Go,* pp. 86–91.

32   Oxford and Asquith, *Memories and Reflections* vol. II, p. 80.

33   Asquith to Kitchener, 23 March 1915, Kitchener Papers, PRO 30/57/82.

34   Kitchener to Asquith, 25 March 1915, Kitchener Papers, PRO 30/57/82.

35   Lloyd George to Kitchener, 25 March 1915, Kitchener Papers, PRO 30/57/82.

36   Oxford and Asquith, *Memories and Reflections,* vol. II, p. 83.

37   Memorandum, Asquith to Kitchener, 8 April 1915, Kitchener Papers, PRO 30/57/82. A copy of this memorandum is preserved among the papers of the Ministry of Munitions, which the name of Admiral Sir Frederick Tudor, the Fourth Sea Lord, is included as the second Admiralty representative on the Treasury Committee. MUN 5/8/172/3.

38   Lloyd George to Balfour, 8 April 1915, Balfour Papers, Add. MSS 49692.

39   Lord Beveridge, *Power and Influence* (London, 1953), p. 124.

3   The May Crisis

1   See Hazlehurst, *Politicians at War,* part II, chapter 3.

2   See Gollin, *Proconsul in Politics,* p. 257. For Bonar Law's efforts to keep the impatient Tory rank-and-file in line, see Robert Blake, *The Unknown Prime Minister: The Life and Times of Andrew Bonar Law, 1858–1923* (London, 1955), pp. 238–40.

3 71 H.C. Deb. 5s, col. 1642, 12 May 1915.

4 This letter is printed in Martin Gilbert, *Winston S. Churchill Companion* Vol. III, Part 2, pp. 891–892.

5 Gollin, *Proconsul in Politics,* p. 258.

6 Lord Fisher wasted no time in making certain that Bonar Law was aware of the altered circumstances at the Admiralty. In the early hours of Saturday 15 May he posted to the Tory Leader an old newspaper cutting in which he underscored the line: 'Lord Fisher was received in audience of the King and remained there about half an hour.' There was no accompanying letter and there was no signature on the cutting. The characteristic handwriting of Lord Fisher, however, was unmistakable, and Bonar Law understood the rather cryptic meaning of the old admiral. See Martin Gilbert, *Winston S. Churchill* vol. III, p. 444. See also, Blake, *Unknown Prime Minister,* p. 243, and Lord Beaverbrook, *Politicians and the War* (London, 1960), pp. 105–6.

7 Lloyd George, *War Memoirs* vol. I, p. 200.

8 A. J. P. Taylor has indicated that Beaverbrook's emphasis of Fisher's place in the crisis was, in fact, meant to 'conceal his own expectation that shells would do the trick.' *Beaverbrook* (London, 1972), p. 93. Stephen Koss, in another recent interpretation has theorized that a cabal of Churchill, Lloyd George, and Balfour was responsible for the fall of the Liberal Government. *Lord Haldane, Scapegoat for Liberalism* (New York, 1969), chapter VII. Cameron Hazlehurst spends no fewer than four chapters (2–5) in his *Politicians at War,* refuting the Koss thesis.

9 See Lord French, *1914,* p. 343.

10 Field Marshal Sir John French was, of course, playing a double game —assuring Kitchener and the Government that he had sufficient munitions to carry out his programmes, while, at the same time, conducting a covert campaign to 'invigorate' a Cabinet he later openly condemned as apathetic toward the munitions needs of the B.E.F. Upon the publication of his book, *1914,* in 1919, Asquith delivered a speech denying French's allegations, which was published in pamphlet form as *The Great Shell Story,* in the same year. See Roy Jenkins, *Asquith: Portrait of a Man and an Era,* (London, 1964), pp. 357–8, for this affair.

11 This letter is printed in Reginald Pound and Geoffrey Harmsworth, *Northcliffe* (London, 1959), p. 475.

12 *The Times,* 14 May, 1915. The headlines of that issue provocatively declared:

NEED FOR SHELLS
BRITISH ATTACK CHECKED
LIMITED SUPPLIES THE CAUSE
A LESSON FROM FRANCE

13   *The History of the Times* (London, 1952) vol. IV, Part I, p. 274. See also Gollin, *Proconsul in Politics*, p. 253.

14   This memorandum is printed in Lord French's *1914*, pp. 358–61.

15   For Asquith's political motives in mid-May 1915, see Gollin, *Proconsul in Politics*, pp. 255–66, and Hazlehurst, *Politicians at War*, Part III, chapter 6.

16   Jenkins, *Asquith*, p. 364.

17   A lengthy excerpt from this letter is printed in Gilbert, *Churchill*, p. 447.

18   Sir C. L. Ottley to Hankey, 2 September 1914, Kitchener Papers, PRO 30/57/80.

19   Crow, *Man of Push and Go*, p. 71.

20   The Master General's behaviour was no secret in Whitehall. G. S. Barnes, an official at the Board of Trade wrote to Lord Buxton on 21 May 1915, 'Von Donop ought to be hung.' Hazlehurst, *Politicians at War*, p. 198, n. 1.

21   Lloyd George to Asquith, Lloyd George Papers, c/6/11/40.

22   His party colleagues agreed that Bonar Law would have made an excellent Minister of Munitions. See Austen Chamberlain to Bonar Law, 20 May 1915, Bonar Law Papers, 50/3/9, and Balfour to Bonar Law, 21 May 1915, Bonar Law Papers, 50/3/17.

23   He wrote to Lloyd George on 26 May 1915: 'Delighted to hear you are coming to help me.' Lloyd George Papers, D/17/6/2. This is all the more remarkable considering Kitchener's reactions to Lloyd George's previous attempts to 'help' him.

4   The Men of Push and Go

1   After a lifetime of acting as one of Lloyd George's closest confidants and advisers, the remarkable Miss Stevenson married him in 1944. She was the first woman to serve as private secretary to a Minister in Great Britain.

2   This amusing story is told in Lloyd George, *War Memoirs* vol. I, p. 213.

3   See Lloyd George, *War Memoirs*, vol. I, pp. 214–15.

4   Lloyd George first employed this phrase on 9 March 1915, in his campaign for the third Defence of the Realm Act. Almost im-

mediately thereafter, Lord Kitchener appointed George Macaulay Booth to organize the Armaments Output Committee and Booth became the first 'man of push and go' in the eyes of the public. See Crow, *Man of Push and Go,* pp. 90–1. Lloyd George genuinely admired Booth's talents but felt the name misapplied to him. 'He was rather a conciliator than a compeller. I found his tact and geniality invaluable....' Lloyd George, *War Memoirs* vol. I, p. 220.

5   Lloyd George had given up the Exchequer and was not yet officially Minister of Munitions. Attorney General until the formation of the Coalition, Simon lent his legal expertise to the constitution of the new Ministry and piloted the Ministry of Munitions Bill in Lloyd George's absence from the Front Bench.

6   MUN 5/10/200/3.

7   MUN 5/10/200/5.

8   See MUN 5/344/260/1.

9   *Ibid.* For the work of Lord Moulton, see below, Chapter IX, Part 3.

10   This letter of 5 June 1915 and the remainder of the great collection of correspondence dealing with transfer of functions which passed between the Ministry and the War Office were collected, printed and preserved as MUN 5/10/200/2.

11   A copy of the act is preserved as MUN 5/12/200/52. The italics are the present writer's.

12   For the later stages of transfer of functions from War Office to Ministry control during Lloyd George's tenure at the Munitions Office, see below, Chapter IX, 'Munitions Technology: The Battle for Weaponry Design'.

13   David Lloyd George, 'The Great Men of Wales,' *The Great Crusade: Extracts from Speeches Delivered During the War,* edited by F. L. Stevenson (London, 1918), p. 34, cited in L. Brooks Hill, 'David Lloyd George as Minister of Munitions: A Study of His Speaking Tour of Industrial Centers', *Southern Speech Journal* [U.S.A.], summer 1971.

14   Even G. A. B. Dewar, who was later to be a firm critic of Lloyd George as Minister, observed the flying tour 'shocked the country to attention.' See his, *The Great Munitions Feat* (London, 1921), p. 34.

15   Speech at Manchester, 3 June 1915, *The Times,* 4 June 1915. These speeches, and others, were later collected, edited, and published by Miss Stevenson as *Through Terror to Triumph* (London, 1915).

16   Addison Diary, entry for 30 May 1915. Addison Papers.

17   See Searle, *The Quest for National Efficiency,* p. 176.

18   Lloyd George, *War Memoirs* vol. I, pp. 216–17. 'There is one thing

we want less than usual, 'he told his listeners at Manchester, 'and
that is Red Tape.' *The Times,* 4 June 1915.

19   See MUN 5/344/260/1.

20   The development of this scheme is outlined in a Ministry of
Munitions staff letter, over the signature of Sir Percy Girouard,
dated 25 June 1915. It is preserved among the Ministry papers as
MUN 5/38/263.3/6.

21   Philipps to Lloyd George, 29 July 1915, MUN 5/38/263.3/12.

22   See MUN 5/8/171/21, Sir Percy Girouard's first scheme for organization for munitions supply, presented to the Armaments Output
Committee, 25 March 1915.

23   Booth found Girouard difficult and 'fearfully self-seeking'. Crow,
Man of Push and Go, p. 112. For Lloyd George's analysis of him
see Lloyd George, *War Memoirs* vol. I, pp. 221–2.

24   Girouard to Lloyd George, 19 July 1915, MUN 4/7056.

25   This remarkable correspondence is preserved in the Lloyd George
Papers: Lloyd George to Girouard, 22 July 1915, D/1/2/16.
Girouard to Lloyd George, 24 July 1915, D/1/2/17. Lloyd George to
Girouard, 24 July 1915, D/1/2/18.

26   The autonomy of the Explosives Supply Department was empha-
sized by the fact that they never left their quarters at Storey's Gate
to join the other supply departments then being gathered to-
gather at the new structure built to house the Department of Agriculture and Fisheries which metamorphosed into Armament
Buildings for the remainder of the War.

27   For the Trench Warfare Supply Department and its important work
in regard both to supply and design of munitions, see below
Chapter IX, Part 4, and Chapter X, Part 6.

28   Each of these transfers brought about a monumental battle between
the War Office and the Ministry of Munitions. See below, Chapter
IX.

29   Lloyd George, *War Memoirs* vol. I, p. 221.

30   See D. N. Chester and F. M. G. Wilson, *The Organisation of British
Central Government: 1914–1964* (London, 2nd edition: 1968), p. 24.

31   Addison, *Politics from Within* vol. II, p. 68.

32   For this survey see *Ibid.,* pp. 68–74. See also MUN 5/344/200/2.

33   There were, however, four 15-inch howitzers, ordered by Churchill
in August 1914, which fired first at the Battle of Neuve Chapelle.
Major-General von Donop expressed doubts that they 'could be
made or would be useful when made'. Winston S. Churchill, *The
World Crisis* (London, 1923) vol. II. p. 62.

34   War Office Progress Books showed that the British Army possessed

119 machine-guns on 4 August 1914. See MUN 5/377/1410.1/1.

35 Dr. Addison reported the request from the Front: 'Send us something or other we can chuck at the Bosch, and send it quickly.' Addison, *Politics from Within* vol. II, p. 113.

36 *History of the Ministry of Munitions* vol. II, part 1, p. 11.

5 National Organisation for Munitions Supply

1 See Chapter II, 'The War in Whitehall', above.

2 Specimens of the correspondence with the many different firms and individuals who wished to aid in the national effort to produce munitions may be found in MUN 5/6/170/5. Perhaps the most curious offer came from the Hong Kong and Wompoa Dock Company of the Crown Colony; see MUN 5/125/1000/55. All offers were not welcome. See Dr Addison's discussion of the 'bandits' who made lavish promises of doing the impossible and providing the unprovidable, *Politics From Within* vol. II, pp. 79–80.

3 For this episode see Duncan Crow, *Man of Push and Go*, pp. 90–1, 97.

4 For the 'A' and 'B' Area scheme, see MUN 5/341/170/1 and MUN 5/142/1121/22.

5 This letter is printed in Crow, *Man of Push and Go*, p. 106.

6 Sir Percy Girouard never actually became a member of the Armaments Output Committee. He did, however, become a Major-General at this time, arguing with the Secretary of State for War that he required the lofty rank in order to deal with the directors of the Ordnance Department, all of whom held that rank already. See *Lloyd George's War Memoirs* vol. II, pp. 52–3 for a wry estimate of the difficulties inherent in dealing with so many Major-Generals.

7 This paper was circulated as M[unitions] C[ommittee] 6. See MUN 5/342/170/11.

8 See Sir Percy Girouard's report of 14 June 1915 to the Minister MUN 5/10/200/2. Sir Percy was, no doubt, influenced by the early success of the National Explosives Factory programme, initiated by Lord Moulton. See Chapter IX, 'Munitions Technology: The Battle for Weaponry Design', below.

9 MUN 5/342/170/2/11.

10 *Ibid.*

11 See Crow, *Man of Push and Go*, p. 116.

12 See Repington, *First World War*, p. 64.

13 Stevenson submitted his plan to Lloyd George on 21 June 1915. See MUN 5/362/1121/2. In this regard, see also Dewar, *The Great*

Munitions Feat, pp. 113–15. In addition to these characteristics, it was felt necessary to appoint Munitions Directors for Scotland and Ireland, who served as lieutenants to the Minister and supervised the Area Offices and Factories and Schemes in their countries. Furthermore, the difficulties in Ireland, which eventually erupted into revolt in 1916, led to the division of the island into two separately administered munitions districts, with Dublin and Belfast as their respective headquarters.

14　For the organization of the Munitions Committees, see MUN 5/142/1121/22.

15　See *Ibid.* and MUN 5/362/1121/2.

16　For the arguments of the Ministry on these points, see MUN 5/362/1121/2. The close central control over Area Organization was a response to the urgency of the need for munitions. Late in the lifespan of the Ministry of Munitions, this was relaxed to a certain degree. See MUN 5/344/200/2.

17　In charge of the survey was the well-known economist, A. L. Bowley. Significantly, aiding in the survey was the last service performed by the local Munitions Committees. See MUN 5/199/1700/4.

18　For the three schemes of production and the Boards of Management which chose each of them see MUN 5/142/1121/22. In this regard see also MUN 5/146/1122/1 and MUN 5/146/1122/5.

19　Despite the initial theoretical responsibility of the Ministry of Munitions to supply armaments to the Navy, in fact, the Admiralty continued to contract for its own requirements throughout the War. The avoidance of competition for machinery, raw materials and labour, therefore, was of supreme importance.

20　See Lloyd George, *War Memoirs* vol. II, p. 37.

21　The most complete source on the various types of National Factories is the *History of the Ministry of Munitions* vol. VIII, Part II, *passim.* For the location of all National Shell, Projectile, Explosives and Filling Factories operated by the Ministry during Lloyd George's tenure there, see MUN 5/146/1122/5.

22　David Lloyd George, in his *War Memoirs,* paid tribute to the armament makers Cammell Laird and Company, which supervised the construction and the day-to-day management of the Nottingham National Projectile Factory and accepted no commission for either service. Vol. II, p. 37.

6 Labour Supply and Control (i)

1 MUN 5/342/170/2/1/a. In this regard see also Humbert Wolfe, *Labour Supply and Regulation* (London, 1923), p. 16, and Mrs. C. S. Peel, *How We Lived Then* (London, 1929), pp. 25–6.

2 Labour Exchange Department, CO Circular 1540, 8 August 1914.

3 Labour Exchange Department, CO Circular 1598, 7 September 1914.

4 Labour Exchange Department, CO Circular 1607, 14 September 1914.

5 These figures were cited by Lloyd George before Lord Crewe's Cabinet Committee which oversaw the Ministry. See Lloyd George Papers, D/3/3/20. They are printed in Wolfe, *Labour Supply and Regulation*, p. 14.

6 MUN 5/322/141/1.

7 Beveridge, *Power and Influence*, pp. 118–19.

8 MUN 5/342/170/2/1/a.

9 For Sir Hubert Llewellyn Smith's evaluation of this meeting and the Reinforcement policy see his memoranda of 23 January and 15 March 1915, MUN 5/9/180/8.

10 See Chapter II above. For this line of argument by the War Office see MUN 5/126/1000/120.

11 J. D. Scott, *Vickers: A History* (London, 1962), p. 101. See also Wolfe, *Labour Supply and Regulation*, p. 19.

12 MUN 5/62/322/8. See also MUN 5/10/180/43.

13 See Woodward, *Great Britain and the War*, pp. 468–9.

14 A copy of this memorandum may be found in MUN 5/9/180/16.

15 See Wolfe, *Labour Supply and Regulation*, pp. 25–6.

16 The text of the Crayford Agreement is printed in G. D. H. Cole, *Trade Unionism and Munitions* (London, 1923), pp. 53–4.

17 These proposals are printed in *Ibid.*, pp. 55–60.

18 See MUN 5/322/141/1/1.

19 For these reports see CAB 37/124/29, CAB 37/124/38, CAB 37/125/12 and CAB 37/125/20.

20 The Shells and Fuses Agreement is printed in Cole, *Trade Unionism and Munitions*, pp. 67–8.

21 The reports of these sessions as well as the text of the agreement may be found in MUN 5/10/180/17 and MUN 5/322/141/1.

22 The minutes of the supplementary Treasury Conference may be found in MUN 5/10/180/42.

23 With Henderson on the Committee were C. W. Bowerman, J. T. Brownlie, John Hill, Frank Smith and William Mosses, who acted

as secretary of both the workers' representatives at the meeting and the Committee itself.

24　In this regard, see Marwick, *The Deluge,* pp. 60–61.

25　Addison, *Politics from Within* vol. I, p. 175.

26　71 H.C. Deb. 55, col. 1201.

27　71 H.C. Deb. 55, col. 2123.

28　Addison, *Politics from Within* vol. I, p. 86.

29　See Llewellyn Smith's memorandum of 9 June 1915, MUN 5/57/320/1. Though unsigned, its authorship is confirmed and excerpts are printed in Lloyd George, *War Memoirs* vol. I, p. 263.

30　See the 'Note' of Owen Smith to Lloyd George, dated 30 November 1915, on this matter of exemptions from Excess Profits Duties, as they were called, preserved among the Lloyd George Papers, D/13/2/3. The final *Rules of Limitation of Profits in Controlled Establishments* of 15 September 1915 may be found in MUN 5/100/360/13. See also in this regard R. W. Matthew's memorandum of 22 May 1915, MUN 5/100/360/3.

31　That some men, hard-faced or not, did well out of the War is undeniable. The firm of Vickers, however, one of the major armaments producers in the world, never achieved the one-fifth in excess of peacetime profits limitations. See Scott, *Vickers,* p. 133.

32　MUN 5/49/300/23.

33　134 firms were declared controlled within the first month following the passage of the Munitions of War Act 1915, and more than 4,000 had been brought under the Act during Lloyd George's tenure at the Munitions Office. See MUN 5/353/360/2. For the significance of the Munitions of War Act and especially the precedent of control over the private sector see Gollin, *Proconsul in Politics* Chapter XII.

34　Perhaps the best published source on Clause 7 remains Wolfe, *Labour Supply and Regulation,* pp. 217–34.

35　The leaving certificate procedure did not, as is often thought, apply only to workers in controlled establishments, but, as declared by Lloyd George in July 1915, to 'any establishment being a factory or workshop; the business carried on in which consists wholly, or mainly in engineering, shipbuilding, or the production of arms, ammunition, or explosives, or of substance required for the production thereof.'

36　The first draft of the Act did not include this provision. In the debate in the Commons following its first reading, the suggestion was made and accepted by Lloyd George that such informal tribunals might be superior in this case to normal courts of law.

37　This Act is printed as Appendix A.

7 Labour Supply and Control (ii)

1 For the work of the Northeast Coast Armaments Committee before the forming of the Ministry, and for Captain Kelly's King's Squad, see MUN 5/362/1121/4.

2 *Ibid.* See also Wolfe, *Labour Supply and Regulation,* pp. 194–5.

3 On 10 June 1915 representatives of the major industrial trade unions, meeting at the Board of Trade, passed a resolution supporting the War Munitions Volunteer scheme. See MUN 5/49/300/36. See the Advisory Committee paper, 'Acceleration of the Supply of Munitions', CAB 37/129/33 and Lloyd George's accompanying memorandum, CAB 37/129/34, both dated 10 June 1915.

4 The minutes of the two meetings of the Minister of Munitions and the trade union representatives to discuss the Volunteer scheme and the Munitions of War Bill, 10 and 16 June 1915, may be found in MUN 5/48/300/4 and MUN 5/48/300/5.

5. More than half of the War Munitions Bureaux were simply Labour Exchanges, renamed in late June. The name-change was Lloyd George's idea.

6 For the War Munitions Volunteer scheme, see the departmental reports found in MUN 5/49/300/23 and MUN 5/49/300/24.

7 For the minutes of this meeting, see MUN 5/57/320/3.

8 For this use of the Volunteers scheme, see the *History of the Ministry of Munitions* vol. IV, pt. 4, p. 33.

9 See MUN 5/69/323/6.

10 MUN 5/348/323/2. See also Lloyd George's impatient letter to Kitchener of 2 July 1915, Lloyd George Papers, D/17/6/15.

11 MUN 5/348/323/2.

12 See MUN 5/57/320/26 and Wolfe, *Labour Supply and Regulation,* pp. 90–6.

13 MUN 5/57/320/3.

14 MUN 5/69/323/6.

15 In this regard, see MUN 5/342/170/2/1/a.

16 The mission, under the Board of Trade's Mr. Windham, sailed in May 1915, after the creation of the Ministry of Munitions, not, as suggested by Wolfe, in early 1915. *Labour Supply and Regulation,* p. 80.

17 MUN 5/342/170/2/1/a.

18 *Ibid.*

19 Labour Exchange Department, C.O. Circular 1686, 4 December 1914, cited *Ibid.*

20   MUN 5/342/170/2/1/a.

21   In this regard, see Wolfe, *Labour Supply and Regulation,* p. 82.

22   The firms were Messrs. Pelabon and Messrs Lahaye, both of which were producing shells by early 1916. See *Ibid.*

23   See 'The Story of Elizabethville', *The World's Work,* June 1918.

24   See Long's report to the Cabinet on Registration Day, CAB 37/132/15.

25   See their reports of 6 and 31 August 1915, in MUN 5/65/322/131.

26   See MUN 5/65/322/131.

27   Trades Union Congress, *Annual Report* 1915, pp. 352–62.

28   For the role of the Advisory Committee in organizing this meeting, see MUN 5/22/242.1/100. For Lloyd George's remarks to the trade union executives see MUN 5/57/320/4.

29   MUN 5/348/324/1.

30   See the confidential memorandum of the DA section of the Labour Department—the section charged with furthering Dilution, MUN 5/72/324/11/9.

31   Circulars L5 and L6 are reprinted as Appendices E and F.

32   See MUN 5/348/324/1.

33   Seventeen ringleaders of the Fairfield strike were found guilty of violating the Munitions of War Act and were fined £10 each. Three refused to pay and were imprisoned, which raised the temperature of the disagreement considerably. Finally, a third party —the shipwrights' union—paid the fine, and both the men and the Ministry of Munitions saved face and claimed vindication. See Wolfe, *Labour Supply and Regulation,* pp. 128–129, and Marwick, *The Deluge,* p. 76. For the reports of Lynden Macassey who, along with Lord Balfour of Burleigh, investigated the matter for the Government, see MUN 5/73/324/15/1 and MUN 5/73/324/15/5.

34   The Shop Stewards were members of the rank and file who spoke for the men in the factories on Clydeside. They were not members of the trade union executive, though their position was recognized by it.

35   *Forward,* a Glasgow Left Wing newspaper, reported in colourful detail the discomfiture of the Minister of Munitions at the St. Andrew's Hall and was officially suppressed under Section 17 of D.O.R.A. Lloyd George blamed the hasty decision on 'panic' within the Labour Department of the Ministry. See Stevenson, *Lloyd George: A Diary,* p. 88. For the Ministry's case against *Forward* and the confidential correspondence behind it see MUN 5/70/324/18.

36   For the reports of the Macassey Commission, see MUN 5/73/324/15/9. A second such body was appointed to facilitate Dilution on Tyneside,

but it was dissolved in May 1915 and its work was taken over by
the Clyde Commission.

37 See Dewar, *The Great Munitions Feat,* p. 269.

38 MUN 5/57/320/26.

39 Millicent Garrett Fawcett, *The Women's Victory and After* (London,
1920), p. 92.

40 MUN 5/57/320/11. For the difficulties encountered by the Training
Department in 1915 and 1916, see MUN 5/76/325/1 and MUN
5/76/325/5.

41 For these volunteer munitions labour programmes see MUN
5/57/320/10.

42 In this connection, see the letter of Sir James Yoxall, M.P., President
of the National Union of Teachers, to Dr. Addison, dated 5 June
1915. Yoxall enquired about the possibility of encouraging
teachers to employ their holidays in the munitions shops. MUN
5/57/320/23.

43 Beginning in October 1916, the Ministry began to publish a
Dilution of Labour Bulletin, which gave monthly figures of place-
ment of unskilled labour. The twenty-two numbers of the *Bulletin*
(publication ceased in October 1918) may be found in MUN
5/73/324/11.

8   'The Women's Part'

1   *Report of the War Cabinet Committee on Women in Industry,* Cmd.
135, 1919.

2   *Ibid.* In this regard see also Marwick, *The Deluge,* pp. 97–8, and
Hurwitz, *State Intervention in Great Britain,* pp. 131–2.

3   Cmd. 135. In this regard see also Peel, *How We Lived Then,* p. 110.

4   Cmd. 135.

5   MUN 5/342/170/2/1/a. Cole, *Trade Unionism and Munitions,* p. 52,
Hurwitz, *State Intervention in Great Britain,* p. 134.

6   MUN 5/342/170/2/1/a.

7   *Interim Report of the Central Committee on Women's Employment,*
Cmd. 7848, 1915.

8   Peel, *How We Lived Then,* p. 26.

9   MUN 5/342/170/2/1.

10 See Beveridge, *Power and Influence,* pp. 121–2.

11 *The Times,* 5 May 1915.

12 Peel, *How We Lived Then,* p. 109.

13 *War Memoirs of David Lloyd George* vol. I, p. 255.

14 *Ibid.*

15 Irene Clephane, *Toward Sex Freedom* (London, 1935), pp. 192–3.

16 See Fawcett, *The Women's Victory*, pp. 91–2.

17 Peel, *How We Lived Then*, p. 60.

18 See MUN 5/329/342/1 and MUN 5/70/324/1. The Ministry advanced Mrs. Pankhurst's group £3,500 to fund the 17 July demonstration. See W. H. Beveridge's memorandum of 11 August 1915, MUN 5/70/324/26.

19 MUN 5/349/342/2.

20 See Cole, *Trade Unionism and Munitions*, p. 87.

21 MUN 5/346/320/2.

22 Circulars L1, L2, and L3 are reprinted as Appendices B, C and D.

23 A. L. Bowley, *Prices and Wages in the United Kingdom, 1914–1920* (London, 1921), p. 186, cited in Hurwitz, *State Intervention in Great Britain*, p. 141.

24 See Cole, *Trade Unionism and Munitions*, p. 104.

25 The Act received the Royal Assent on 27 January 1916, the same day on which the first compulsary Military Service Act became law.

26 Special regulations, which sometimes differed from L2 and L3 were from time to time enforced in the National Factories, where the Ministry had greater control. See MUN 5/81/342/6.

27 See MUN 5/349/342/1.

28 Cmd. 135, and Wolfe, *Labour Supply and Regulation*, p. 296.

29 For the terms created to describe the women munitions workers, see Hurwitz, *State Intervention in Great Britain*, p. 135.

30 A first-hand account of the life of a middle-class Munitionette is Monica Cousens, *Mr. Lloyd George's Munitions Girls* (London, 1917).

31 MUN 5/348/324/1.

32 *Ibid.*

33 This Circular is reprinted in Cole, *Trade Unionism and Munitions*, pp. 107–108.

34 These statistics are taken from Wolfe, *Labour Supply and Regulation*, pp. 169–170. For more comprehensive figures of numbers of women employed in industry, see MUN 5/71/324/34.

35 *War Memoirs of David Lloyd George* vol. I, p. 302.

36 Newman already served as Chairman of the Sub-Committee of Canteens of the Central Control Board for Liquor Traffic. He was a champion of the 'Efficiency Movement' in Britain before the War and a disciple of Sir Robert Morant. See G. R. Searle, *The Quest for National Efficiency* (Oxford, 1971), pp. 243–244.

37 Rowntree had visited Lloyd George at his home in Walton Heath in November 1915 and pleaded with him not to abandon his

life-long commitment to 'democracy' in his quest for the organization of munitions production. The Minister of Munitions assured his guest that this was impossible. Shortly thereafter, of course, Rowntree was appointed to head the Welfare Section and himself blend the old Liberal tenets of social reform with the newer principles of State control. See Stevenson, *Lloyd George: A Diary*, p. 76.

38   Wolfe, *Labour Supply and Regulation*, pp. 180–181.

39   *Ibid.*, pp. 185–186. The Central Control Board was created under the Defence of the Realm (Amendment) (Number 3) Act of April 1915 to regulate closely the trade in wine and spirits. 'Drink' was, of course, a passionate cause of Lloyd George at that time, and the limitations they placed upon strength and availability of alcoholic beverages, as well as upon closing hours of public houses, remain today among the most long-lived alterations to British life which stemmed from the First World War.

40   See Yates, *The Women's Part* ch. VII, 'The Growth of the Industrial Canteen'.

41   *Ibid.*, pp. 37–44.

42   Despite the general approval of women's munitions efforts, as late as 1916 there were still occasional murmurs in the press about the unsuitability of women wearing trousers, even while on duty in a munitions factory. See Peel, *How We Lived Then*, p. 112.

43   For the myriad duties of the welfare supervisors, see MUN 5/93/346/113.

44   MUN 5/93/346/107.

45   Yates, *The Women's Part*, pp. 45–51.

46   MUN 5/352/346/2/1.

47   See Lloyd George, *War Memoirs*, vol. I, p. 306.

48   Dewar, *The Great Munitions Feat*, p. 322.

49   Marwick, *The Deluge*, p. 103.

9 Munitions Technology: The Battle for Weaponry Design

1   This letter, along with all correspondence relevant to transfer of functions between the War Office and the Ministry of Munitions, is printed and may be found in MUN 5/10/200/2.

2   See Llewellyn Smith's letter to the War Office of 2 July 1915, MUN 5/10/200/2. This transfer was made only because the War Office did not possess sufficient staff to carry out inspection of munitions

made in the new factories or by new contractors. The War Office
retained control over specifications.

3   See Addison, *Politics from Within* vol. I, p. 75.

4   *Ibid.*, p. 76.

5   Lloyd George, *War Memoirs* vol. II, p. 53.

6   See the Departmental memorandum of 10 June 1918, MUN 5/152/
1122.11/7.

7   See Lloyd George's letter to Sir Frederick Donaldson, the Chief
Superintendent of Ordnance Factories, of 25 August 1915, MUN
5/152/1122.11/7.

8   In addition to Black and Geddes, the committee included G. M.
Booth, Sir Charles Ellis, Sir Sothern Holland and Vincent Raven.
MUN 5/152/1122.11/23.

9   For Lloyd George's appreciation of the two men, see his *War
Memoirs* vol. II, p. 53–4. The first Minister of Munitions believed
that a poorly-run system could stifle a competent man until he was
no use to a well-run one; he saw Donaldson as a case in point.

10 Addison, *Politics from Within* vol. I, p. 77.

11 See MUN 5/120/800/6, a Ministry analysis of munitions design
theory.

12 Long extracts from this letter are printed in Lloyd George, *War
Memoirs* vol. II, pp. 88–89.

13 See the entry for 15 November 1915 in Stevenson, *Lloyd George:
A Diary*, p. 72.

14 This memorandum of 6 November and a second memorandum on
the transfer of design authority may be found in MUN 5/10/200/2.
Each is dated simply 'November 1915'. See also Addison, *Politics
from Within* vol. I, pp. 76–78.

15 Lord Oxford and Asquith, *Memories and Reflections* vol. II, p. 132.
The Prime Minister did indeed 'break his fall'; see von Donop's
letter to Kitchener, of 29 November 1915, *Kitchener Papers*, WO
159/4, in which he described the meeting.

16 This printed version, dated 27 November 1915, may be found in
MUN 5/10/200/2.

17 This more complete version, undated and marked 'secret', may
be found in MUN 5/120/810/3. It is printed in Lloyd George, *War
Memoirs* vol. II, p. 90.

18 See the *Annual Report of the President of the Ordnance Board for the
Year 1915,* for the Director's letter of 26 November, 1915. A copy
is preserved in MUN 5/120/810/6.

19 The Board was reinstated after the War. Curiously enough, when
the powers of the Master General were restored post-War, the

man who exercised them was Major-General DuCane, who succeeded von Donop in 1920.

20 This long letter is printed in Lloyd George, *War Memoirs* vol. II, pp. 92–3. See also the candid evaluation of this crisis by Colonel Repington, who interviewed DuCane on 3 December 1915. *The First World War,* pp. 76–7.

21 See the letter from the Ministry to the War Office of 27 February 1916. See also the minutes of the War Committee for 26 January 1916, CAB 42/7/13, and the paper presented on the matter of the transfer of munitions· design to the Ministry on 1 February 1916, by Lieutenant-Colonel Hankey, CAB 42/8/1.

22 See MUN 5/357/700/1/b.

23 CAB 37/130/22.

24 For this correspondence see MUN 5/10/200/2. See also the correspondence collected in MUN 5/43/263.8/7. Save for research on what were to become known as tanks (in which the Ministry and the Admiralty had become partners by this time), the Admiralty had transferred to Lloyd George's authority all research on land warfare weapons not already transferred to the War Office.

25 See MUN 5/357/700/1/b. The advisory panel of Section A41 grew both in size and prestige at this time, for such luminaries as the former Chief Superintendent of Ordnance Factories and the Director of Artillery were added to it. It was a last ditch defence to prevent the small branch from being absorbed into the Ministry of Munitions.

26 See Lloyd George, *War Memoirs* vol. II, pp. 83–6. One of these men, Colonel H. E. F. Goold-Adams, later succeeded Moir as Controller of Munitions Inventions.

27 MUN 5/43/263.8/7. This letter is also printed in Lloyd George, *War Memoirs* vol. II, pp. 83–5.

28 MUN 5/43/263.8/7. See also MUN 5/357/700/1/b.

29 MUN 5/117/700/2.

30 MUN 5/117/700/3. Almost 50,000 invention ideas were received by the Munitions Inventions Department by the end of the War. See MUN 5/119/700/6/9.

31 See MUN 5/117/700/1.

32 See the fascinating series of monthly reports of the Munitions Inventions Department in MUN 5/119/700/6/1. See also Addison *Politics from Within* vol. I, pp. 123–5.

33 See Lloyd George, *War Memoirs* vol. II, pp. 48–51 for the role of Professor Weizmann. See also Addison, *Politics from Within* vol. I, pp. 160–1.

34   Moulton to Lloyd George, 16 June 1915, Lloyd George Papers, D 10/2/2. This letter is printed in Lloyd George, *War Memoirs* vol. II, pp. 43–4.

35   In regard to the use of amatol, see MUN 5/194/1520/11.

36   After some debate about the proper name of the new weapon, it was finally decided that, while it was technically a trench howitzer, the term trench mortar meant essentially the same thing. See MUN 5/196/1610/1.

37   The Master General was well aware of the need for mortars in France. W. R. Robertson, then Lieutenant-General and Quarter-master General with the B.E.F., wrote to von Donop on 4 November 1914 in regard to these weapons: 'What we want is *something,* the best you can do quickly, and not wait until we get the perfect article.' WO 159/15.

38   MUN 5/384/1610/4.

39   *Ibid.*

40   For Stokes' own description of the technical evolution of his weapon, see *The Ministry of Munitions Journal* No. 6, May 1917, pp. 165–7.

41   Ordnance Board Minute 13160, cited in MUN 5/384/1611/1.

42   MUN 5/384/1611/1.

43   MUN 5/384/1610/5.

44   MUN 5/384/1610/4.

45   This demonstration at Wormwood Scrubs was remarkable in that both the Stokes gun and a Killen-Strait caterpillar tractor were seen by Lloyd George, Churchill and their companions. The latter device, of course, was an experimental step in the direction of the tank.

46   See MUN 5/384/1611/1 and Lloyd George's *War Memoirs* vol. II, p. 79, for this employment of 'special funds'.

47   MUN 5/384/1610/4.

48   Lieutenant F. A. Sutton, a mortar specialist, had been invalided home from the Dardanelles campaign in May 1915. He almost immediately became involved with the campaign to gain approval for the Stokes mortar. See his candid 'Notes', a remarkable memoir of this period. MUN 5/384/1610/7.

49   MUN 5/384/1611/1.

50   MUN 5/195/1600/11.

51   The name applied to the weapon, as it neared completion in late 1915, was meant to disguise its purpose; the vehicle was originally called a landship. The code, however, lead to certain rather amusing circumstances: more than once, supply departments

within the Ministry demanded of the Tank Supply Department immediate delivery of the water or petrol or compressed gas tanks they had ordered. After the invention made its debut in battle, the confusion ended.

52   See Lord Hankey, *The Supreme Command: 1914–1918* (London, 1961) vol. I, pp. 227–8. See also Major-General Sir Ernest Swinton, *Eyewitness* (London, 1933), pp. 59–62, and Swinton's memorandum of 26 December 1918 on his role in the development of the tank, MUN 5/211/1940/13.

53   This memorandum is·printed in Hankey, *Supreme Command* vol. I, pp. 244–50.

54   See Sir Albert Stern, *Tanks, 1914–1918: The Log Book of a Pioneer* (London, 1919), *passim,* and Sir Murray Sueter, *The Evolution of the Tank* (London, 1937), chapter I. See also Tennyson–d'Eyncourt's memorandum of 18 September 1916, on his committee's role in tank development, MUN 5/211/1940/13.

55   Winston S. Churchill, *The World Crisis* (London, 1923) vol. II, p. 69. See also Churchill's memorandum to Asquith of 5 January 1915, MUN 5/210/1940/11.

56   MUN 5/391/1940/2. See also B. H. Liddell Hart, *The Tanks* (London, 1959) vol. I, pp. 26–9.

57   Churchill, *World Crisis* vol. II, p. 66.

58   Swinton's paper is preserved in MUN 5/211/1940/13.

59   See MUN 5/391/1940/2, and Liddell Hart, *The Tanks* vol. I, p. 35.

60   See MUN 5/391/1940/2.

61   *Ibid.*

62   Liddell Hart, *The Tanks* vol I, p. 45.

63   See MUN 5/391/1940/2 In this regard, see also Liddell Hart, *The Tanks* vol. I, p. 46.

64   Tennyson–d'Eyncourt's letter of 14 February 1916 is preserved in MUN 5/211/1940/13.

65   The question of who actually 'invented' the tank became a hotly contested issue between late 1917 and the close of 1920. A special committee called the Royal Commission on Awards to Inventors was appointed to settle the matter. The minutes of its proceedings, between 1 and 22 November 1920, and the mass of depositions, testimony and memoranda employed in their deliberations may be found in MUN 5/210/1940/22 and MUN 5/211/1940/35–37. Major awards were eventually made to William Tritton, the builder, and Walter Wilson, the major designer of 'Mother Tank'.

66   Edward L. Katzenback Jr., 'The Mechanization of War, 1880–1919', in *Technology in Western Civilization* vol. II, (edited by

Melvin Kranzberg and Caroll Purcell Jr. New York, 1967), pp. 548–9. Sir Basil Liddell Hart has written: 'A weightier charge against the military chiefs of 1914–1918 is that they failed so lamentably in their technical sphere. For here there is no excuse.' *Through the Fog of War* (New York, 1938), p. 162.

67   Sueter, *Evolution of the Tank,* p. 227.

10   Delivering the Goods

1   See MUN 5/344/200/2.

2   See *History of the Ministry of Munitions* vol. I, part 1, p. 38, for the development of the Boulogne Programme.

3   Copies of this correspondence are preserved as MUN 5/177/1200/3.

4   Kitchener did not reveal his intention to field seventy divisions until the Calais Conference in July. For these figures see MUN 5/177/1200/19.

5   *Ibid.*

6   Acting as the Ministry's buying agent in America at this time was the House of Morgan, the great merchant bankers. A new partner was added to the firm to manage the Ministry's business; he was Edward Stettinius, later the American Secretary of State.

7   MUN 5/177/1200/19.

8   See the Cabinet Paper circulated by Kitchener on 6 October 1915, CAB 37/135/8.

9   The 'Synopsis of Evidence' given before the Cabinet Committee on the Coordination of Military and Financial Effort is preserved as CAB 37/141/38.

10   Owen, *Tempestuous Journey,* p. 295. A somewhat less delicate version of the same story is told by Lloyd George's eldest son: 'It's the end of the bloody committee,' said father. 'That's the last we'll ever see of that bunch.' Earl Lloyd-George, *Lloyd George* (London, 1960), p. 151.

11   See the one-page 'Note by the Secretary of State for War' CAB 37/142/17.

12   See Charles Ellis' report to the Minister of 22 August 1916 which gives these figures, MUN 5/177/1200/15. See also Dewar, *The Great Munitions Feat,* p. 126.

13   See MUN 5/344/260/5.

14   In 1915 alone, for example, Beardsmore received £700,000, Vickers £800,000, and Coventry Ordnance £300,000. The new plant laid down by the manufacturers remained State property.

15   MUN 5/177/1200/21. For complete figures of artillery, shell and

machine-gun production during this period see Appendix G.

16   For these figures see MUN 5123/1000/24 and MUN 5/177/1200/12.

17   MUN 5/123/1000/24.

18   MUN 5/177/1200/13.

19   See MUN 5/189/1410/27 and MUN 5/189/1410/3. Total guns supplied under these contracts with renewal or continuation options would have been but 8,300.

20   It was calculated by the War Office at this time that the life expectancy of machine-guns was six months and that provision, therefore, had to be on a yearly two-for-one basis. Repair facilities and actual experience proved this estimate pessimistic.

21   Part of Geddes' memorandum of the meeting with Kitchener is printed in Lloyd George, *War Memoirs* vol. II, pp. 65–7.

22   A facsimile of Geddes' note which Kitchener initialled is printed *Ibid*.

23   *Ibid*. These figures would have placed sixty-four guns with each battalion—a rather grandiose prospect in mid-1915, which would have seemed outrageous to the War Office at that time. Before the end of the War, the Ministry supplied machine guns on the basis of a War Office requirement of eighty guns per battalion.

24   Robertson, the first British Field Marshal to rise from the ranks, had been Quartermaster General and, later, Chief-of-Staff at G.H.Q., France. He forced upon the Government as a condition of his appointment as C.I.G.S. his view that he, not the Secretary of State for War, should be the chief adviser on strategy to the Cabinet. Likewise he demanded, and received, the authority to issue orders to the field commanders—another power formerly reserved for the Secretary of State.

25   MUN 5/377/1410.1/2.

26   See Addison, *Politics from Within* vol. I, p. 114.

27   For this correspondence, see MUN 5/195/1600/15.

28   *Ibid*. See also MUN 5/195/1600/16.

29   See MUN 5/195/1600/15.

30   While the Ministry had been responsible for grenade production for only one month of that time, it was the source of well over half the grenades produced in the year. It is remarkable that the War Office handed this requirement over to the Ministry with great reluctance.

31   MUN 5/195/1600/2.

32   MUN 5/195/1600/11.

11 Epilogue

1 Chester and Willson, *The Organization of British Central Government*, p. 83.

2 See *The History of the Ministry of Munitions* vol. XII, parts 4, 5 and 6, which deal with the provision of mechanical transport vehicles, railway equipment and agricultural machinery, respectively.

3 In February 1915, Asquith created a Joint War Air Committee to coordinate efforts to supply air stores. It was unsuccessful and was replaced in April by the Air Board, under Lord Curzon. After Lloyd George became Prime Minister, he strengthened the powers of the Board and raised it to Ministry rank. The Air Ministry was not created until January 1918 and the Royal Air Force was officially constituted on 1 April of that same year.

4 Dewar, *The Great Munitions Feat*, p. 188.

5 MUN 5/344/200/6.

6 *Ibid.*

7 Churchill's Munitions Council consisted of the following members:

> *Member 'F' (Finance),* Sir Herbert Hambling
> Finance, Munitions Works Board, Controlled Establishments, Munitions Contracts, Lands, Central Stores, and Salvage

> *Member 'D' (Design),* Major-General F. R. Bingham
> Design, Inspection, Trench Warfare Design, Munitions Inventions

> *Member 'S' (Steel and Iron),* John Hunter
> Iron and Steel Production, Factory Construction

> *Member 'M' (Materials),* E. W. Moir
> Non-Ferrous Metals, Scrap Metals, Development of Mineral Resources, Government Rolling Mills, Transport: Railways, Overseas, and Trench Warfare, Forwarding and Receiving, Railway Materials, Cranes, Optical Munitions, Potash

> *Member 'X' (Explosives),* Sir Keith Price
> Explosives Supply, Trench Warfare Chemical Supplies, Mineral Oil Production, Royal Gunpowder Factory at Waltham Abbey

Member 'P' (Projectiles), James Stevenson
Area Organization, Gun Ammunition and Filling, Trench
Warfare Ammunition: Filling and Supply (other than
trench), Small Arms Ammunition, Munitions Gauges,
Central Clearing Bureau, Timber

Member 'G' (Guns), Glyn West
Gun and Carriage Supply and Repair Guns, Machine-Guns
and Pistols, Rifles and Bayonets, Royal Small Arms Factory
at Enfield, Royal Ordnance Factory at Woolwich

Member 'E' (Engines), Arthur Duckham
Aeronautical Supplies, Petrol Engines Supply, Mechanical
Transport, Mechanical Warfare, Agricultural Machinery,
Electric Power Supply, Machine Tools, Stampings and
Castings

Member 'A' (Allies), Sir Frederick Black
Munitions Supply to Allies

Member 'L' (Labour), Stevenson Kent
Labour Regulations, Labour Supply, Housing, Welfare

Secretariat.
Council Secretariat, Parliamentary and General, Legal,
Requirements and Statistics, Establishment, Special
Intelligence, Priority.

Soon after the constitution of the Council a new Group was
added:

Member 'R' (Requirements and Statistics), Walter Layton
Requirements and Statistics

In February 1918, the 'E' Group was divided and newly created
as:

Member 'A' (Air), Sir William Weir
Aeronautical Supplies.

In July 1918, one further Council position was created:

Member 'W' (Warfare), Major-General J. E. B. Seeley
Remainder of former 'E' Group, plus Trench Warfare
Supplies and Inventions.

See Churchill, *The World Crisis* vol. II, pp. 5–11 and 283–4.

8   *Ibid.,* p. 10.

9 Among the strongest supporters of the creation of some form of central stores department was Churchill. See Chester and Willson, *The Organization of British Central Government,* pp. 225–6, and *The History of the Ministry of Munitions* vol. II, part I, ch 4. The idea was also supported by the 1918 Machinery of Government Committee, chaired by Lord Haldane. See their *Report,* Cmd 9230.

10 Just before leaving the Ministry in July 1916, Lloyd George ordered the preparation of 'a systematic record of the origin and work of the Ministry of Munitions . . . [which was to serve in part] as a guide for any future action.' MUN 5/219B. This was the origin of the *History of the Ministry of Munitions,* which was more or less complete by 1922. Eight of the twelve volumes of the *History* were available to the public in numerous libraries throughout Britain before the beginning of World War II, though it was never actually published for sale. The remaining four volumes were made available in similar fashion after the War. For the writing of the *History* see Denys Hays, 'The Official History of the Ministry of Munitions', *Economic History Review* vol XIV, no. 2. G. A. B. Dewar, the former editor of *The Saturday Review,* requested permission of the Ministry in December 1918 for access to Departmental papers to prepare a book on the work of the Ministry. G. I. H. Lloyd, the chairman of the editorial committee of the official history ruled: 'It should be understood that he is not entitled to have access to official records. The only privilege he will receive will be facilities for visiting munitions factories, or interviewing individual officers of the Department (obtaining specific authority in each case). His materials should be submitted for censorship before publication.' (Lloyd to Masterton Smith [secretary to the then Minister, Winston Churchill], 9 December 1918. MUN 5/1/1/11.) In 1921, Dewar's *The Great Munitions Feat* was published. In regard to the place of the Ministry in munitions supply planning during the inter-War years, see J. D. Scott and Richard Hughes, *The Administration of War Production* (London, 1955), pp. 68–78.

11 See *The Report of the Committee on the Amalgamation of Services Common to the Navy, Army and Air Force,* Cmd. 2649. Though the report was presented in 1922, it was not published until 1926. Cited in Chester and Willson, *The Organization of British Central Government,* p. 227.

12 Of Beaverbrook's work at the Ministry of Aircraft Production, A. J. P. Taylor has written: 'He deliberately started from scratch as Lloyd George had done with the Ministry of Munitions. The precedent was much in Beaverbrook's mind. Indeed, Sir Walter

Layton, a survivor from the Ministry of Munitions, was among the first of those whom Beaverbrook consulted on 11 May. . . . Now he intended to fight the Air Ministry as Lloyd George had fought the War Office. . . .' The passage continues and points out the differences between the two Departments. It is significant, however, how acute was Beaverbrook's sense of Lloyd George's achievement. *Beaverbrook* (London, 1972), pp. 415–16.

13 The first Minister of Production was, again, Lord Beaverbrook. He resigned almost immediately, however, and his place was taken by Oliver Lyttelton.

14 See M. M. Poston, *British War Production* (London, 1952), p. 252.

15 Eric Geddes told A. J. Sylvester, Lloyd George's secretary at the time, in 1932 of the Minister's techniques for recruiting men of push and go: 'His methods were strange to everybody. He interviewed applicants with a crowd of secretaries and hangers-on around him. He considered you much as a casual labourer at the docks would be treated.
'He asked me [Geddes said to Sylvester] if I knew anything about munitions. I did not. He asked me what I could do. I said I had a faculty for getting things done. 'Very well,' said he, 'I will make you head of the department.' ' *Life with Lloyd George: The Diary of A. J. Sylvester* (edited by Colin Cross (London, 1975), p. 84.

16 For Lloyd George's views of the 'slugs' who neither pushed nor went, see Tom Clarke, *My Lloyd George Diary* (London, 1939), p. 192.

APPENDIX A

An Act to amend the Munitions of War Act, 1915.

[27 January 1916]

Be it enacted by the King's most Excellent Majesty, by and with the advice and consent of the Lords Spiritual and Temporal, and Commons, in this present Parliament assembled, and by the authority of the same, as follows:

Part I

1. The Minister of Munitions may by order declare any establishment or establishments belonging to or under the control of His Majesty or any Government Department in which munitions work is carried on to be a controlled establishment or controlled establishments as the case may be, and thereupon the provisions of the Munitions of War Act, 1915 (hereinafter referred to as "the principal Act"), and this Act relating to controlled establishments shall apply to such an establishment or establishments subject to such modifications and exceptions necessary to adapt those provisions to such an establishment or establishments as may be specified in such order.

2. Subsection (2) of section one of the principal Act shall have effect as if after the words "in any case in which they think fit may" there were inserted the words "and in the case where the difference is a difference between an employer and persons employed which appears to the Board of Trade a bona fide difference and which the Board have failed to settle by such steps as aforesaid, shall within twenty-one days from the date of the report."

3. (1) Where a workman has entered into an undertaking with the Minister of Munitions under section six of the principal Act, and was at the time of entering into that undertaking in the employment of any employer, then if that employer within the period of six weeks from the date of the undertaking dismisses that workman from his employment, he shall be guilty of an offence under the principal Act, and shall be liable to a fine not exceeding five pounds, unless he proves that there was reasonable cause for dismissing the workman.

(2) It is hereby declared that where the fulfilment of any workman of any contract is interfered with by the necessity on his part of complying with an undertaking entered into by him under section six of the principal Act, that necessity is a good defence to any action or proceedings taken against that workman in respect of the non-fulfilment of the contract so far as it is due to the interference, and he shall be entitled to enter into such an undertaking notwithstanding the existence of such a contract.

(3) Section six of the principal Act shall apply to a workman who had before the passing of the principal Act entered into an undertaking of the nature mentioned in that section in like manner as if the undertaking had been entered into in pursuance of that section.

4. Where a person who has been temporarily released from naval or military service for the purpose of employment on or in connection with munitions work, or a workman who has entered into an undertaking with the Minister of Munitions under section six of the principal Act or to whom the section is applied by this Act, has been assigned to any employer, and that employer has entered into an undertaking with the Minister of Munitions as to the class or description of work on or in connection with which the person or workman so assigned to him is to be employed, then, if the employer acts in contravention of or fails to comply with any of the provisions of the undertaking, he shall be guilty of an offence under the principal Act and liable to a fine not exceeding five pounds.

5. (1) Section seven of the principal Act shall have effect as if for sub-sections (1) and (2) of that section the following two sub-sections were substituted:—

"(1) A person shall not give employment to a workman who has within the last previous six weeks, or such other period as may be provided by order of the Minister of Munitions as respects any class of establishment, been employed on or in connection with munitions work in any establishment of a class to which the provisions of this section are applied by order of the Minister of Munitions, unless he holds a certificate from the employer by whom he was last so employed or from a munitions tribunal that he is free to accept other employment.

"(2) If any workman or his trade union representative complains to a munitions tribunal, in accordance with rules made with respect to those tribunals, that an employer has unreasonably refused or neglected to issue such a certificate as aforesaid, that tribunal may, after examining into the case, if it thinks fit, itself issue such a certificate or order the issue of such a certificate by the employer."

(2) Where a workman employed on or in connection with munitions work in any establishment of a class to which the provisions of section seven of the principal Act are for the time being applied by an order made thereunder is dismissed or discharged by his employer, the employer shall forthwith give him such a certificate as aforesaid, and if he fails to do so, a munitions tribunal may, in addition to issuing or ordering the issue to him of such a certificate, order the payment to him by the employer of such sum, not exceeding five pounds, as the tribunal may think fit, unless the tribunal is of opinion that the workman was guilty of misconduct for the purpose of obtaining dismissal or discharge.

This subsection shall apply to a workman who applies for a certificate on the grounds that he has for a period of more than two days been given no opportunity of earning wages, or who leaves his employment on account of conduct on the part of the employer, or any agent of the employer, which would justify the immediate termination by the workman of his contract of service, in like manner as if he had been dismissed or discharged by his employer.

(3) Where a contract of service with a workman employed on or in connection with munitions work in any establishment of a class to which the provisions of section seven of the principal Act are for the time being applied by an order made thereunder is terminated by dismissal, and less than one week's notice, or wages in lieu of notice, has or have been given, the employer shall, subject to the provisions of this subsection, within twenty-four hours of giving notice of dismissal to the workman report the matter in such manner as may be prescribed by rules made by the Minister of Munitions, and such rules shall provide for the determination by a munitions tribunal (in case of difference) of the amount, if any, and not in any case exceeding five pounds, which is to be paid by the employer to the workman in lieu of notice, and for the payment of the sum so determined to the workman, unless the tribunal is of opinion that owing to the discontinuous or temporary nature of the employment or misconduct of the workman

the employer had reasonable cause for dismissing the workman without a week's notice:

Provided that nothing in this subsection shall apply to workmen engaged in ship repairing, or to any class of workmen exempted in the prescribed manner on the ground that the circumstances of their employment were such that the provisions of this subsection ought not to apply to them.

(4) The provisions of section seven of the principal Act which prohibit the giving of employment to workmen in the circumstances mentioned in that section shall not apply so as to prevent the giving of employment to a workman in a controlled establishment to which he has been assigned by the Minister of Munitions in pursuance of section six of the principal Act.

(5) In determining whether the grant of a certificate has been unreasonably refused for the purposes of section seven of the principal Act as amended by this section, a munitions tribunal shall take into consideration the question whether the workman has left or desires to leave his work for the purpose of undertaking any class of work in which his skill or other personal qualifications could be employed with greater advantage to the national interests, and whether the employer has failed to observe the conditions laid down in the fair wages clauses required by resolution of the House of Commons to be inserted in Government contracts, and whether the workman has left or desires to leave his work because he has recently completed a term of apprenticeship or period of learning his trade or occupation and desires to obtain the full standard rate of wages applicable to fully qualified workmen in his trade or occupation.

(6) The Minister of Munitions may make rules for carrying section seven of the principal Act as amended by this section into effect, and in particular may by such rules provide—

(a) for the issue, form, custody, duration, delivery up, and replacement in case of loss or destruction of certificates;

(b) for the issue of certificates to persons not engaged on or in connection with munitions work;

(c) for prohibiting the insertion in a certificate issued by an employer of any matter other than the prescribed particulars;

and may provide for any breach of such rules being punishable as an offence under the principal Act with a fine not exceeding five pounds.

(7) This section shall not come into operation until such date as may be fixed by the rules made thereunder.

6. (1) Where female workers are employed on or in connection with

munitions work in any establishment of a class to which the provisions of section seven of the principal Act as amended by this Act are for the time being applied by an order made thereunder, the Minister of Munitions shall have power by order to give directions as to the rate of wages or (subject, so far as the matter is one which is dealt with by the Factory and Workshops Acts, 1901 to 1911, to the concurrence of the Secretary of State) as to hours of labour, or conditions of employment of the female workers so employed.

(2) Any directions given by the Minister of Munitions under this section shall be binding on the owner of the establishment and any contractor or sub-contractor employing labour therein and the female workers to whom the directions relate, and any contravention thereof or non-compliance therewith shall be punishable, in like manner as if the order in which the direction is contained was an award made in settlement of a difference under Part I of the principal Act.

(3) No direction given under this section shall be deemed to relieve the occupier of any factory or workshop from the obligation to comply with the provisions of the Factory and Workshops Acts, 1901 to 1911, or of any orders or regulations made thereunder, or to affect the liability of any person to be proceeded against for an offence under the Employment of Children Act, 1903, so however that no person be twice punished for the same offence.

7.   The Minister of Munitions shall have power by order to give directions as to the rate of wages, hours of labour, or conditions of employment of semi-skilled and unskilled men employed in any controlled establishment on munitions work being work of a class which, prior to the war, was customarily undertaken by skilled labour, or as to the time rates for the manufacture of complete shell and fuses and cartridge cases in any controlled establishment in which such manufacture was not customary prior to the war; and any direction so given shall be binding on the owner of the establishment, and any contractor or sub-contractor employing labour therein, and the workers to whom the directions relate, and any contravention thereof or non-compliance therewith shall be punishable, in like manner as if the order in which the direction is contained was an award made in settlement of a difference under Part I of the principal Act.

8.   (1) The Minister of Munitions may constitute special arbitration tribunals to deal with differences reported under Part I of the principal Act which relate to matters on which the Minister of Munitions has given or is empowered to give directions under the last two preceding sections, and the Board of Trade may refer any such difference for settlement to such tribunal in lieu of referring it for settlement in

accordance with the First Schedule to the principal Act.

(2) The Minister of Munitions may also refer to a special arbitration tribunal so constituted, for advice, any question as to what directions are to be given by him under the said sections.

(3) The tribunal to which matters and questions relating to female workers are to be referred under this section shall include one or more women.

9. (1) The expression "munitions work" for the purposes of the principal Act and this Act means—

(a) the manufacture of arms, ammunition, ships, vessels, vehicles, and aircraft, and any other articles or parts of articles (whether of a similar nature to the aforesaid or not) intended or adapted for use in war, and of any other ships or vessels, or classes of ships or vessels, or parts of ships or vessels, which may be certified by the Board of Trade to be necessary for the successful prosecution of the War, and any metals, machines, or tools required for any class specified in an order made for the purpose by the Minister of Munitions, required for, or for use in, any such manufacture or repair as aforesaid; and

(b) the construction, alteration or repair of works of construction and buildings for naval or military purposes, and of buildings in which munitions work is or is intended to be carried on, and the erection of machinery and plant therein, and the erection of houses for the accommodation of persons engaged or about to be engaged on munitions work; and

(c) the construction, alteration, repair, or maintenance of docks and harbours and work in estuaries in cases where such construction, alteration, repair, maintenance or work is certified by the Admiralty to be necessary for the successful prosecution of the war; and

(d) the supply of light, heat, water, or power or the supply of tramways, facilities in cases where the Minister of Munitions certifies that such supply is of importance for the purpose of carrying on munitions work, and the erection of buildings, machinery, and plant required for such supply; and

(e) the repair of fire engines and any other fire brigade appliances in cases where the Minister of Munitions certifies that such repair is necessary in the national interest.

(2) In section three of the principal Act there shall be added after the words "affecting employment on", in both places where those words occur, the words "or in connection with," and in the same section the words "the manufacture or repair of arms, ammunition,

ships, vehicles, aircraft, or any other articles required for use in war, or of the metals, machines, or tools required for the manufacture or repair in this Act referred to as" shall be repealed.

(3) This section shall not come into operation until the time fixed by rules made under section five of this Act as the date for the commencement of that section.

10. At the end of section nine of the principal Act the following proviso shall be inserted—

> "Provided that the power of making an order applying section seven of this Act to any dock shall rest with the Minister of Munitions and not with the Admiralty."

11. Subsection (2) of section four of the principal Act shall read as if the words "or to any agreement existing before the establishment became a controlled establishment, between the owner of the establishment and an employee with regard to any periodical increase of remuneration" were inserted after the words "nineteen hundred and fifteen."

12. For removing doubts it is hereby declared that the expressions "workman" and "workmen," wherever they occur in the principal Act and this Act, include not only persons whose usual occupation consists in manual labour, but also foremen, clerks, typists, draughtsmen, and other persons whose usual occupation consists wholly or mainly in work other than manual labour.

13. Subsection (4) of section fifteen of the principal Act shall be read as if the words "of the second class" were struck out.

14. For section twelve of the principal Act the following section shall be substituted—

> "12. If any person makes any false statement or representation or gives any false certificate, or furnishes any false information—
>
> (a) for the purpose of evading any provision of this Act; or
>
> (b) in any proceedings before any munition tribunal, arbitration tribunal, referee, or board of referees under this Act or the rules made thereunder; or
>
> (c) to the Minister of Munitions or any officer employed by him, for the purpose of obtaining or retaining employment, or of obtaining or retaining the services of any workman;
>
> or if any person alters or tampers with a certificate given under section seven of this Act, or personates or falsely represents himself to be a person to whom such a certificate has been given, or allows any other person to have possession of any such certificate issued for his use alone, he shall be guilty of an offence and liable on conviction under the Summary Jurisdiction Acts to imprison-

ment with or without hard labour for a term not exceeding three months or to a fine not exceeding fifty pounds."

15. Where non-union labour is introduced during the war into any class of work in a controlled establishment in which it was the practice prior to the war to employ union labour exclusively the owner of the establishment shall be deemed to have undertaken that such introduction shall only be for the period of the war, and if he breaks or attempts to break such an undertaking he shall be guilty of an offence under the principal Act and liable to a fine not exceeding fifty pounds; but subject as aforesaid such introduction shall not be deemed to be a change of working conditions.

16. (1) In subsection (1) of section eleven of the principal Act, which specifies the matters in respect of which owners of establishments in which persons are employed are, if required by the Minister of Munitions, to give information, the following paragraph shall be inserted after paragraph (c):—

> (cc) the cost of production of the articles produced or dealt with in the establishment, and the cost of the materials used for such production, and the names and addresses of the persons by whom such materials were supplied or who are under contract to supply them.

(2) If any person, except as authorised by the Minister of Munitions, discloses or makes use of any information given under section eleven of the principal Act, as amended by this or any subsequent enactment, he shall be guilty of a misdemeanour and on conviction be liable to imprisonment with or without hard labour, for a term not exceeding two years, or to a fine, or to both imprisonment and a fine.

17. (1) An inspector appointed by the Minister of Munitions for the purposes of the principal Act shall have power to enter at all reasonable times the premises of any establishment (other than a private dwelling-house not being a workshop) for the purpose of ascertaining whether it is desirable to put in force as respects any establishment or any person employed therein any of the powers of the Minister of Munitions, whether under the principal Act or otherwise, or for the purpose of obtaining any information in connection with the supply of munitions, and to make such examination and inquiry as may be necessary for any such purpose and the owner of the establishment and every person engaged in the management or direction of the establishment shall furnish to any such inspector all such information, and shall produce for inspection all such registers, wages books, and other similar documents, as the inspector may reasonably require.

(2) If any person wilfully delays or obstructs an inspector in the

exercise of any power under this section or fails to give such information or to produce such documents as aforesaid, he shall be guilty of an offence under the principal Act, and shall be liable to a fine not exceeding ten pounds.

(3) Every inspector shall be furnished with a certificate as to his appointment, and on applying for admission to any premises for the purposes of this section shall, if so required, produce such certificate.

18. (1) All offences which are by or under this Act made offences under the principal Act, other than those for which the maximum fine exceeds five pounds, shall be deemed to be offences with which munitions tribunals of the second class have jurisdiction to deal.

(2) Rules under section fifteen of the principal Act shall provide—

(a) that in proceedings before a munitions tribunal the chairman shall, before giving his decision, consult with the assessors, and in all cases where the assessors are agreed he shall, except as respects questions which appear to the chairman to be questions of law, give effect to their opinion in his decision;

(b) that where the person or persons by or on behalf of whom or against whom the complaint is made in any proceedings before a munitions tribunal is or are a female worker or two or more female workers, the assessor or one of the assessors chosen from the panel of persons representing workmen shall be a woman.

(3) Decisions of munitions tribunals shall be subject to appeal to such judge of the High Court as may be appointed by the Lord Chancellor for the purpose on any ground which involves a question of law or a question of mixed law and fact, or on any other ground that may be prescribed in rules made by the Lord Chancellor, in such cases and subject to such conditions and in such manner as may be specified in such rules, and whether by means of the statement of a special case for the opinion of the judge or otherwise; and those rules may provide for such appeals in any classes of cases specified therein being heard and determined in a summary manner and for the fixing, remission, or reduction of any fees and scales of costs, and as to the manner in which effect is given to the decision of the judge, and the decision of the judge on any such appeal shall be final and binding on all munitions tribunals.

In the application of this provision to Scotland "High Court" shall mean Court of Sessions, "Lord Chancellor" shall mean Lord President of the Court of Sessions, "rules made by the Lord Chancellor" shall mean Act of Sederunt.

In the application of this provision to Ireland "Lord Chancellor" shall mean the Lord Chancellor of Ireland.

(4) In the case of a company being guilty of an offence under the principal Act, every director, manager, secretary, or other officer of the company, who is knowingly a party to the contravention or non-compliance constituting the offence shall also be guilty of the offence and liable to the like fine as the company.

(5) In subsection (3) of section fifteen of the principal Act after the words "so far as relates to offences" there shall be inserted "and the enforcement of orders."

19. In subsection (3) of section five of the principal Act, after the words "affords no standard of comparison" there shall be inserted the words "or that no such average exists," and after the words "if he thinks just, allow," there shall be inserted the words "or require"; and in paragraph nine of the Second Schedule of the principal Act, for the word "fourth," there shall be substituted the word "third."

20. The Minister of Munitions may make arrangements with any other Government department for the exercise and performance by that department of any of his powers and duties under the principal Act or this Act which appear to him to be such as could be more conveniently so exercised and performed, and in such case the department and the officers of the department shall have the same powers and duties for the purposes as are by the principal Act and this Act conferred on the Minister of Munitions and his officers.

21. For the purposes of proceedings under section two of the principal Act, a certificate of the Board of Trade purporting to be signed by the President or a secretary or assistant secretary of the Board of Trade, or by a person authorized for the purpose by the President that a difference to which Part I of the principal Act applies has or has not been reported to the Board, and, in cases where such a difference has been reported, as to the date on which it was reported, shall be admissible as evidence of the facts therein stated.

22. (1) Where a munitions tribunal dismisses any case under the principal Act or this Act, and it appears to the tribunal that the proceedings were vexatious or frivolous, the tribunal shall, unless it sees good cause to the contrary, award costs to the person against whom the complaint is made, and the costs so awarded shall, unless good cause to the contrary appears, include such sum as compensation for the expenses, trouble, and loss of time incurred in or incidental to the attendance of the person against whom the complaint is made before the tribunal as to the tribunal may seem just and reasonable.

(2) Where a referee or board of referees to whom a matter has, under subsection (3) of section five of the principal Act, been referred by the

Minister of Munitions on the requirement of the owner of an establishment, considers that the requirement was unreasonable, the referee or board of referees may order that any costs payable by the owner of the establishment shall be paid out of the amount of profits divisible under the principal Act.

23. The Arbitration Act, 1889, shall not apply to any reference to any referee or board of referees under the principal Act or this Act or the rules made thereunder.

24. Where the Minister of Munitions makes an order revoking any order previously made by him under section four of the principal Act, the order so revoked shall, if that order has not been in operation for more than three months and was made under a misapprehension and the revoking order so directs, be treated for all or any of the purposes thereof as if it had never had effect.

25. Rules and regulations made under the principal Act as amended by this Act shall not be deemed to be statutory rules within the meaning of section one of the Rules Publication Act, 1893.

26. In subsection (2) of section twenty of the principal Act, which relates to the duration thereof, the words "Part I of" shall be repealed.

27. This Act may cited as the Munitions of War (Amendment) Act, 1916, and shall be construed as one with the principal Act, and the principal Act and this Act may be cited together as the Munitions of War Acts, 1915 and 1916.

APPENDIX B

CIRCULAR LI.

(November, 1915)

Ministry of Munitions of War,

6 Whitehall Gardens,

London, S.W.

Sir,—I am directed by the Minister of Munitions to enclose for your information copy of the recommendations of the Munitions Labour Supply Committee with reference to—

(a) The employment and remuneration of women in munition work of a class which prior to the War was not recognized as women's work in districts where such work as customarily carried on.

(b) The employment and remuneration of semi-skilled and unskilled men on munition work of a class which prior to the War was customarily undertaken by skilled labour.

I am to inform you that the Minister has decided to adopt the Committee's recommendations as regards munition factories for which the Ministry is responsible, and also to commend them to the favourable consideration of other employers engaged on munitions work.

I am sir, your obedient servant,

H. Llewellyn Smith

APPENDIX C

CIRCULAR L2.

Payment of Women not on Recognized Women's Work
Ministry of Munitions
Munitions Labour Supply Committee

Recommendations relating to the employment and remuneration of women on munition work of a class which prior to the War was not recognized as women's work in districts where such work was customarily carried on.

(Note. These recommendations are on the basis of the setting up of the machines being otherwise provided for. They are strictly confined to the war period and are subject to the observance of the provisions of Schedule II of the Munitions of War Act.)

1. Women of 18 years of age and over employed on time, on work customarily done by men, shall be rated at £1 per week, reckoned on the usual working hours of the district in question for men in engineering establishments.

    This, however, shall not apply in the case of women employed on work customarily done by fully skilled tradesmen, in which case the women shall be paid the time rate of the tradesmen whose work they undertake. Overtime and night shift and Sunday and holiday allowances payable to men shall also be made to women.

2. Where women are prevented from working, owing to breakdown, air raid, or other causes beyond their control, they shall be paid for the time so lost at the rate of 15s. a week as above, unless they are sent home.

3. Women shall not be put in piece work or premium bonus systems until sufficiently qualified. The period of qualification on shell work shall not, in general case, exceed three to four weeks.

4. Where women are employed on piece work they shall be paid the same piece work prices as are customarily paid to men for the job.

5. Where women are engaged on premium bonus systems the time allowed for a job shall be that customarily allowed to men for the same job, and the earnings of the women shall be calculated on the basis of the man's time rate.

6. Where the job in question has not hitherto been done on piece work or premium bonus system in the establishment, the piece work price, or the time allowed, shall be based on a similar job previously done by men, on piece work or premium bonus system as the case may be.

7. Where in the establishment in question there are no data from previous operations to enable the parties to arrive at a piece work price or time to be allowed, the price or the time to be allowed shall be so adjusted that the women shall receive the same percentage over the time rate of the class of men customarily employed on the job, as such man would have received had he undertaken the job on piece work or premium bonus system as the case may be.

8. The principle upon which the recommendations proceed is that on systems of payment by results equal payment shall be made to women as to the men for an equal amount of work done.

9. Piece work prices and premium bonus basis times shall be fixed by mutual agreement between the employer and the woman or women who perform the work.

10. On piece work, every woman's time rate, as per Clause 1 hereof, shall be guaranteed irrespectively of her piece work earnings. Debit balances shall not be carried forward beyond the usual weekly period of settlement.

11. On premium bonus systems, every woman's time rate as per Clause 1 hereof shall in all cases be paid.

12. Overtime and night shift and Sunday and holiday allowances shall be paid to women employed on piece work or premium bonus system on the same conditions as now prevail in the case of men in the district in question for time work.

13. Piece work prices and premium bonus time allowances, after they have been established, shall not be altered unless the means or methods of manufacture are changed.

14. All wages and balances shall be paid to women through the office.

15. Any question which arises as to the interpretation of these recommendations shall be determined by the Minister of Munitions.

October 1915.

APPENDIX D

CIRCULAR L3.

Payment of Men on Skilled Work
Ministry of Munitions
Munitions Labour Supply Committee

Recommendations relating to the employment and remuneration of semi-skilled and unskilled men on munitions work of a class which prior to the War was customarily undertaken by skilled labour.

(Note.—These recommendations are strictly confined to the war period and are subject to the observance of Schedule II of the Munitions of War Act.)

GENERAL

1. Operations on which skilled men are at present employed, but which by reason of their character can be performed by semi-skilled or unskilled labour, may be done by such labour during the period of the War.

2. Where semi-skilled or unskilled male labour is employed on work identical with that customarily undertaken by skilled labour, the time rates and piece prices and premium bonus times shall be the same as customarily obtain for the operations when performed by skilled labour.

3. Where skilled men are at present employed they shall not be displaced by less skilled labour unless other skilled employment is offered to them there or elsewhere.

4. Piece-work prices and premiums bonus time allowances, after they have been established shall not be altered unless the means or method of manufacture are changed.

5. Overtime, night shift, Sunday and holiday allowances shall be paid to such machinemen on the same basis as to skilled men.

Time ratings for the manufacture of complete shell and fuses and cartridge cases, where not hitherto customary.

6. Where the manufacture of this class of munitions was not customarily undertaken by the establishment prior to the War, the following time ratings shall apply:

(a) Semi-skilled and unskilled men of 21 years of age and over, when, engaged as machinemen on the above manufacture, shall be paid a time rate of 10s. per week lower than the time rate for turners, including war bonuses, engaged in the engineering trade of the district, but in no case shall the rate paid to such men be less than 28s. per week of the normal district hours. This rate also includes all war bonuses already granted.

(b) Where a semi-skilled or unskilled man of 21 years of age and over has had no experience previously of the operation he is called upon to perform, his starting rate shall be 26s. per week, which shall be paid during his period of training, but such period shall not exceed two months from the date on which he commenced work as a machineman.

(c) The time rates payable to setters up shall be not less than as follows:

Setting up of fuse-making machines, 10s. per week over the current district time rate for turners. Setting up of shell-making machines, 5s. per week over the current time rate for turners.

These extras are in addition to any war bonuses which have been granted.

INTERPRETATION

7. Any questions which arise as to the interpretation of these recommendations shall be determined by the Minister of Munitions. October 1915.

APPENDIX E

REPORT ON DILUTION OF LABOUR
Central Munitions Labour Supply Committee

REPORT TO MINISTER OF MUNITIONS re DILUTION OF SKILLED LABOUR

I. Minister's Circular to Controlled Establishments.

In his circular letter to the controlled establishments the Minister stated that he had reason to believe that skilled workmen were being employed in too large a proportion to semi-skilled or unskilled workmen.

He further stated that he was convinced that it would be quite impossible to satisfy the urgent and prospective demand for skilled workmen unless their employment is strictly limited to work for which their special skill is essential and which cannot be performed in whole or part by semi-skilled or unskilled labour, either of men or women.

II. Interim Report by Committee.

In their Interim Report the Committee, following on the above action by the Minister, submitted an outline of a scheme for dilution of skilled labour by the introduction of semi-skilled and unskilled male and female labour.

III. Interim Report Accepted by Minister.

The Minister having accepted their proposals on this point, the Committee submit, for the consideration of the Minister, the details of the scheme of dilution.

IV. Conditions of Employment.

The terms upon which labour to be introduced in accordance with the schedule is to be employed are contained in Circular Letters L2 and L3 attached hereto.

The terms as hereto laid down do not, however, cover cases of males under 21 years of age and females under 18 years of age. It is understood that the Ministry desire to give further consideration to the proposals of the Committee on these points before issue.

V. Standardisation of Working Conditions and Procedure.

The Committee are of opinion that it would be in the general interest if notes were issued from time to time for the information and guidance of controlled establishments.

These notes should advise how points covered by the Act coming within the scope of the Committee's reference should be dealt with, should give to those concerned the benefit of any useful information possessed by the Ministry, and should be of such a nature generally as would encourage the employers and workpeople to seek advice from the Ministry on contentious points and so avoid differences arising as far as possible.

In order to obtain information as to questions which might be a source of difference, the Committee have interviewed representatives of several leading firms who have had experience of dilution of skilled labour. The Committee have embodied in the notes appended hereto the principal points brought out at these interviews, and they now submit these notes for approval and issue by the Minister.

VI. Dilution Scheme Proposed.

1. The principle of the scheme is that no skilled man should be employed on work which can be done by semi-skilled or unskilled male or female labour.

2. The principle cannot be applied to all establishments in the same degree—for example, in a shop doing repetition work the scheme is generally applicable, whereas in a marine engineering or repairing works the scheme would be applicable to a less extent.

3. It will be necessary to have a special survey of shops by fully qualified technical inspectors, as far as possible specially conversant with the employment of semi-skilled and female labour, who could advise the Ministry on the extent to which the dilution could take place, and assist the employers in the process.

4. (a) The returns on the schedules issued with C.E.I. and 3–8 forms should be divided into

    (i) Cases in which it seems clear that some men are available for enrolment and transfer.

    (ii) Cases requiring special attention.

(b) Class i. cases will be referred to the Local Labour Exchange manager—acting as labour supply officer of the Ministry—to visit the works and arrange for the enrolment of the men. He will report any action taken to the local Advisory Board at a joint meeting, bringing before them also for further action those cases in which there have been insufficient enrolments. Objections raised by the workmen to the dilution of skilled labour shall be reported by the labour supply officer to the Minister, who shall, if the question is purely a local question, remit the same for settlement by the labour officer in conjunction with the local Advisory Board. He will, whenever this seems advisable, be accompanied to the works by a representative of the local Advisory Board to assist in securing enrolments.

(c) Class ii. cases will be, according to the circumstances in each case, referred either to the superintending engineer or to the labour officer, or to a special investigator from the Ministry, as may be deemed necessary. In each case the objective of the visit will be to clear the way for subsequent enrolment and transfer. The labour supply officer will, whenever convenient, accompany the engineer or other special investigator for this purpose.

(d) All officers visiting the works for the purposes specified above will be furnished with warrants showing their authority, and the way will have been prepared for them by the circular to the firms.

(e) The transferance will be undertaken locally by the labour supply officer, and the men will be transferred to firms indicated to him by the Ministry as being establishments in which the need is most urgent. In determining the urgency of any firm's requirements the Ministry should have regard amongst other considerations to the extent to which dilution has taken place in the establishment in question.

(f) Men will be enrolled on the existing War Munitions Volunteer terms, and disputed questions as to subsistence allowances and other payments to them will be referred to the Labour Advisory Boards at joint meetings with the labour supply officers.

5. The skilled workmen released should be dealt with in the following sequence:

(a) Arrangements should be made for working full 24 hours per day as far as practicable on all machines.

(b) The extra requirements of the district should be satisfied.

(c) Any volunteer workmen who are working in the district and belong to another district should be returned if possible to their district of origin and replaced by men released as a result of dilution.

(d) Only the surplus then available should be sent to other districts.

(e) The foregoing shall not apply to demands for labour certified by the Minister as urgent.

6. Returns regarding the number of machines of the various classes in the various factories should be examined in order to check the views of firms regarding the dilution, and enable the technical inspector to arrive at a conclusion on that subject.

7. Where it is found that firms are not running full day and night shift owing to lack or orders for munition work, the matter should be taken up with the Director-General of Munitions Supply, so that if possible further orders may be issued. Similarly in cases where the cause is lack of material, etc.

8. The Central Committee should be kept posted by the local officers, through the Department, of all difficulties and questions of importance arising out of the dilution of skilled labour.

9. Executive action by the Ministry should be subject to the advice and assistance of the Central Committee, in so far as it affects questions of policy relating to the dilution of skilled labour.

10. The services of the Local Labour Advisory Boards should be fully taken advantage of in respect of local difficulties which may arise out of the dilution of skilled labour.

VII. Recommendation.

The Committee recommend the foregoing to the favourable consideration of the Minister, and are of opinion that the scheme of dilution as now submitted should, as approved, be put into operation as early as possible.

VIII. Appendices.

Appendix A. Proposed notes for the guidance of controlled establishments.

Appendix B. Printed documents L2 and L3 relating to wages of semi-skilled and unskilled male and female labour.

(Signed) Chairman of Munitions Labour
October 25th, 1915.   Supply Committee

APPENDIX F

CIRCULAR L6.

NOTES FOR GUIDANCE OF CONTROLLED ESTABLISHMENTS

A. Alterations in Working Conditions.

Schedule II, paragraph 7, provides: 'Due notice shall be given to the workmen concerned, wherever practicable, of any changes of working conditions which it is desired to introduce as the results of the establishment becoming a controlled establishment, and opportunity for local consultation with workmen or their representatives shall be given if desired.'

Procedure. The Minister is of opinion that the following procedure should be adopted by a controlled establishment when any change is made in working conditions:

1. The workmen in the shop in which a change is to be made should be requested by the employer to appoint a deputation of their number, together with their local Trade Union representative if they desire, to whom particulars of the proposed change could be explained.

2. At the interview the employer, after explaining the change proposed and giving the date when it is to come into operation, should give the deputation full opportunity of raising any points they desire in connection therewith, so that if possible the introduction may be made with the consent of all parties.

3. Should the deputation be unable at the interview to concur in the change, opportunity should be given for further local consultation when representatives of the Trade Unions concerned might be present.

4. It is not intended that the introduction of the change should be delayed until concurrence of the workpeople is obtained. The change should be introduced after a reasonable time, and if the work-

people or their representatives desire to bring forward any question relating thereto they should follow the procedure laid down in Part I of the Act.

5. It is not desirable that formal announcement of the proposed change should be put on the notice board of the shop until intimation has been given as above to the men concerned or their Trade Union representative.

While this is so the Minister is of opinion that it will be consistent with prudence that every endeavour should be made by employers to secure the co-operation of their workpeople in matters of this description.

Any difficulties experienced by either employees or workpeople should be at once referred to the Ministry in order that an immediate endeavour may be made to find a satisfactory solution.

B. Shell Work.

It would appear desirable that women under 18 years of age should not be employed on shells over six-pounders.

C. Women on Skilled Work.

The Minister is of opinion that before female labour is hereafter employed in the highly skilled branches of the engineering trades the proposal of the employer in question should be submitted to the Ministry for approval.

D. Working Hours.

The desirability of working the three-shift system, as compared with the two-shift system, when this is otherwise feasible, has been referred by the Minister to the Committee appointed by him regarding industrial fatigue and hours of labour for consideration and report.

E. Sunday Work.

This question has also been referred by the Minister to the Committee above named.

F. Superintendence of Female Labour.

The Minister is of opinion that where females are employed they should be supervised by a forewoman, who should act as intermediary between the workers and the shop foreman or manager.

G. Provision of Overalls and Caps.

In the interest of safety the Minister recommends that female workers should be supplied by the employers with caps and overalls and that suitable arrangements should be made for the necessary washing of these.

H. Night Shifts.

It appears desirable that where two shifts are in operation female labour should, as far as is reasonably practicable, be employed on the day shift rather than on the night shift.

I. Suitable Occupations.

While it is not possible at this stage to indicate fully the occupations in which women may be employed, the following may serve as a guide:

(i) Hand work.—Inspection and viewing, especially those processes which do not involve the use of appliances of precision. Assembling, welding (mechanical) small parts. Armature winding. Taping armature coils. Armament core building. Painting and varnishing of shells.

(ii) Machine work.—Automatic machines. Semi-automatic machines, where operations are within the limits of a woman's physical capacity. Generally, work of suitable dimensions and of a repetitive character.

(iii) Storekeepers and timekeepers.

J. Accommodation for Females.

It is essential that suitable lavatory and cloak room accommodation, with the necessary female attendants, should be provided for the exclusive use of female labour employed.

K. Suggestions.

The Minister will be glad to receive any suggestions for incorporation in subsequent issues of these notes, and particularly will be glad to receive a note of the difficulties any establishments may have experienced in connection with their labour, and what measures were adopted to adjust the difference. The Minister feels that it is important that all firms should have as much information as possible of the experience of others so that they may benefit thereby.

APPENDIX G

MUNITIONS PRODUCTION

Artillery Deliveries, June–December 1915

[These figures of gun production refer to actual deliveries. See MUN 5/177/1200/21.]

18-pounder guns	1,904
(repaired for service)	100
4.5 inch howitzers	416
60-pounder guns	104
6-inch howitzers	4
8-inch howitzers	39
9.2-inch howitzers	14
12-inch howitzers	20
15-inch howitzers	1

Artillery Deliveries, January–June 1916

18-pounder guns	1,020
4.5-inch howitzers	682
60-pounder guns	293
6-inch howitzers	184
8-inch howitzers	18
9.2-inch howitzers	76
12-inch howitzers	16
15-inch howitzers	11

Artillery Deliveries, July 1916–June 1917

18-pounder guns	1,379
(repaired for service)	745
4.5-inch howitzers	531
(repaired for service)	101
60-pounder guns	556
(repaired for service)	240
6-inch guns, MK. XIX★	5
(repaired for service, MK. VII) . .	66
6-inch howitzer	737
(repaired for service)	55
8-inch howitzers	148
(repaired for service)	24
9.2-inch howitzers	159
(repaired for service)	33
12-inch howitzers	32
(repaired for service)	1

★The MK. XIX 6-inch gun was a new weapon introduced in 1917. The MK. VII, the older version, accounted for those 6-inch guns repaired for service. Gun repair was not considered an urgent matter until late in 1916; thereafter, it received high priority, with the conversion of several National Projectile Factories to repair facilities.

Shell Deliveries, August–December 1914

[MUN 5/183/1300/130]

CALIBRE	NUMBER	TONNAGE
18-pounder gun	850,000	1,457
4.5-inch gun	175,000	3,719
60-pounder gun	33,000	1,137
6-inch gun	9,700	514
8-inch howitzer	nil	
9.2-inch howitzer	nil	
12-inch howitzer	nil	
15-inch howitzer	nil	
AGGREGATE TOTALS★	1,363,700	21,269

★These charts include the most important classifications of shells; the aggregate totals include all natures of shells supplied to the Army.

Shell Deliveries, January–June, 1915

CALIBRE	NUMBER	TONNAGE
18-pounder gun	1,491,426	18,642
4.5-inch howitzer	173,023	3,676
60-pounder gun	98,771	3,402
6-inch gun	4,300	227
6-inch howitzer	50,365	2,507
8-inch howitzer	1,930	185
9.2-inch howitzer	9,275	1,275
12-inch howitzer	nil	
15-inch howitzer	nil	
AGGREGATE TOTALS	2,278,105	36,460

Shell Deliveries, July–December 1915

CALIBRE	NUMBER	TONNAGE
18-pounder gun	4,070,344	50,879
4.5-inch howitzer	520,496	11,060
60-pounder gun	130,965	4,512
6-inch gun	19,454	1,032
6-inch howitzer	127,771	6,363
8-inch howitzer	39,158	3,759
9.2-inch howitzer	24,178	3,324
12-inch howitzer	4,474	1,545
15-inch howitzer	847	567
AGGREGATE TOTALS	5,380,102	90,077

Shell Deliveries, January–June 1916

CALIBRE	NUMBER	TONNAGE
18-pounder gun	10,073,809	125,922
4.5-inch howitzer	2,060,578	43,786
60-pounder gun	460,159	15,852
6-inch gun ⎱ 6-inch howitzer ⎰	431,238	21,576
8-inch howitzer	109,938	10,554
9.2-inch howitzer	95,110	13,078
12-inch howitzer	14,749	5,096
15-inch howitzer	3,261	2,188
AGGREGATE TOTALS	13,995,360	248,694

Shell Deliveries, July–December 1916

CALIBRE	NUMBER	TONNAGE
18-pounder gun	22,789,232	284,865
4.5-inch howitzer	5,602,011	119,043
60-pounder gun	1,846,207	63,601
6-inch gun 6-inch howitzer	2,375,527	106,494
8-inch howitzer	614,636	59,005
9.2-inch howitzer	693,885	95,408
12-inch howitzer	59,740	20,640
15-inch howitzer	4,225	2,834
AGGREGATE TOTALS	35,407,193	775,263

Machine Gun Production: August 1914–December 1916

[These figures refer to machine-guns produced domestically.
See MUN 5/377/1410. 1/2]

MONTH/YEAR	VICKERS GUN	CUMULATIVE TOTAL
Aug. 1914	7	—
Dec. 1914	6	266
March 1915	109	555
June 1915	185	976
Sept. 1915	328	1,709
Dec. 1915	381	2,617
March 1916	525	3,986
June 1916	559	5,521
Sept. 1916	688	7,740
Dec. 1916	747*	10,100

*previous month, 1,006

MONTH/YEAR	LEWIS GUN	CUMULATIVE TOTAL
Aug. 1914	—	—
Dec. 1914	2	8
March 1915	—	47
June 1915	244	510
Sept. 1915	500	1,496
Dec. 1915	948	3,658
March 1916	1,626	7,580
June 1916	1,424**	12,628
Sept. 1916	1,606	18,728
Dec. 1916	2,060***	25,273

**previous month, 2,271
***previous month, 2,758

MONTH/YEAR	HOTCHKISS GUN	CUMULATIVE TOTAL
(no production August 1914–November 1915)		
Dec. 1915	9	9
March 1916	200	354
June 1916	279	1,016
Sept. 1916	456	2,269
Dec. 1916	544	4,165

INDEX